THE VIEW FROM THE HIGH BOARD

Richard Williams is the chief sports writer of the *Guardian*. His other books include *The Death of Ayrton Senna*, *Racers*, which was shortlisted for the William Hill Sports Book of the Year Award, and *Enzo Ferrari: A Life*.

For I. M. W. and J. H. W.

Richard Williams

THE VIEW FROM THE
HIGH BOARD

Writings on Sport

First published in Great Britain
2003 by Aurum Press Ltd
25 Bedford Avenue, London WC1B 3AT

Design by Roger Hammond

Many of these pieces first appeared in an earlier
form in the *Guardian*, *Independent*, *Independent
on Sunday* and *Condé Nast Traveler*.

A catalogue record for this book is available
from the British Library.

ISBN 1 85410 936 7

1 3 5 7 9 10 8 6 4 2
2003 2005 2007 2006 2004

Typeset in Minion and
Trade Gothic by M Rules
Printed in Great Britain by
MPG Books Ltd, Bodmin

CONTENTS

The North Wheatley Cricket Club XI, *circa* 1950. The Rev. I.M.
Williams, the author's father, is fourth from left in the top row.

INTRODUCTION

Sometimes I think that I'm happiest in an empty stadium in the hours before the action begins, when the place is filled with a sense of what might be about to happen. Or even when the contest is all over and the stadium has emptied, leaving only the memory of what took place. Sport exists in the anticipation and the recollection as well as in the moment, which is what makes it so rich and incremental a pleasure.

Wherever it is I have to be in the course of my work as a sportswriter, I try to get there early and let my imagination work. Time spent in reconnaissance, as General Clausewitz wrote, is never wasted. But mostly it's for the sheer pleasure of soaking up the atmosphere: the resonances of history written and still to come. The Indianapolis motor speedway at 4 o'clock on a May morning, an hour or two before dawn breaks over grandstands that will shortly be bursting with half a million people, is a place already loud with ninety years' worth of echoes. Wimbledon's Centre Court, on the day before the tournament begins, is a great Elizabethan theatre awaiting its cast while the stagehands erect the last bits of scenery. Walking down the course at Cheltenham on Gold Cup morning, reaching the point where the track bottoms out and turns sharp left into the long uphill drag to the line, you can feel the thunder and the panic to come. Even a brand new stadium, such as those in which the 2002 World Cup games were played in Japan and South Korea, is waiting for the first page of history to be written.

Any of this stuff also represents a useful antidote to the cynicism that will occasionally seep even into the most naturally enthusiastic spirit when, as often happens nowadays, the commerce gets in the way of the sport. When the late Mark McCormack spotted the potential for persuading multinational companies that televised sport offered a new and highly effective way of marketing their wares, he made it possible for many people to be properly rewarded for their efforts. But the scale of those rewards, and the importance of safeguarding the marketing opportunities, eventually came close to obliterating the real meaning and value of the exercise. That's why the antidote has become increasingly useful.

Occasionally, too, I try to stay late. Then I can catch the sun setting through the tall pines of Augusta National after the US Masters has been won and lost, the red dust of the Georgia hills refracting its rays as the last spectators wander back to their cars and the lights go on in the old clubhouse. Or the silence that settles over the autodrome at Monza when the helicopter traffic has been stilled and you can wander out on to the track and see what the driver sees as he exits the Parabolica and streaks past the pits: a surreal back-projected panorama of mountains at the far end of the main straight. Or I might be a witness to the exhaustion of the riders in the Tour de France preparing for an evening in an Alpine ski station, having a meal and trying to get the day's agony out of their bones while the technicians check over their bikes.

Sport is all this, in addition to the actual running and jumping and kicking and hitting, and I never felt it more keenly than one afternoon in 1992 when I walked up the steps to the high board above the Montjuic pool in Barcelona, the site of the Olympic diving competition. Never having dived in my life for anything other than a dropped £5 note, I felt I had no way of empathizing with what Fu Mingxia, the tiny thirteen-year-old Chinese girl, had just done to win a gold medal with such spectacular grace. But I thought if I climbed those steps and saw the world as she saw it in the moments before she made her weightless plunge, then it might give me a bit more of an understanding of her achievement.

So did I learn anything? In technical terms, no. It didn't help me do anything other than try to describe how she looked when she was falling through the air or how she behaved when she was invited to talk about it. But I believe that anything bringing the observer closer to the practitioner's experience eventually produces a dividend, even if it cannot be identified or quantified. When you see how small the patch of water looks from the high board, you cannot help but feel closer to the diver.

We spectators tend to observe the games from afar, like gods. We watch the plays unfolding as if from a coach's blueprint, and often we can identify the mistakes almost before they happen. It is easy to forget that the participant sees things quite differently. There is the discomfort, for a start: the heat, the sweat, the screaming pain as lactic acid collects in the muscles, the driving rain, the bone-hard ground, the wind, the fear, the scrape of thighs and shoulders on gravel, the punch that drives out breath and fills the mouth with blood. But there is also the ability of the very greatest performers to stand in the middle of mayhem and identify patterns as they form, and then to make that moving geometry work for them. That is what makes the intelligence of a Barry John or a Zinedine Zidane so remarkable. It is what made Michael Jordan able to think in four dimensions: looking at a space crowded with bodies, instantly calculating the precise moment at which there would be a hole there and launching himself towards it while twisting up towards the basket. The closer you can think yourself into what the performer experiences, the closer you are likely to get to a true description of what he or she is doing.

If these were some of the things I hoped to see when I started writing about sport, I also had a more prosaic desire to cover events that concluded with a definite result. This was the biggest difference between sport and music, which was the subject I'd previously spent most of my time writing about. With sport, you could take a result and work backwards. A score line or a set of timings made everything much simpler. Sport offered the opportunity to describe events that unfolded in clear (although sometimes complicated) narrative terms, and it seemed that the men and women who took part revealed their characters through the manner in which they competed much more straightforwardly than musicians did. To put it bluntly, the sweetest music is sometimes made by the most obnoxious people, and vice versa (examples available on request); in sport, by contrast, the way people play the game is generally also the way they are as human beings, which makes it legitimate to discuss how someone's performance is affected by his or her character. What I hadn't been expecting was the way modern sport would lead those responsible for its coverage into the contemplation of so many areas coming under the general heading of moral debate. And that makes it an even more interesting, if frequently uncomfortable, place to be. No longer is the result always the bottom line. Sometimes there is a layer of meaning that can never be a matter of simple victory or defeat.

The last few years in sport have been full of examples of philosophical questions overshadowing the business of straightforward games-playing. Michael Atherton's perennial vulnerability to the bowling of Glenn McGrath, for instance, commanded much less attention than the dirt-in-the-pocket affair at Lord's in 1994, which opened up discussions on whether it was acceptable for an England cricket captain to indulge in a little mild gamesmanship and, by extension, whether this reflected a decline in the nation's probity. The attention Eric Cantona attracted when he helped Manchester United to win the English league title for the first time in a quarter of a century was nothing compared to the interest in his retaliation to the insults of a Crystal Palace fan in 1995, highlighting not just deteriorating standards of public behaviour on both sides of the touchline but also, seen from the Frenchman's perspective, a more general erosion of respect, good manners and so on in national life. When Glenn Hoddle dropped Paul Gascoigne from England's 1998 World Cup, Sheryl Gascoigne's much-photographed facial bruises brought the question of spousal abuse into the arena. Hoddle may have laughed when I told him at the time that he wielded more moral influence on the nation than the Archbishop of Canterbury, but it was true; and when he was dismissed after clumsily discussing his belief in reincarnation, he may have glimpsed a distorted version of that notion. Gascoigne's difficulties with alcohol, along with the similar experiences of Tony Adams, Paul Merson and others, dramatized the widespread problem of addiction, usefully drawing public attention both to successful forms of therapy and to the difficulty of ensuring a favourable outcome in all cases. When Mike Tyson bit a chunk out of Evander Holyfield's ear and then went round the other side for a second helping, we had to ask ourselves questions about our willingness to be spectators of such depravity. Michael Schumacher's ruthless tussle with Damon Hill exposed the way that even potentially lethal gamesmanship is sometimes tacitly condoned by a nexus of special interests. The scenes on the 17th green at Brookline during the 1999 Ryder Cup were discussed in terms of the American presumption of the right to triumph, no matter who or what gets trampled on in the process. The brief bout of industrial action by England's rugby squad in 2000 told the nation that the ethos of amateurism, the central pillar around which the Victorians had built just about all the major sports a hundred years earlier, had finally been demolished and cleared away, and that there would be no room in the future for hypocrisy on that score: no more gentlemen and players, no more rich man in his castle, poor man at his gate.

With the exception of money, and specifically the salaries of English Premier League footballers, nothing brings more agitation to the moral debate than the question of drugs. I know where I stand on the issue: drugs should have no place in sport, and I have great admiration for those athletes, such as Paula Radcliffe, who campaign against them, sometimes even at a cost to their own popularity in the locker room. The activities of US track and field administrators in covering up positive tests on their top athletes are worthy only of contempt. Any coach or doctor who condones the use of human growth hormone for performance-enhancing reasons should be put in jail. But there are enough grey areas to make it hard for any open-minded commentator to give a hard and fast ruling on every case.

Racing cyclists, to take the most obvious example, exist in a culture that has its roots in systematic doping of various sorts: not so much to make the riders go faster as to reduce the extraordinary degree of pain involved in chasing up and down mountains all day. For fifty years nobody minded much. Then, when the outside world started to object, they minded a bit. Now the use of steroids, growth hormone and blood-doping, all potentially life-threatening, has crept into the culture and is proving difficult to eradicate. But to invite enthusiasts to switch off their engagement with the sport until and unless all traces of doping are removed is to expect too much. I feel the same. I don't like the fact that some cyclists dope, perhaps even a majority of them, but it won't stop me watching the races any more than I would petition for the results of past heroes known to be dopers to be struck from the record. That is, admittedly, a difficult moral position to defend.

In one important respect, covering sport today is not the pleasure it was for earlier generations. The possibility of establishing decent communications with leading sportsmen and women has become vastly more difficult since television took a central role in the promotion of sport, bringing global audiences, multinational sponsors, agents, marketing departments and public relations experts along with it.

The effect of these forces has been to create what Gene Collier, a former sportswriter for the *Pittsburgh Post-Gazette*, memorably called 'an impenetrable sense of entitlement' among the athletes, a sense of specialness that does nothing for whatever quotient of modesty they may have possessed in their natural state. It is unsurprising, since hardly a minute of the day goes by when someone does not wants a piece of them. So it is enormously refreshing when, every now and then, one of them turns out to be an unspoiled person with considered views on matters both within and beyond sport. And, conversely, how enormously depressing it can be to see so many young athletes reduced to an artificially restricted range of responses, devoid of truth or insight – a restriction nowhere more obvious than in England, for some reason.

In this job you see a lot of things that could make you cynical: young footballers who would rather stay in bed than meet Nelson Mandela, to offer but one recent example. Yet for all the damage inflicted by the excesses of the celebrity culture, the authentic thrill keeps coming back: the thing you might have glimpsed, long ago, in Neil Harvey's cover drive or John McEnroe's angled volley or Joe Montana's arm, now reappearing in different forms. Probably covered with logos and communicating only in press conferences, but the same in essence.

Some things have definitely changed. Motor racing, for instance, has seen much of its charm smothered by advanced technology at the same time as losing its ability to kill its participants on a regular basis: a fair exchange, no doubt. The power of today's tennis players has deprived the game of some, although by no means all, of its poetry. In other cases, however, these are indeed the good old days, or at least as good as the old days. To witness Zidane, Ronaldo, Raul and Luis Figo stroke the ball around in the white of Real Madrid is to see players who refuse to bow to the imperatives of modern football, with its restricted spaces and banal compromises. To watch Clive Woodward's England rugby team overcoming the southern hemisphere giants at home and away has been to see an old game touching new heights of organization and imagination. And sometimes greatness comes from a completely unexpected direction, as it did with the 2003 Boat Race, when the nation's annual game of Pooh sticks turned into a titanic battle of wills from beginning to end. How I wished I'd been there, instead of taking a day off and watching it on the television. There's a lesson never too late to be learnt: if you have the chance, just go.

Now it's the day after Wimbledon. Not a great tournament this year, by and large, although Roger Federer announced himself as an important talent. But there was definitely something to write about in the latest women's singles final between the Williams sisters, whose rise has been among the most compelling and inspiring phenomena of my time as a sportswriter. An injury to one of the sisters compromised the final both as a contest and a spectacle, which meant that there was even more to be said than usual, and not just by those who refuse to believe that a match between two siblings – make that two black siblings with a noisy father – can be anything other than a set-up.

Before the match I was pleased to note the presence in the royal box of Maria Bueno, who won the championship in 1959, 1960 and 1964, and who was the first woman tennis player to make an impact on me. Bueno comes back every year from her home in Brazil, drawn to a theatre in which she became an immortal. She is in her sixties now but still recognizably the gamine figure who scampered around this same lawn forty and more years ago, taking it out on the likes of Darlene Hard and Margaret Smith.

I find it hard to say which I found more moving: the struggle of Venus Williams to overcome an injury that destroyed her attempt to regain her title, or the simple fact of Bueno's presence, a reminder of the essential continuity of sport. And I feel very lucky that I don't have to make a choice.

Richard Williams
London, 2003

THE VIEW FROM THE HIGH BOARD

FU MINGXIA
Not Like Us

I T TAKES HALF an hour to climb out of the centre of Barcelona, up the hundreds of steps past the ornamental fountains and the baroque National Palace, through the dusty park with its face-painters and hair-plaiters, past the giant sculptured radio mast, the great Olympic stadium and the Joan Miró museum, to the Piscina de Montjuic. It's a breathless ascent, and when you get to the top you find that there are still forty-eight more steps to climb.

These are the four flights of wooden stairs, bordered by shiny steel handrails, which lead on to a blue-carpeted platform 10 feet long and 4 feet wide. It's like being in the starting hut of the Hahnenkamm or on the viewing platform of the Empire State: there's a sudden urge to close your eyes and hold on tight to something solid. And, if you can conquer the vertigo, there's a view that Fu Mingxia will never forget as long as she lives.

Did Fu take the chance to look out over the towers of Gaudi's Sagrada Familia to the distant hills and the sea? Maybe not. Maybe the only thing she saw, as she stood motionless above the city of

Barcelona, was a patch of bright blue water 33 feet below. Eight times she climbed those steps in her progress to the gold medal in the high-board diving final last week, and eight times we saw a tiny body spinning through the air, held against the sky as it twisted and turned, slicing first the air and then the surface of the water with an economy that seemed to leave the elements undisturbed.

Eight times she launched herself, and eight times she moved further ahead of her rivals, who waited behind her on the steps to the platform, lounging against the rails with a self-absorbed nonchalance, like a *tableau vivant* from a 1930s edition of *Vogue*.

An hour or so later, we were asking questions of the bronze medal winner, a feisty, all-American girl called Mary Ellen Clark, when an urchin in a white singlet and shorts squirmed through the crowd and found a seat on the small stage. There was a little buzz, and although we continued for a minute or two to address our questions to Ms Clark, both she and we knew that the focus had shifted, in more senses than one.

Fu Mingxia is 13 years old, 'almost 14'. Still glowing from her exertions, she looked less like an Olympic champion than a child who had just come in from playing on the neighbours' lawn.

Mary Ellen Clark had already been diving for seven years by the time Fu was born. But it was one of those days in sport, one of those days of maximum unfairness, when experience counts for nothing. Even the American's own coach, Ron O'Brien, had told us that watching Fu reminded him of nothing less than the effect Greg Louganis had on the sport in the early 1980s. 'He took it to another level, and so has she,' he said, and shook his head at the memory of 'that damn back three-and-a-half twister' with which she had paralyzed the opposition in the sixth round of the final. Along the platform, Mary Ellen's face seemed to be registering relief that this wasn't a problem she'd be facing for much longer.

Then it was Fu's turn. To begin with, there were questions about her training routine at the Beijing diving academy. Was it true that she did a lot of dry-land work, like standing somersaults, and also that she practises in the pool under unusual conditions, such as during rainstorms or with her fellow pupils shouting at her and banging dustbin lids, as a way of developing her powers of concentration? Yes, she said, her serious little face breaking into a child's smile: 'If you can dive in the middle of a storm, you can dive even better when the weather is fine.'

Fu went on to tell us, through an interpreter, that her chief ambitions were to work on her consistency, to increase the degree of difficulty of her dives and to learn to relax during competitions, and there were relieved sighs in the interview room when an American reporter cut through the mundane technical stuff and got to the serious business.

'Since a lot of young people around the world are going to want to know about you,' he said, drawing a deep breath, 'I'm going to ask you this: what are you going to do with your medal, what's your favourite food and what do you like to do when you're not diving?'

His colleagues, who knew that here was the real story, couldn't resist chuckling gratefully at the gentle self-parody. Fu, who can't have got the joke, said she hadn't had time to think about the medal, but she liked eating lots of ice-cream and she enjoyed music and maths and books. No one showed much interest in following up the mention of maths and books, but there was a lot of concern to get her to be more precise about the music. Did she mean she enjoyed Western pop music?

'I like listening to Niagara,' she said, via her interpreter. Much furrowing of brows. Niagara? Some new heavy-metal band unknown to the middle-aged press corps? 'And Madonna,' she added. The joy of her listeners was hilarious to behold.

In a week when the *Wall Street Journal* was running a major article about the dubious benefits of the complete and conclusive Americanization of global culture, here was a perfect example of its effects. The relief with which we greeted the news that a 13-year-old Chinese celebrity admires a Western pop star demonstrated the degree to which we are only really comfortable with foreigners who can show that they are exactly like us.

In some ways, the twenty-fifth Olympiad of the modern era is chiefly a celebration of how, over the last four years, the world has been made safe for the giant multinational corporations. Where Marx and Lenin once held sway, now the people's aspirations are defined by Nike and Panasonic. And here in Barcelona, the marriage of competition and commerce is being consummated.

Thus Coca-Cola can use its status as a main sponsor of the

Games to proclaim, mystifyingly, that it is 'sharing the Olympic ideal'. What sporting ideal, exactly, can a soft drink share? Thus, too, Mary Ellen Clark could tell us that she plans to spend her time after retirement from competition repaying her debt to the McDonald's Corporation, whose backing enabled her to pursue a full-time training regime in Fort Lauderdale, Florida, after her university studies had been rewarded with degrees in public health and physical education. She could not resist pointing out the contrast with her rival. 'We,' she said, meaning the athletes of the free world, 'have to work in order to be able to compete.'

But what is work? And how, now that the Eastern bloc has disappeared, and with it the conquering armies of Soviet and East German athletes, will the teams from the United States and their noisy, flag-waving supporters respond to the new reality of competition with a world that now shares its own value-system? How will they manage without the layer of ideological conflict that for so long provided a springboard for sporting aggression? The US is used to telling the world that the American Way is the better way, that the American Dream is the better dream. Better than whose, now that everyone is following the way and dreaming the dream?

The answer may be in the 4 feet 11 inches, 92-pound frame of Fu Mingxia. What the youngest winner of an Olympic gold medal since 1936 told us about her life came as a shock to the Western mind.

Where did her parents live, we asked. What do they do? How often does she see them? She comes from Hubei province, she replied, from the city of Wuhan. Her parents are workers. And she sees them twice a year, when she goes home from the diving academy. Sometimes, in their holidays, they make the journey to see her – a thousand kilometres, eighteen hours by railway.

'Workers?' We suspected an incomplete translation. 'What do they do?' Fu Mingxia looked serious for a moment, then smiled her child's smile and said she didn't know.

Here, if they want it, is the new opposition to America's imperial ambitions. Here is a nation of a billion people whose sports coaches, such as Yu Fen, sitting next to Fu Mingxia on the press conference platform, can take a child from her home at the age of eight and turn her into the most efficient diving machine ever seen.

*

Two days after Fu's triumph, Mark Lenzi faced the press at the Piscina de Montjuic with his gold medal hanging around his neck. A 24-year-old ball of muscle from Fredericksburg, Virginia, born on the Fourth of July, Lenzi had just won the men's springboard title for himself and for the US of A.

On the platform beside him were two people wearing vests embroidered with his name and with the stars and stripes. Bill and Ellie Lenzi, Mark's parents, were in the mood to celebrate and were delighted to give their own interviews to journalists who couldn't penetrate the mob surrounding the new champion.

Ellie, who was also wearing stars and stripes earrings, works in a restaurant; Bill is a supervisor at the local US Navy base. A classic blue-collar couple. Their boy had always been keen on sport: baseball, soccer, wrestling. In fact, he had won a college scholarship on the basis of his wrestling prowess until, inspired by Louganis's exploits, he gave it up to become a diver. His parents, with three other children to bring up, couldn't afford to send him to college without a scholarship, and weren't pleased by his decision. 'We had a falling out,' Bill Lenzi told me, 'and he lived away from home for a while.'

Eventually, though, they were reconciled, and the father began to drum up support for his son. 'I wrote to thirteen millionaires in Virginia, asking for sponsorship. Five or six of them replied but none of them came through. Now I'm hoping that this means he'll get some endorsements, to make his life easier.'

It was when he talked about his son's adolescence that the differences between the lives of the American boy and the Chinese girl were most starkly defined. 'We let him alone,' the American parent explained. 'We tried to give him what he wanted, we let him make his own decisions and we tried to be there when he needed us.'

Fu Mingxia was back in the pool every day after her high-board triumph, practising for tomorrow's springboard event. Turning the foot-wheel to adjust the board back to maximum flex after the heavier girls had been using it, she pulled off a series of perfect dives.

The other girls, with their muscled shoulders and thighs, seemed to use their own force to break the surface of the water. Fu just dropped, bending gravity to her will, entering the water like a fast and silent blade. It reminded me of something the defeated Mary Ellen Clark had said, shaking her head in admiration: 'She just doesn't miss a lot.'

That precision was the quality Yu Fen spotted when she watched the ten-year-old Fu at a gymnastics class in Wuhan. 'She stood out,' the coach said. 'When that happens, you rely on your intuition. I had a hunch about her.' Yu Fen's hunch took Fu away from her family and to Beijing. She has been there ever since, training in the morning and doing her academic lessons in the afternoon, preparing for the career that reached its first climax in Barcelona.

The world has changed, and will change again. These Games are not like any that most of us can remember. But although Beijing may now have the biggest McDonald's in the world, little Fu Mingxia is not exactly like us; not at all.

MY FATHER'S GAME

M Y EARLIEST MEMORIES of my father have nothing to do with his place of work, which was the fifteenth-century church on the other side of our rectory lawn, or even the vegetable garden, which was where he seemed to spend most of his time. Cricket is what I think about when I remember him as a young man. I think of him smoothing linseed oil into the blade of his bat and knocking the compressed mud and grass from the steel studs of his leather boots. I remember him putting on his flannels and his white shirt and sweater, and sometimes his college blazer, before walking down the hill, past the church on the left and a farm on the right, and turning into the lane that led to the cricket field.

The village was called North Wheatley, a place of old red-brick farms, orchards and strawberry fields in north Nottinghamshire. When we arrived I was two years old and my father was surprised to discover that there was no longer a cricket club for him to join. He had played at school and college in Wales, and when I was born he was playing regularly in the Yorkshire Council League. Within a short time of our arrival in the village, he had begun to explore the possibility of organizing a team.

According to the brittle, yellowing pages of the old minutes book, the reconstituted North Wheatley Cricket Club's earliest matches were played in 1949 on a meadow borrowed from a farmer, with a public footpath running across the pitch and, at one end, a patch of stinging nettles untouched on the farmer's strict orders where the slip cordon should have been. Soon the fledgling club moved to another borrowed field, this one unimpeded by pathways or nettles. Here, beside Low Pasture Lane, my father cut a proper square and dressed it with Nottinghamshire marl, the reddish mixture of clay and lime that deadened Trent Bridge pitches for a generation. He mixed the marl with fresh cow dung, which helped settle the track but also tended to engulf the players in a noxious miasma. Most of them, being country people, were unperturbed. This dressing eventually produced a wicket of impeccable docility until, after twenty or thirty overs, it started to break up, at which point things would get interesting.

A member of the newly formed committee was sent to the nearest town to buy, on the club's behalf, four bats, a set of stumps and bails, three pairs of batting gloves, two pair of pads, a pair of wicketkeeping gloves with inners, four balls and a scorebook: total cost £32 18s 10d. My father organized the purchase from British Railways of an old wooden passenger carriage, which was delivered to the ground for use as a pavilion at a cost, in his recollection, of no more than £20, including delivery. The club entered a local league and the team sheet was posted weekly in the window of the village shop. The following year my father took over as captain; two years later he assumed the chairmanship; before we left the village, in the summer of 1955, the team were winning trophies.

More than the cricket itself, I remember from that time the curious weight in a child's hands of the old, rough-edged rectangular metal plates with painted numbers that were propped against a trestle to indicate the score, and I remember, when things got dull, going fishing for tiddlers with a friend in the beck that ran alongside the ground.

Not long ago, wanting to know if cricket was still going on in North Wheatley, I talked to the secretary, who told me that the club was doing well. So well, in fact, that they now had a semi-professional overseas player, a New Zealander. This notion drew an incredulous chuckle from my father, who had coached local farmhands and blacksmiths in the game's most basic arts in order to get the original team together. The secretary told me that the current pavilion building, the eventual replacement for the railway carriage, was itself about to be replaced by a new clubhouse, pending the result of an application for national lottery funding. Most of the playing members, he added, now came from outside the village, but the current rector, the latest of my father's successors, was the 2nd XI scorer and his wife made the teas. The track was still basically well behaved, perhaps thanks to those early applications of marl and dung.

I grew up watching my father bowling his outswingers and off-cutters, moving the fielders around into the positions whose names he taught me, and batting with just a little bit too much bottom hand (my own principal flaw).

He played football for the village, too, and tennis at a club not far away. Only rugby, his main sport during his youth in Wales, was no longer available to him. At every ball game he played, including billiards, table tennis and golf, he showed a natural technical ability and a shrewd tactical brain. Of them all, however, it seemed that cricket was the closest to his heart, probably because it combined cunning of eye, hand and mind with a relationship to the elements: soil, air, degrees of moisture. A village parson's life is a relatively relaxed one, at least to the outside observer's eye, and I think he felt that the time spent getting the cricket club off the ground and fulfilling the various duties of captaincy and chairmanship were as much a part of his pastoral function as giving communion to the sick or counsel to the bereaved. And I would guess that he was absolutely right.

When I was eight, not long after we left North Wheatley, he taught me how to bowl a leg-break. Just about every day in the summer he took guard in front of a tree on the lawn of our new house and invited me to bowl at him from a distance of 18 yards. On his instructions I would make my approach round the wicket, bringing the well-worn full-sized ball out from behind my back in an attempt to produce a delivery that would pitch just outside the leg stump, draw him into a false stroke and zip across to remove his off bail, or at least take the outside shoulder of his bat for a potential catch by an imaginary wicketkeeper. Sometimes it worked, and I can still remember the feeling of pleasure. Sitting in a press box almost forty years later and watching Shane Warne dismiss Mike Gatting with a ball that would plausibly be described as the greatest ever bowled in Test cricket, I rather wished I hadn't decided, at the age of nine, that fast bowling was a better idea. My father had known what he was doing: whereas would-be speed merchants were ten a penny, leg-spinners were pearls beyond price.

Where he probably went wrong was in taking me to see Ray Lindwall playing for Richie Benaud's Australians one day in 1956, when I was nine. Far more than England's Frank Tyson, Brian Statham and Fred Trueman, Lindwall was a sight to sear young eyeballs. As, not many years later, was Wes Hall in his majesty, followed by the curly-haired, dark-browed John Snow, who also wrote poetry. So I started to take a longer run and to polish one side of the ball on my flannels and to practise the art of making a curled V with the forefinger and middle finger, fitting the ball into the crook so that the angle of the seam determined its behaviour in flight. Getting an outswinger right was the most satisfying result, depending not just on delivering the ball from the hand properly, with the seam angled as if both hands of a clock were stuck at five minutes to five, but on doing so with a proper body action: body fully sideways on, left arm flung high in the delivery stride, eyes looking over the left shoulder and firmly pinned on the batsman's off stump. Pitching it on a good length came naturally, as of habit, thanks to my father's tuition, and it was probably enough to compensate for the fact that I was not quite as quick as I dreamed of being.

If all this makes it sound as though I was obsessive about the game, that would be far from the truth. I looked out for my favourite players and played endless games of Owzat at school, but cricket occupied a place in my life no more prominent than football or motor racing or music. Quite a lot less prominent than music, actually. But I liked the fact that it was something I could do reasonably well without a fuss being made, and I suppose that being good at it was important, in the light of my father's enthusiasm and expertise.

But there was more to it that that. There was a personal feeling that had nothing much to do either with the game itself, in the sense of a contest between twenty-two men, or with doing something to please my father. What I think I really loved was marking out my run, turning and running in off fourteen paces, digging the ball in on a good length and beating the bat. I loved dropping into a rhythm and bowling long spells on a warm day without taking off my sleeveless sweater. The hotter I became, the more fluent and relaxed I felt. I loved turning at the end of the follow-through to see the marks of my boots on the grass going all the way back to the start of my run, darkening as the overs piled up and the grass bruised. I loved walking away to my fielding position at the end of an over and taking a breather while thinking about what I had just done and what I wanted to do next. I loved being the one with the responsibility for disrupting the static tableau vivant of a cricket field, starting my run-up in the knowledge that I would be setting batsmen, fielders, umpires and scorers in motion. And I hated being taken off.

Eventually I got to play in the same side as my father, when his diocesan team were a man short for a midweek match during the school holidays. It happened quite often. I wasn't called upon to do much more than field and bat at number eleven, but he'd given me good cricketing habits – stay alert, walk in with the bowler, aim your throw at a point six inches above the bails, always catch a dropping ball with your hands high, where you can see them – so I don't think I let him down, any more than his dog did. (A sweet-natured labrador, she would lie down just outside the boundary, waiting for the end of the innings or his dismissal; he often said that she knew when he was out before the umpire's finger had gone up. She would bring lost cricket balls and baby rabbits for his inspection with equal tenderness.) Later my father and I played occasionally for the same village side, and there was an occasion when, with thirty-five years separating us, we opened the bowling together. I suppose I thought that if I ever had a son, he and I would do the same thing.

*

And so it was that, well into adulthood, bowling a cricket ball was the thing that came most easily to me. Then one day, without warning, it stopped, taking a piece of me with it. And the day it stopped, my father was a spectator.

That had never been a frequent occurrence. I remember his quiet pleasure when he watched me take eight wickets for a handful of runs in a match at a friend's house when I was twelve or thirteen, against boys from much posher schools than mine. He wasn't there on the humid Saturday afternoon when I took five wickets cheaply in my first appearance for the school's 2nd XI at an away match, an idyllic day spoilt only when I was reported by the father of another boy (who had gone wicketless) for smoking behind the pavilion and snogging with my girlfriend on a grass bank in the shade of the geranium bushes while our batsmen were knocking off the runs. This was the culmination of a year of difficulties with authority, and on the following Monday morning, instead of hearing my bowling analysis intoned by the headmaster when he read the weekend's results at the end of assembly, I was expelled. A master was deputed to march me into off to collect my belongings and I was left at the back gate to wait for my father, who had been summoned by telephone. 'You fool,' he said as I got into the car.

But even after Miles Davis and Martha and the Vandellas had come along to claim an unhealthy slice of my attention, cricket kept its place in my life. Not long after I moved to London I started to play for a club in the Surrey suburbs, near where I lived. The first shock was that if you took five wickets, or, much less likely in my case, scored fifty runs, you were expected to buy a jug of beer. Where I had just come from it was the other way round: if you did well, the beer was bought for you. And league cricket was still a novelty in the south, to be viewed with considerable suspicion. I played there for five or six years, until life and work got in the way and I could no longer guarantee to be available for the whole of any particular Saturday.

I don't think my father ever came to watch me play in those days, not even when we opened a new clubhouse with a charity match and I got a chance to bowl at Denis Compton. By then my parents had moved down to Oxfordshire, not so far away, but I suppose in my father's view – if he thought about it in these terms at all, which I doubt – cricket was still something that you did as a matter of course, part of life's routine, and not something so remarkable that it required the attendance of family spectators. By the time he turned up, on the day cricket left me, I was playing occasional matches for a team of journalists: friendly matches, with nothing at stake except collective enjoyment and pride in individual performance. And, perhaps, a vague feeling that we were maintaining some sort of a link with an inherited culture.

It happened on a Saturday afternoon at an Oxford college ground, half an hour's drive from my parents' home. The match was less than an hour old, I was six or seven overs into my opening spell and I'd taken four wickets. It was a warm midsummer day and I was enjoying myself. Once I'd bagged a few wickets, my father's presence became an extra source of pleasure. But then, as I bowled the first delivery of a new over, it all went wrong.

The ball left my hand, but instead of curving away from the batsman before pitching on a good length, it rose almost vertically above my head. That was a bit of a shock. Although, on a hot day, a worn leather cricket ball can sometimes momentarily stick to your fingertips as you release it, this was very different. I was somebody who couldn't remember having bowled a wide in his life, but this was as wide as a wide could get. There were a couple of amused smiles as I picked the ball up and went back to my mark.

With the next delivery, I nearly shattered my own toecaps. Once again, after a perfectly normal approach to the wicket, the ball came out of my hand in a totally unexpected direction – and at almost exactly 180 degrees to the trajectory of its predecessor. All its momentum gone, it dribbled a few yards down the pitch and stopped well before reaching the batsman. I think the umpire called a no-ball. There were a couple more chuckles and a few strange looks. So I went back and tried again. Same sort of thing. And again and again. The batsmen affected not to notice anything amiss as concerned expressions replaced the smiles on the faces of the fielders. The captain asked me what was wrong. I don't know, I said. It must have looked ludicrous. Eventually I got through the over. The captain was considerate enough to give me another one, because he couldn't believe it either. But the same thing happened again, only worse. From a promising position for our team, the score had shifted strongly in favour of the opposition, and two overs of wides and no-balls from me had done it. Enough was enough.

My father was equally puzzled. He didn't say much, beyond suggesting that perhaps it had been caused by tiredness, but then he hadn't said much on the morning I got kicked out of school either. But this time I felt a much more profound sense of shame at the spectacle with which I had presented him. School had been my own affair. This, however, seemed like a betrayal of his gift to me.

I used to keep a note of my bowling figures, probably as some sort of reassurance. But that day I didn't even go and look at the scorebook. I was thinking too hard about what had gone wrong, trying to find a reason for it and working out what to do to make sure it never happened again.

In that respect, failure was total. I turned up for the following weekend's match hoping that it had been an aberration. Wrong again. The one over I was allowed, the first of the match, reproduced the phenomenon in all its particulars. I spent the rest of the match in a fog of misery and uselessness.

I went to the nets, where it became apparent that something had broken down. Even released from the pressure of a match, my line and length were completely awry. Whatever I tried, I couldn't get the act of bowling to feel right. It was as if my body were refusing to stretch a particular muscle that allowed me to bring my shoulders round and the right arm down on line of the off-stump. But nothing was actually hurting, except my pride. It could hardly have been a matter of age: my father had bowled into his late fifties. In the nets I concentrated as hard as I could, and every now and then I produced a delivery that mimicked the old characteristics. But mimicry is what it was. It didn't feel natural, it didn't feel good and it certainly didn't feel as though I could produce it on demand.

I found myself thinking, for the first time in my life, about what my hand was doing as it released the ball. I could feel the skin of my fingertips, the roughness of the ball, the stickiness of the sweat. But that only made it even worse. There was an extra decision to be made as the ball was released, where before nothing more than instinct and muscle memory had been needed. When ball and fingers parted company, there was something like a sudden flare of white light in my head: it was a moment during which I had no control over anything.

That was the end of me as a fast bowler. I didn't want to stop playing altogether, so I tried to recreate myself as a cricketer by bowling off-spin, as my father had done more frequently after reaching his fifties. Leg-spin was out, since it needed a degree of precision I had commanded at the age of eight but no longer possessed. Off-spin, however, with a conventional action, seemed to hold out the possibility of regaining some sort of control.

It did, to a degree, and I played as a spin bowler for a season. But the word to describe what I was doing was mediocre, and I hated everything about it. I missed the sweat and the rhythm and the darkening footmarks, and the feeling of getting a ball to climb past the batsman's shoulder or jag back through his guard and into his stumps. Taking a wicket with an off-break felt like cheating, somehow. I missed coming off the field feeling exhausted but happy, taking off my boots and padding around the pavilion in my stockinged feet and drinking a few cups of tea while our batsmen got padded up. I missed going to examine the scorebook and seeing my name at the top of the bowlers' list with a row of Ms and Ws, indicating maiden overs and wicket maidens, alongside it. I missed what I'd been doing for thirty years too badly to settle for a lesser alternative.

Trying to work out what it meant suddenly to become bad at something at which I had been at least reasonably competent, I tended towards the belief that the problem had some metaphysical basis. If it wasn't age, was it a result of my rather rackety life and perhaps even some sort of judgement on it? If I'd settled down properly, concentrated on doing the garden and the odd jobs around the house, perhaps I would still have been bowling a dozen brisk overs on a Saturday afternoon into my late fifties. On the other hand, there might have been some perfectly plausible physiological explanation, nothing to do with the mind at all.

They call it the yips, but personally I don't like giving it a name at all, since that conveys the assumption that those who experience similar symptoms necessarily share a diagnosis. What happened to me felt like my own problem and nobody else's. Maybe I should have looked harder for a cure, but there were other things to be getting on with and I concluded, somehow, that if I couldn't solve it for myself, then I would just have to live with it, or rather without it. Cricket was something you just did, as I had always done it. It wasn't something you took with you to the analyst's couch and tried to sort out.

So by the time I had a son of my own, I hadn't played a serious game of cricket for years. We didn't have the sort of garden, incorporating a suitable tree, that had been so important in my childhood. And work meant that I wasn't around all that much, anyway. My son's school was good at rugby and football but, to my sorrow, hopeless at coaching cricket. I took him to Lord's when he was too small to know what was going on, and I took him to the Oval to see Warne and McGrath, the Lindwall of a later generation, when it was too late to make any difference. He grew up without absorbing any of the stuff that had been rubbed into my grain long before I reached my teens.

All this makes me feel a bit of a failure, in quite a significant way. Like a lot of people of my age in England, I let a lot of elements of tradition slip through my fingers. Growing up in the 1960s, there were plenty of distractions. Our lives were being formed into new shapes by a completely different set of influences. It was a special time and I can't imagine a better one. But it certainly inflicted its share of collateral damage, and this was mine. I made no contribution. I failed to enable the next generation to participate in that continuous experience, or at least to give them the chance of making their own decision. So when I think about cricket, I don't think about the days when I took five, six, even eight wickets. I think about what I couldn't and didn't do.

But the village cricket club my father helped to start in Nottinghamshire is still there. In a recent survey of the county's cricket grounds, mostly a catalogue of closures over the last fifty years, a local cricket historian describes a visit to the ground on Low Pasture Lane. 'The whole is a credit to the village,' he reports.

DAVID DUVAL
The Right Spot

THERE WAS NO shortage of expressive figures and interesting characters stomping up and down the fairways and the leader board at Royal Lytham yesterday. There was Ian Woosnam, with his sideways look of suppressed rage, like a robin from whom a magpie has just snatched a worm. There was Alexander Cejka, who swam across a river to escape communism at the age of nine. There were men wearing their emotions as prominently as the logos of their equipment manufacturers, like Colin Montgomerie and Sergio Garcia. Men looking as if they have seen everything life has to offer, like Miguel-Angel Jiménez. Men greeting misfortune with a smile and a puff on a Cuban cigar, like Darren Clarke.

David Duval was not one of these men. His trademark is a pair of wraparound sunglasses, from behind which no glint of character or temperament is allowed to emerge. His back is straight, his swing is unfussy. His emotions are kept in some inner recess, where they cannot interfere with the business of hitting a golf ball. He is patient, laconic, stoic and self-effacing. And yesterday evening

David Duval became, with absolute justice, the winner of the Open championship.

It was his first major tournament victory in the eight years since he turned professional, and in most people's view it was long overdue. Not least, it provided some recompense for his ordeal last year at the hands of his friend Tiger Woods. The number one and number two in the world, they went head to head in the final round of the Open at St Andrews. Duval's two handicaps were an injured back and a deficit of six shots to a certified genius. On the front nine of the Old Course he bravely cut that margin in half. But bogeys at the 11th and 12th, followed by the nightmare of all nightmares in the Road Hole bunker, drove him down to sixth place and out of sight as Woods revelled in his coronation.

Yesterday it was the other guy's turn. And Duval won in the way champions do, the way Woods did last year, by starting quietly and turning up the pressure gradually, making the pars and taking the birdies as they came until, when he entered the finishing straight, there was no question about the verdict.

The difference was that he had to emerge from a pack. His first two rounds at Royal Lytham gave him scores of 69 and 73, for an aggregate of level par. At that point, Colin Montgomerie was seven shots ahead of him. 'I wasn't hitting the ball well in the first two days,' said Duval, 'but I was making every putt, and that kept me alive. In the last two rounds I started hitting the ball well and I was still making every putt. I played real well and I feel real good about that.'

Duval is what the Italians call a *figlio d'arte*, born to the calling. His father and uncle are golf professionals, and he spoke yesterday of how, in his childhood, he would switch the television on early in the morning to watch the Open championship, fascinated by how different it was from the game his father had taught him – 'all dust and grass flying, no lakes'.

As he clutched the claret jug yesterday, he told the crowd thronging the grandstands and the 18th fairway a charming story about his first visit to Britain, to play the Scottish Open in 1995. On the 12th hole he had to hit his second shot out of a gorse bush 170 yards from the pin. He got it out and a spectator shouted: 'Well played – what a wonderful golf shot.'

'That made me feel really good about golf over here,' he said. 'It seemed like the national sport.'

Born in Jacksonville, Florida, twenty-nine years ago, Duval's victory is the twenty-fifth by a US golfer in the fifty-six tournaments since the Open championship resumed at the end of World War II. Until yesterday, his own record was most remarkable for his win in the 1999 Players championship, which some regard as the fifth major. When he finished second in the US Masters in 1998 after leading by three strokes with three holes to play, and finished runner-up in the same tournament again this year to Woods, he seemed to reinforce the doubts often voiced by those who called him the nearly man of golf, a player unable to translate his period as the world's number one into the currency of the four titles by which golfing greatness is measured.

There is no doubt that his failure to capture a major weighed heavily on this quiet, uncharismatic, likeable man. Yesterday, however, he discovered the truth about golf. 'You know what? It's a silly old game,' he said. 'Today I was just trying to hit it solid and move it forward and then going to hit it again. It sounds stupid. But it's funny how much is made about it, because we're playing a game. I've made it a lot bigger than it is, too, at times. Maybe that's some of the reason I feel so good today. Maybe I finally realized that it's just a game.'

But being brought up in a world of golf also has its advantages. Earlier in the week, Duval took two almost identical putters – one was an eighth of an inch longer than the other – and swapped their shafts. Then he chose the one he liked better and bent it a little. 'I worked really hard on it,' he said, 'until finally I got it to where it was looking a little bit like I wanted it to.' He could have been a garage mechanic's son fiddling with a carburettor, or a fisherman's son tying a fly.

When they gave him the freshly inscribed claret jug, he looked for his own name and for that of Woods. 'I got to see where his name is,' he said, 'and I like the position of my name right below his. It looks like it's in the right spot.' Now, he said, with remarkable humility, he knew how the golfers of previous generations had felt, the ones who had beaten Jack Nicklaus and Tom Watson.

'They knew they'd beaten the best player,' he said. 'You can argue if he's the best player ever or the best player of his generation, whatever it may be. Time will tell that. You know, I beat them all this week and I played really good. It feels wonderful.'

As he walked up the 18th fairway, the crowd engulfed him like a tidal wave. When he emerged, he walked to his ball with only the most discreet raising of the right hand in acknowledgement of the traditional ovation. The sunglasses came off after he had sunk the final two-foot putt.

He was certainly smiling, but still there was only a single small wave of salute. No punching the air, no grimacing, no leap of triumph. Did the crowd expect more? Either somebody, long ago, taught this man how to behave in victory, or he possesses enormous reserves of natural dignity. What a treat it was to see.

THE ROBLEDOS
The Boys from Chile

THERE'S A PENNANT hanging on my wall, stained with age. It carries a picture of a dark-haired man in a white and black football shirt. 'Jorge Robledo', it says, and 'Colo Colo', which is the name of the biggest football club in Chile. That's where it came from, more than forty years ago, a gift to my grandfather from the dark-haired man.

I knew about the Robledo brothers before I was even old enough to kick a football. They were mythical creatures, half-English and half-Chilean, and I knew about them because they had gone to the South Yorkshire school where my grandfather was the headmaster. And, as seemed to be the way of my grandfather's pupils, they kept in touch.

So it was big news in the household when two of them, George and Ted, were transferred together from Barnsley, their local league club, to Newcastle United in 1949, and even bigger news when George, the elder of the two, starred in the 1951 FA Cup-winning team, laying on the first of Jackie Milburn's goals in the 2–0 victory over Blackpool. The following year he returned to Wembley to face Arsenal, this time with his brother Ted also in the team, and scored the only goal of the match to acquire his second Cup winner's medal and a lasting place among the legends of St James' Park. Newcastle's team sheets – and Barnsley's, too, come to that – have been full of foreign names in recent years, but in their time the Robledos, although they spoke with Yorkshire accents, represented an authentically exotic addition to English football in the post-war years.

George and Ted are long dead. George's medals are in the museum at St James' Park, donated by his widow, who lives in Chile. Ted's medal is in a London suburb, in the house of a third brother, Walter, who poured a cup of tea the other day and filled in some of the details of an extraordinary saga.

My grandfather had told me a few things about how their mother was not much more than a girl when she left Yorkshire to work in South America, and how she had returned by herself with three small sons to bring up. He told me about George and Ted, and also about Walter, the youngest – who might, he said, have become the best footballer of the lot had he not suffered from poor eyesight in an age before the invention of lightweight contact lenses.

Today, Walter dismisses that notion. He didn't care so much for football, he says. Yes, he played it, wearing glasses. 'But when people used to say, "It runs in the family," that put me off.' There is a powerful impression that, irrespective of his feelings for the game, he wanted to make his own independent mark on the world. Which he was to do with a resolve surely inherited from his remarkable mother.

Elsie Oliver was 18 years old when she left her home in West Melton, a village in the south Yorkshire coalfields, soon after World War I, and travelled to Argentina to take up a position as the governess to the children of an English mine manager. When the family were transferred to Iquique, in the north of Chile, she went with them. There she met and married Aristides Robledo, the mining company's chief accountant, and within a few years she had produced three sons, starting with George, born in 1926, and Edward, who arrived two years later.

Her third child had just been born when she decided to return home. It was 1932, so perhaps her decision was influenced by economic difficulties induced by the effect of the worldwide recession on the mining industry and by Chile's political instability. But perhaps, although she never said so, it was something to do with the state of the marriage. At any rate, Aristides stayed behind, never to see his wife or two of his sons again.

George was five, Ted was three and Walter was six weeks old when they and their mother arrived in Liverpool on the *Reina del Pacifico*, a liner of the Pacific Steam Navigation Company, en route to West Melton. Elsie's parents were both dead by the time she returned, and she took over a shop from which an uncle had sold hardware and timber, turning it into a general store. She brought up the boys with the help of relatives, and when they were too old for the village school she sent them to the George Ellis Senior School at Brampton, where my grandfather, Harold Steer, was the headmaster, and my mother taught English.

Prowess at ball games soon marked George out, along with a fond interest in my mother's younger sister, Elisabeth. In 1938–39 the school team won six championships, thanks largely to his goals. When they posed for the team photograph, with their two football masters, Maurice Field and Fred Kay, and their trophies, my grandfather took his place behind them.

George played a few games for Barnsley and Huddersfield Town as an amateur during the war, and signed professional forms at Oakwell in 1943, when he was 16. Angus Seed, Barnsley's long-serving manager, had spotted his talent. 'Angus was a good manager and he knew players,' says Johnny Steele, an inside-forward in that side. 'He saw George's potential.' On the opening day of the first post-war season, in his league debut, George scored all the goals in a 3–0 defeat of Nottingham Forest.

According to Steele, George was not a natural footballer. But, at just under 5 feet 11 inches, he had a good strong physique, and he was willing to work hard to turn himself into an effective player. 'There wasn't a lot of fancy stuff in his play, but he was good in the air and he was an effective finisher. He was a natural sportsman and he worked hard to become a good player. He was a great fellow, a hell of a nice person.'

Ted followed George to Oakwell in 1947. An inch or two shorter, he played right-half. 'Another good strong player, no mug,' Steele says. But Ted lacked George's outgoing character. 'You could tell Ted lacked a father. He used to follow me round and wait outside the ground for me. Sometimes I couldn't get rid of the boy. I felt like a father to him. But fortune didn't smile on them, did it?'

For a while it certainly did. George had scored 47 goals in 114 Second Division and FA Cup appearances for Barnsley when, in January 1949, an approach came from Newcastle United, the giants of the North East. They wanted George and were willing to pay £26,500 to get him. But George insisted that they should also take Ted, who had made only five appearances for the Yorkshire club, and Newcastle agreed.

'George was the one who insisted that the two of them should stick together,' Walter remembers. 'Ted went along with it because he was the easy-going type, but really he didn't care.' In fact, Newcastle got the whole Robledo family. Elsie went, too, and took Walter, finding him a local school at which to complete his studies. The four of them took up residence in a house rented by the club.

George went straight into the side and quickly established a mutually fruitful partnership with the great Milburn, who wore the No. 9 shirt. George's team-mates christened him 'Pancho', and at the end of his first full season at St James' Park his origins were recognized by a call to join Chile's national team in Brazil for the 1950 World Cup. He played in all three Group Two matches, losing 2–0 in the Maracanà to the England of Wright, Finney and Mannion, and going down by a similar score to Spain. So Chile were already out of the competition when they beat the United States – England's conquerors – by 5–2 in Recife, with George opening the scoring.

George was now a hero in Chile, and it seems to have been during one of his visits that he had his sole encounter with his father, the only one of the brothers to do so. In the lives of Ted and Walter, Aristides was never much more than an old wedding photograph.

Besides news of that meeting, George also brought back from South America a pair of the new low-cut rubber-studded boots, but failed to persuade his English team-mates to give up their traditional heavyweight footwear, which they wore at Wembley in 1951 and 1952.

By the time of the second Wembley final, Ted had joined his brother in the team. George hit thirty-three goals that season, to Milburn's twenty-eight, including two in a famous 3–0 demolition of Arthur Rowe's Spurs, the reigning champions, at White Hart Lane in the fourth round of the Cup. The final itself was a less splendiferous affair, since Arsenal, captained by Joe Mercer, were forced to play for more than an hour with ten men after the loss of the injured Wally Barnes, their right-back, and both sides were affected by the imbalance. 'You're a set of babies,' Joe Harvey, the Newcastle skipper, told his team at half-time. 'You're feeling sorry for Mercer's lot. You'll feel even sorrier for yourselves if I don't get that cup.' Five minutes from time, George ran on to Bobby Mitchell's left-wing cross and headed the winning goal in off the post.

There had been repeated inquiries from Chilean clubs, and at the end of the 1953 season George and Ted set sail, again accompanied by Elsie and Walter, for Chile, to join Colo Colo of Santiago, five times national champions. 'They were offered much more money than they'd been getting under the maximum wage at Newcastle,' Walter says. 'Our fares were paid, we were given a very nice club house and there were good bonuses.' Aristides had died shortly before their return.

George and Ted won two league titles during their five years with Colo Colo, and both of them regularly represented Chile. They appeared together in the side beaten 1–0 by Argentina in the final of the 1955 South American Cup in front of 65,000 people in Santiago's Estadio Nacional. In the records of Chilean football they are listed as 'Jorge' and 'Eduardo', leading to the assumption that their names were anglicized after their arrival in Yorkshire. Not so, Walter says. They were indeed baptized in Chile, but by a Presbyterian minister who recorded their names as George Oliver Robledo and Edward Oliver Robledo.

Although both men finished with Colo Colo at the end of the 1957 season, they went on to pursue separate destinies. George played a season for the O'Higgins club in Rancagua before taking a job coaching the football team of a US-owned copper mining corporation. Later he moved with his Chilean wife, Gladys, and their daughter, Elisabeth, to the resort of Viña del Mar, near Valparaiso, where he worked as a sports master at an English school, St George's College, while becoming a director of both Colo Colo and O'Higgins. When Chile hosted the World Cup in 1962, he was a member of the organizing committee and acted as a liaison officer with the England squad.

Easy-going Ted, who had married a well-known Chilean dancer, decided to give English football another try, but two matches for Notts County in the autumn of 1957 represented the sum of his attempt. 'Ted played in a less glamorous position and he was not a self-publicist,' Walter says. 'He was tough and a hard worker, and his passing was good. A good team man, reliable and accurate. But George was the one who scored the goals.' Ted returned to Chile, but his marriage was failing and he began working on oil rigs, eventually finding his way to the Persian Gulf.

Walter had struck out on his own, leaving Chile for the US when his education was over. A job with a mining company in Montana had led to a posting back to Chile, and he prospered. When he wrote to my grandmother on hearing of his old headmaster's death in 1972, it was from a fine London address, in Holland Park.

By that time, however, tragedy had struck his own family. One night in 1970, a few days after returning to the Gulf from a visit to England, Ted went missing from a ship, the *Al Sahn*, sailing out of Dubai. There was said to have been a fight with the ship's captain, although no one who knew him believed that the introspective Ted could have provoked such a confrontation. The captain was charged with murder but acquitted. Walter went twice to the Gulf to look for the truth, but his brother's body was never found and the circumstances of the death remain unresolved.

The formidable Elsie, who had returned to England, died in the mid-1970s. George, so disturbed by Ted's fate that he could not bring himself to join Walter's investigation, died of a heart attack at home in Viña del Mar in 1989, aged 63. He was full of honours, if not of years, in the country of his birth, and large crowds attended his funeral in Santiago.

At the end of our conversation I asked Walter about my grandfather, to whose Yorkshire home George Robledo proudly sent that pennant almost half a century ago. 'He taught us that we were English and what it meant,' the youngest of the Robledo brothers said. 'He taught us discipline and fair play. All the things that were important.'

ERIC CANTONA
A Man of Two Halves

APRIL 1994

'THERE ARE JUST two Eric Cantonas,' Michel Platini said. '*L'un qui existe et l'un qui s'exprime* – the man himself and the man who talks. Do you see what I mean?'

Platini, the greatest French footballer of all time, was trying to explain the character of a man whose career he has salvaged twice and whose complex temperament he can probably claim to understand better than most. For when Eric Cantona arrived in England two years ago, no one had seen anything like him – either of him, in Platini's definition. The man himself had become established in France as the most charismatic footballer of his generation. But the man who talks had a reputation for being unable to avoid trouble, and had walked out on French football with the words of a disciplinary tribunal hanging in the air: 'You can't be judged like any other player. Behind you there is a trail of the smell of sulphur.' When he signed with Leeds United in January 1992, speaking barely a word of English, nobody was seriously expecting him to stick around.

Two years later, he is still here. Last week, moreover, he became the first non-British winner of the Professional Footballers' Association's player of the year award. But the other Cantona was also on view – as the first man to win the award while banned from playing the game. While his Manchester United team-mates challenged for the honours in the season's climactic games, Cantona was sitting out a suspension for violent conduct on the pitch. The whiff of sulphur had arrived at last.

The ambiguity of his temperament is one of the reasons why he became a folk hero almost as soon as he set foot on an English pitch. Tall, haughty and private in manner, he seemed to abide by none of the usual rules of domestic football culture. He was interested in poetry and philosophy, he painted colourful abstracts in an expressionist style, he listened to the music of anarchist troubadours. He admired Nicolas de Staël, Arthur Rimbaud, Jim Morrison, Mickey Rourke and Isabelle Adjani. In his spare time he went back home to Provence to shoot birds in the hills or accepted an invitation to model clothes for Paco Rabanne in Paris. His wife, Isabelle, took a job teaching French at Leeds University, and neither she nor their small son, Raphaël, was exposed to public view. These things added to the impression, already created by his ferocious gaze and his disdainful response to the criticism of referees, that he lived by the old maxim: never apologise, never explain.

But the fans took to him as they had taken to no other footballer since Gazza, and to none before that since Best. They loved Cantona's imperious posture – head up, back ramrod-straight and feet splayed at ten to two, like a ballet dancer. They loved his stealth and his incessant use of the backheel – a risky device, frowned on by most English coaches, but one that can alter the whole pattern of play in an instant. They loved his spectacular goals. They even loved the way he wore the collar of his number 7 football shirt turned up. And his team-mates loved the unselfish way he would seek them out with a pass like a sudden dagger-thrust. They were impressed, too, by his habit of staying behind after training to hone his skills still further.

What both fans and team-mates liked best, however, was the success he brought. Within four months of his Leeds debut, the club had won the championship for the first time since 1974. But only weeks after the start of the next season, amid rumours of dressing room conflicts, he was being hurriedly sold across the Pennines – to Manchester United, Leeds' bitterest rivals. Six months later his new club had won the championship for the first time since 1967. Most people thought that Cantona had made the difference.

On the terraces at Leeds, a chant had begun soon after his arrival. In time it transferred itself to Old Trafford and thence to the playgrounds of Britain, where it now accompanies a children's game: 'Ooh-ahh Cantona, ran away with the teacher's bra ...'.

It was Platini who persuaded him that the future might lie in England. But what had convinced Platini that this subtle Gallic temperament might find a congenial environment among the rosbifs and their crash-bang football? 'It's a country where you play football and don't talk too much,' Platini replied. 'If you want, you can go to the pub after the match and be quiet. In England your life is your life.' In other words, a place where not being able to talk – at least, with anything but your feet – might be a real advantage.

Cantona can certainly express himself in words. 'I dream of lightness, harmony and pleasure,' he writes in his autobiography, describing his philosophy of the game. 'The music of football today is nothing but heavy metal.' But during his career in France, his eloquence was the problem. It had started in 1988, soon after his first big-money move, a £2 million transfer to the star-studded Olympique Marseille club, itself an expensive vehicle for the political ambitions of the media magnate Bernard Tapie.

After scoring goals in both his first two games, Cantona was left out of the French national squad by a manager who said that he was 'in poor form'. He responded by telling a national television audience that the manager was 'practically a shitbag'. This was rewarded with a one-year ban from international selection, rescinded only when the manager in question, Henri Michel, was sacked and Platini appointed in his stead.

Platini, who had not really known Cantona before then, found that he had unexpected qualities. 'As a man, he's honest and open,' he said last week. 'Frankness is very important to him. He doesn't like false values. He judges a man according to his honesty. For him, football really is a game – *de joie, de fête.*'

But the Platini-inspired rehabilitation didn't put an end to the difficulties. One night in 1989 Cantona threw his Marseille shirt to the ground during a charity match, provoking a ticking-off from Tapie: 'This doesn't match up with my idea of football in general and of football at Olympique Marseille in particular,' the president said, suspending him from the team. Later in 1989, after Tapie had sold him to the less glamorous Montpellier, there was a post-match row in the dressing room, during which Cantona threw his boots at the face of a team-mate who had criticized his efforts.

The climax to this crescendo of abrasive behaviour came on 15 May 1990 when, back at Marseille once more, he responded to an unfavourable refereeing decision by hurling the ball at the official. He made a sort of apology to the disciplinary committee, was suspended for a month, responded by telling each member of the committee to his face that they were idiots, and had his sentence doubled.

At that moment he decided to hang up his boots. By his own account, he spent weeks walking the beaches of the Camargue. He read, he painted, he listened to the music of Léo Ferré and William Sheller, he played with his son, and he thought about the future.

'But I missed everything,' he concluded eventually. 'The smells and the ambience of the dressing room, the feeling of belonging to a group, of winning together. And then Michel Platini came to speak to me. He understood everything. He knew that I had to get away.'

At Old Trafford, Cantona has been playing to an adoring audience in a ground once described as 'the theatre of dreams'. Cosseted by an indulgent management, the man whose career had taken him to Auxerre, Marseille (twice), Martigues, Bordeaux, Montpellier, Nîmes and Leeds – seven clubs in seven years – seemed to have found his platform at last. But suddenly, towards the end of last year, the other Cantona took the stage.

In November he insulted the referee when Manchester United were eliminated from the European Cup in Istanbul, and was struck by a Turkish policeman's baton as he left the pitch. In December he kicked a Norwich City defender in response to a foul and in

January, retaliating to another foul, he put his heel into the face of a second Norwich defender – going unpunished for both offences. Last month, however, he was sent off twice in four days – first for stamping on the chest of a Swindon Town defender who had tried to hold him back, and then for a couple of much less serious offences against Arsenal players.

The Swindon incident, for which he received a three-match suspension, was generally held to be indefensible, but the feeling inside football was that he was unlucky at Arsenal. The rules nevertheless decreed that his suspension was extended to five matches – which meant that whereas in the previous season his presence had brought serenity to a tense, neurotic team, enabling them to complete their championship bid, now he had become a symbol of a side showing signs of unease under the pressure of retaining their title.

The old headlines were dusted off – 'Eric le Terrible', 'Crazy Cantona' – and the speculation began over whether these incidents would be enough to drive him out of English football. In Paris the daily sports paper *L'Equipe* ran a page under the banner: '*L'Angleterre contre Cantona*'.

For once, Cantona kept his thoughts to himself. In his autobiography, however, he records his own reaction to such outbursts. 'In reality,' he says, reflecting on the time he threw the ball at the ref, 'that gesture was a natural part of my personality. I take responsibility for it. There are perhaps more beautiful or more ugly personalities. You need a particular talent only to want to please. I don't have this talent …'.

Honesty and pride are the words you hear most often in conversation with French football people who know Cantona well. 'He's a wholehearted man,' said Alain Migliaccio, his former agent. 'Someone who's open, loyal, sensitive. A generous man, and an impulsive one, who won't put up with injustice. If you're open and loyal with him, he's open and loyal with you. If you're dishonest with him, he's … well, not dishonest, but *méchant* … no, not *méchant* … aggressive with you. He wouldn't know how to be dishonest.'

'He's not like others,' said Gérard Houllier, a close friend of Cantona, who succeeded Platini as the national manager and is now the technical director of the French football federation. 'That's probably what I found attractive in his temperament. If I wanted to define him, I'd say that he's an island of freedom, generosity and pride. He's mentally very strong, very solid. He dares to say things that sometimes people don't care to say.'

It seems clear that there are two Eric Cantonas in senses other than the one Platini intended. There are the English Cantona and the French Cantona, for instance. The English version is 'very private', according to Gary McAllister, a former Leeds team-mate. 'Really quiet,' added Kevin Sharp, another Leeds player, 'not saying a lot, always on his own, reading a book or staring out of the window.'

Sharp, a 19-year-old, himself spent a year at Auxerre, one of Cantona's former clubs, which meant that he was one of the few Leeds players able to hold a real conversation with the Frenchman. As for the French Cantona, Sharp heard about him from his Auxerre team-mates: 'He was talked about as a very dominating character, on and off the field.'

Gérard Houllier also describes a more outgoing Cantona who, on trips with the French team, 'talks with his room-mate, or goes from room to room, plays cards, listens to music … he's not just hidden away in his corner. And he was very helpful with the younger players who had just come into the team. The image is of an individualist, but that comes from those who don't take the trouble to know him accurately. He's totally the opposite of that, believe me.' This, clearly, is the Cantona whom Aimé Jacquet, the new French manager, has made captain of the national team.

Even Cantona himself sometimes sees a second Eric, whenever he watches *Les Guignols de l'Info*, France's nightly version of *Spitting Image*, in which his puppet-caricature is called 'Picasso' and spends its time spouting pseudo-philosophical nonsense. 'It's amusing,' he writes. 'But what I find strange is the new and distorted picture it can give of someone in public life. Picasso can leave the stage exasperated and use words like "whore" and "fuck" … Picasso can paint a red card and show it to himself … On this show, a gesture or words previously considered reprehensible or unreal suddenly become funny, comical, and in some strange way accepted by public opinion as how I really am.'

The second of Albert Cantona's three sons, Eric Cantona was born twenty-seven years ago in Caillols, just outside Marseille. Half-Sardinian and half-Spanish, he grew up in the foothills of the Massif de la Sainte Baume. The family's house had once been simply a mountain cave, briefly used by the occupying Nazis as a lookout post. But in 1955 Cantona's paternal grandfather arrived from Sardinia with his wife and occupied the cave, using his mason's skills to build a house above and around it as the years passed. His other grandfather was a Spanish Republican Army officer who had fought against Franco and fled, also with his wife, to exile in France, where he was interned by the Vichy government before settling after the war in Marseille.

The young Eric lived the enchanted life of a Provençal country boy. His father, an amateur goalkeeper, taught his sons to play football and took them out shooting lark, thrush and woodcock. 'Nature intoxicated him,' Eric was to write. 'Our pleasure came from the colours of dawn, the smell of the wood and the soil, and the soothing sounds of nature.' Albert Cantona was also a keen painter, with a studio in the house, and he shared his interest with his second son, who grew up an admirer of Munch, de Sta'l and the Fauves. Like most Provençal artists, of whatever status, Eric Cantona has a special fondness for the dramatic interplay of colour in his canvases, which he sometimes donates to charity auctions.

Eric was still in primary school when he joined the football club of Caillols, a celebrated nursery for young players. 'It was obvious from the start that Eric was something special,' Yves Cicculo, the club president, said last week. 'He had all the qualities of a player. At nine he was playing like a 15-year-old. When he was with us, we won lots of tournaments – and I can honestly say that he alone made the difference.'

What was the nine-year-old Cantona like?

'Exactly as he is today. Hot-headed but a genius. He's always been his own man.'

Did he get into trouble in those days?

'I have to admit that he was a little difficult occasionally. He knew he was better than anyone else. And there were sometimes difficulties with the other lads. It wasn't serious. It was all in the cause of his football. And the Eric Cantona that I see on the television today, *c'est bien lui*. He hasn't changed.'

At 14 he came under the wing of Guy Roux, the manager of Auxerre, a French first division club with which he signed as a junior and then as a full professional. 'I remember we had a meal with his mother and grandmother when he joined us,' Roux said last week. 'And I told them, he will play for France. He was like a matchstick, but he had class and he saw the game very clearly. He was always trying things. When they came off, it was magnificent – but often it didn't and he gave the ball away. That was his principal fault. We had to teach him more discipline. He was mischievous, sometimes difficult, but children at that age are. There was nothing we couldn't deal with.'

In his instinctive reaction to adversity, Cantona continues to show a quality that some might call childish, although others might justify it on the grounds that his offences are committed in response to the foul deeds of others – and if Eric Cantona earnt his living as a painter, for instance, how would he be expected to react if another artist kept coming up and smearing a rag across his canvas?

'He knows when he's done wrong,' Gérard Houllier said. 'He doesn't try to escape that. He doesn't try to find false reasons.' Patrick Battiston, the former international fullback who manages Bordeaux, described Cantona to me as *très fair-play*, a man who only commits fouls when provoked.

An English view is a bit blunter. 'He's always had a mad head on him,' said Kevin Sharp, whose experience in Auxerre has given him an insight into the cultural differences that might have played a part in the Frenchman's troubles. 'There's always been the odd dirty tackle,' Sharp observed. 'He can be a bit sly – you'd never get someone from England doing some of the things he does. That annoys some players.'

Perhaps the key to Cantona's behaviour is something he said last year: 'When times are difficult, I tell myself, "I'm just passing through."' It's the sort of existentialist attitude that can get him out of trouble, to his own satisfaction if no one else's, and it finds an echo in his reaction to charges that he sets a bad example to his young fans: 'My reply is that I think one should stop treating the heart and soul of youngsters as clay to be modelled in whatever fashion you like. I'm not there to educate anyone. I don't see that as my role. They should be able to work things out for themselves. Children go where they find sincerity and authenticity. In my way of working, of carrying out my career, I don't betray anyone and they know it. I don't consider that it would be better to teach them to deny their own emotions for the benefit of the established order. Is it through teaching people to be submissive that they become adult citizens?'

He is not the only rebellious French genius making a success of exile in England. At Covent Garden, the ballerina Sylvie Guillem has been the principal guest artist since she flounced out of the Paris Opera Ballet after a row with the management. Tall, haughty and private in manner, Guillem spends little time with her Royal Ballet colleagues. She turns up for her five hours' rehearsal a day, performs at night and disappears in her black Issey Miyake overcoat and her high Doc Marten boots to be with her boyfriend, a French photographer.

Her rare interviews always contain suggestions of a careful disengagement from the processes of fame, a disinclination to play the usual publicity games or to accept the customary responsibilities of celebrity. When she arrived in London and launched a series of blazing rows with choreographers and costume designers, nobody seriously thought she was in it for the long haul. But six years later she's still here, still glaring and stamping her foot and doing things that make her audiences gasp with rapture. If we can hang on to 'Mademoiselle Non', as she is known to the headline writers, maybe we can also keep 'Le Brat' – which is what the tabloids christened Cantona.

It will take more than money, although he can't be too unhappy with the £6,000 or so that he receives each week from Manchester United. 'Money has not changed my life,' he said, 'and it will never change it. You may find it odd that I should think that happiness does not come from being able to buy a car that one wants or in having money in a bank account. I don't. It's all a matter of upbringing. My brothers and I were never given many presents. My parents weren't rich enough to rush off to the shops, but it was also a matter of choice on their part.' His wife, he adds, 'has always preferred books to sports cars'.

The Cantonas appear to have other imperatives. Eric, Isabelle and five-year-old Raphaël live in Leeds' Roundhay Park, in the unprepossessing semi rented for them when they arrived in England two years ago. 'The house and the district are definitely not plush or exclusive,' Cantona writes, 'making the atmosphere very pleasing to me. Many of our neighbours are Pakistanis or West Indians, as well as English. They are straightforward, friendly and generous. I prefer by far our little English house with its wild piece of garden to those vast Victorian houses among which I'm sure I would soon get fed up.'

'Fed up' is a phrase that tends to recur in Cantona's discourse, usually followed by 'moving on'. 'I'm someone who'll always move on,' he told *L'Equipe*, 'even though it may be later rather than sooner. I've learnt to live day by day. And I'm naturally a curious person. Every day I need to find something new, even simple things. It's this permanent state of curiosity that enables me to progress.'

A year ago he said that if Manchester United won the championship and France reached the World Cup finals, he would retire at the end of 1994. The first part came gloriously true, but a couple of shock defeats cost France their place in America this summer. So he may want to try again in 1998 – when the World Cup will be held in France. He has also muttered something about wanting to finish his career in Prague ('An interesting city,' Michel Platini says with an affectionate laugh, 'but I don't think he can make much money there').

'This isn't 1950,' English football's principal guest artist once said. 'You don't have to spend twenty years with the same club.' But he likes England: 'the strong bond that exists between a football club and the public, the weight of tradition. Football here is alive, and people make you really feel it. I thought England could make me more effective, more pragmatic. From that point of view, I've not been disappointed.'

JANUARY 1995

YOU DIDN'T HAVE to look very long and hard at Mr Matthew Simmons of Thornton Heath to conclude that Eric Cantona's only mistake was to stop hitting him. The more we discovered about Mr Simmons, the more Cantona's assault looked like the instinctive expression of a flawless moral judgement.

No, I'm sorry, I'll start that again. After all, this is still supposed to be a civilized society, in which the first duty of a sporting hero is to provide an example for children. And Mr Simmons, 20 years old, a double-glazing fitter with an alleged history of neo-Nazi sympathies and a conviction for attempted robbery with violence, was merely exercising the inalienable right of the English football fan as he played his historic role in the last temptation of Eric Cantona.

That right, as it has been described to me on several occasions this week, involves the ritual humiliation of opposition players. Acquiring the ability to ignore such systematic abuse is one of the tests of character faced by those who wish to play professional football in England. It is a test that Eric Cantona has clearly failed.

A year earlier his friend Gérard Houllier had defined him to me as 'an island of freedom, generosity and pride.' But Cantona's insularity was breached last Wednesday night by a set of circumstances that the fates were always going to arrange for him one day. Now he has become not merely a martyr to his own myth, but also a scapegoat for one of the ills that still afflict English football.

At Selhurst Park, Cantona had been complaining throughout the match about the challenges from Crystal Palace's defenders. Nothing new there. Attackers create, defenders destroy. With respect to such obvious exceptions as Bobby Moore, Franz Beckenbauer and Gaetano Scirea, if defenders were better footballers, they'd be playing in another position. In order to keep things relatively even, the game is so arranged that the destroyers get away with persistent illegality while the attackers are supposed to cultivate a saintly forbearance. But in Cantona's case, if he is a genius, he is certainly not a misunderstood one: throughout the Premiership, defenders understand all too well how to get at him through his fatal weakness.

At 8.57 p.m. on Wednesday, three minutes into the second half of a scrappy game, Cantona was tackled from behind by his marker, Richard Shaw. The linesman flagged; the referee did nothing. A minute later the infuriated Cantona aimed a sly retaliatory kick at

Shaw. It's something he's done many times before in similar circumstances, and it marks him out from the general run of British professionals. This time the referee paid attention and Cantona was heading for the early bath.

According to the view of those who defend the manners of English football crowds, Matthew Simmons was guilty of nothing more than getting full value for his £300 season ticket when he rushed down to the touchline from his seat in the eleventh row of the main stand at Selhurst Park to tell Cantona that he was 'a French bastard' who should 'fuck off back to France'. (Or something to that effect: for 'bastard', according to some reports, substitute 'wanker'.) The speaker himself couldn't remember his exact words: 'I might have sworn at him – I'm not sure,' he told the *Sun*, which had bought the rights to his side of the story. 'But whatever I said, it never gave him any excuse to do what he did. Cantona was the lunatic, not me.'

Hearing the words in question, and seeing their author gesticulating obscenely at him, Cantona misunderstood the conventions of English football, failed to turn the other cheek and thus broke the understanding that such displays are, in the apologists' usual terminology, 'part and parcel' of the game.

Since the success of the long campaign to curtail hooliganism at English football grounds, the noisy dishonouring of opponents seems to be the lout's last liberty. In my view, the ugliest sound in the English game is the shrill hiss of derision that nowadays routinely greets a missed shot at goal by a player of the visiting team. It isn't funny or charming, or even traditional. It's the distilled essence of hatred and a reminder that the existence of all-seater grandstands with decent lavatories doesn't guarantee a mass conversion to the higher emotions. Perhaps that should be the next object of the campaign to improve football culture, and perhaps *l'affaire* Cantona might be its catalyst.

It is not an impossible task. Human beings are not irreversibly programmed to display rancour towards their opponents at football matches. The European Cup finals of 1992, at Wembley, and 1994, in Athens, were the most enjoyable football nights I can remember, for the ambience created by the supporters. The stakes could hardly have been higher, yet the fans of Barcelona (on both occasions), Sampdoria and Milan found a way of supporting their teams, of accepting defeat or victory, without needing to experience any emotion darker than disappointment. The expression of hatred is no more intrinsic to an exciting football match than the crumbling terrace or the disgusting beefburger. In this connection, Crystal Palace's action in banning Matthew Simmons for the remainder of the season is a thoroughly appropriate response.

At the moment, however, Simmons is still ahead of the game. Cantona, suspended by his club until the end of the season, has been fined an undisclosed sum, said to be the maximum amount permitted under the terms of his contract. Manchester United's value as a publicly quoted company fell in the forty-eight hours after the Crystal Palace game from £79.6 million to £77.2m. At a special incident room at Addington police station in south London, several policemen and women are devoting their full-time attention to the task of interviewing witnesses to the incident. And Mr Simmons is better off to the tune of whatever Rupert Murdoch's people have paid him, which could be £500 or £5,000 or £50,000 (on Friday the editor of the *Sun* declined my invitation to confirm the nature of their agreement or to disclose the amount of any fee he may have paid).

Such is the nature of our society, a society from which Cantona, of course, has taken a share of the profits in a way that makes it even harder to mount a plausible defence of his conduct. For his part in the notorious Nike advertising campaign, he has been paid several hundred thousand pounds to go with his £500,000 salary.

When I saw the cinema advertisement last September, I thought he should have been charged there and then with bringing the game into disrepute. 'I have been punished for striking a goalkeeper,' he said to the camera, in modishly grainy monochrome. 'For spitting at supporters. For throwing my shirt at a referee. For calling my manager a bag of shit. I called those who judged me a bunch of idiots.' A pause. A wry half-grin. 'I thought I might have trouble finding a sponsor.'

Yes, very funny. And very stylish. Advertising people naturally fell over each other in the rush to acclaim the piece. But in the real world, even those of us who have enjoyed watching Cantona's half-baked existentialism flourish in the unlikely context of English football found this hard to stomach. Nike's diabolically clever exploitation of unsporting behaviour had finally gone beyond the limits of acceptability.

But there was not a word from the Football Association, who could have used the opportunity to make an important point, quietly but firmly. When the ad was removed from the cinemas, it was at the insistence of the Advertising Standards Authority, on the grounds of its use of the word 'shit'.

This time, of course, Nike simply can't lose. At last they've found a way to overcome the principal threat to their campaigns, which is the basic uncertainty of sport. In the past they have often been tripped up by hubris. Ian Wright sneered, 'Gary who?' and proved he couldn't score goals for England. Sergei Bubka fell flat on his face at the Barcelona Olympics. Quincy Watts's running shoe disintegrated in Stuttgart. But the irony of the Cantona brouhaha – and, in ad-man's terms, its magic – is that the scandal can only reinforce the message of the campaign. Reporters who rang the company this week to ask if Nike planned to terminate the footballer's contract were not merely wasting their breath but missing the whole point.

The obvious parallel is with John McEnroe, the original Nike bad boy, whose outbursts of vicious rage (usually directed at middle-aged line judges) were equally reprehensible and similarly appeared to be out of his own control. When Jimmy Connors made semi-obscene gestures or put an opponent off by wasting time, it was the product of cold calculation. When McEnroe exploded, it was at the prompting of inner voices. This made it more frightening and somehow pitiful. And genuinely tragic, too, since it was combined with a transcendent sporting gift. Cantona is not a McEnroe in world terms, although in the environment of the English league he can look like one, which is why we sincerely mourn his fate and try our best to find reasons for his aberrant behaviour.

Like a lot of people, I found myself spending a few awkward minutes on Thursday morning trying to explain the events of the previous night to an eight-year-old who has always been encouraged to take pleasure from Cantona's presence among us. It wasn't easy. But I finished by saying that although we wouldn't be seeing him for a while, because he'd probably be suspended and that would be only right, I hoped he would be back next season, and we'd go and see him then. Because, whatever he did on Wednesday night, I don't believe that Eric Cantona is one of the bad guys.

UNLICENSED BOXING
A Real Night Out

BY THE TIME I get the car parked under a decent streetlight on the main drag, somewhere there's a chance that the wheels might still be on it at the end of the night, the queue outside the Ritzy is stretching along Streatham High Road, round the corner and halfway down the next street. It's three deep, and buzzing. Rented mini-buses are drawing up by the kerb like stretch limos at a Hollywood première, disgorging a dozen people at a time. There's still an hour to go, but if you haven't got a ticket, you can forget it. Two and a half thousand people will get in tonight, and around five hundred will be disappointed. In south London unlicensed boxing is a proper night out.

Inside the Ritzy, crowding the bars and balconies under the complicated high-tech dancefloor lights, the audience breaks down like this. About 80 per cent are young white men, under 35, mostly in jeans and leather bomber jackets. Another 10 per cent are their dads: hard nuts in their 40s and 50s, in the sort of gear described in disco dress-code language as 'smart casual'. Quite a lot have smudged noses and overhanging eyebrows. Five per cent are young black men, ranging from cool to extremely cool. And five per cent are girls: sexy girls with thin faces and stringy blonde hair.

Two of these girls are right behind me now, shouting loud enough to burst their replica Wonderbras.

'Wasss-oo-ooo!' they're chanting. 'Wasss-oo-ooo! Wasss-oo-ooo!'

They're cheering a man whose name is Russell, Russell Ford, a welterweight from Dartford. He's fighting Wayne Weeks, a southpaw from Woolwich with a tattoo of his own likeness on his left shoulder blade.

It seems like a normal enough fight. Four rounds of two minutes each, a bow-tied referee, three judges at ringside, a doctor and a couple of paramedics nearby, an ambulance outside, the nearest neuro-surgery unit informed of the event a week ahead. But it isn't. Tonight's event has been organized by a promoter who has been refused a licence by the British Boxing Board of Control, which means that to most people he and his promotion are outside the bounds of decent conduct.

Boxers need board licences, too, and Wayne Weeks is one of maybe only three or four fighters on this bill who have held one at some time. It's hard to tell, since three of them are fighting under pseudonyms. At this late stage of his career, Weeks probably isn't bothered about getting his licence back. But 'The Duke', 'Tyson' and 'Eddie Kidd' may be thinking that the board's disciplinary committee would not be impressed by their appearance here.

The man the boxers are working for tonight is Reg Parker, a squat, powerfully built 33-year-old who runs a health club, a security firm and a heating business from an office above the World of Leather showroom in Eltham, at the eastern extremity of the South Circular. To get there from central London means a drive through Bermondsey and Camberwell, past the famous gyms – the Henry Cooper, the Thomas à Becket – of the Old Kent Road: a journey through some of the myths and legends of London boxing.

If you say 'unlicensed boxing' out loud, you get two kinds of reaction. Insiders, protective of what's left of the sport's reputation, start to get very twitchy. Everyone else thinks you're talking about some sort of criminal activity. Which isn't true. The British Boxing

Board of Control makes the rules, issues licences and has an official-sounding title, but it is a limited company, not a government organization. Its view is that boxing is best run by a single body, and that body is itself. Not everybody agrees.

When he was 18, Reg Parker was an unlicensed boxer. Egged on by his mates, he took half a dozen bouts as a middleweight, culminating in a thrashing at the hands of Albert Hillman, a top-of-the-bill fighter. 'That was a fight I took the day before. His opponent had pulled out. I was promised all kinds of money, but at the end of the evening I ended up with a hundred and fifty quid. And I got a severe beating. Basically, I should never have been in with him.'

In those days, Parker says, it was a rough game, and mismatches were common. 'There were no weigh-ins, no doctors or paramedics, it was a game of chance. And you had a few old boys, people who were past their sell-by dates.' But he was making good money as a heating engineer, with excellent prospects, and he was too smart to imperil that by turning pro. When he started his own gym in 1983, he began to think of putting on fights himself.

As his first headliner he hired Lenny McLean, a heavyweight who'd been a big draw on south London's unlicensed circuit in the 1970s but had been retired for six or seven years. Parker himself had been a fan of McLean. 'I put him in against a gypsy feller from north London. When people saw Lenny's name on the posters, the house sold out. But then it went haywire. When the referee brought them together, all of a sudden the gypsy's gone boom – he's nutted Lenny. Just like that. No bell, nothing. So Lenny's smashed him to the floor. Kicking him, smashing him … we all had to jump in and pull Lenny off.' Unfortunately for Parker, a television crew was there, working on a programme about boxing licences. 'It went out on *News at Ten*. Which is why the board have always tried to give me a bad name.'

Parker has put on thirty-odd unlicensed promotions since then, the audiences growing all the time. They like the fact that the top ticket price is £35, which puts you within gumshield-spitting range, and they probably like the illusion of being on the margins of the law, too. Parker is sometimes cagey about the details of forthcoming promotions, saying that he's had venues mysteriously cancelled at the last minute. (He claims to have booked a London football ground for an open-air promotion in August, but won't say which one.) So word of mouth, in the pubs and gyms, is the way the news gets around south London.

At the beginning of last year, in fact, Parker decided to go legit and applied to the board for a promoter's licence. But the secretary of the southern area council, Simon Block, wrote back saying that they had considered his request and turned it down. There was no interview, no appeal. 'The board does not give reasons for the refusal of a licence,' Block said last week when I asked him about it. As I understand it, the reason for the secrecy is that their decisions are sometimes based on judgements that can only be made on subjective grounds and wouldn't necessarily stand up to legal scrutiny – a judgement on a boxer's competence, say, as opposed to one based on his verifiable medical condition. But this, of course, merely fuels Parker's belief in an establishment plot. His response to the refusal was to form his own body with its own rules and regulations. So last week's bill at the Ritzy was the launch promotion of the United Boxing Organisation, Reg Parker's very own board of control.

'When professional boxing started,' he says, 'it was basically a high-society sport, right? The Queensberry rules, the National Sporting Club, the Lonsdale belt. It was people who didn't come from the street. Now, when was the last time you saw a society gentleman in the ring? You tell me. Where does boxing come from now? From the street, that's where.

'I could give you a thousand people that they've pulled licences on, all because their face don't fit. Professional fighters that have got into trouble, ended up getting a bit of bird, yeah? Six months in prison, say. Then he comes out. Got to earn a living. All he knows is boxing. So he's got to box. If he don't box, he's got to go and thieve something and end up back in prison. So what does he do? He goes and sits in front of a little body of men who think they're closer to God than anyone else. "You've been a bad boy." "Well, I've paid my debt to society." "You go away, prove you can behave yourself for another six months, then come back and apply again." Is that justice?'

Parker believes that the board imposes unreasonable conditions, particularly on the relationship between a boxer and his manager. 'The majority of people going into the fight game haven't had a very good education, and they get used. But if you get a boxer educated, then he realizes that the boxer employs the manager. The manager doesn't employ the boxer.' The evidence he adduces, however, seems unreliable. He tells me categorically that the board is insistent on boxers signing contracts with managers for a minimum of three years and giving them a flat 25 per cent of their earnings. According to Block, though, the board's rules say that three years and 25 per cent are both statutory maximum figures, with no stipulated minimum. And that certainly damages Parker's argument, if it doesn't destroy it.

'Cay-boo-ooo!' It's the last bout of the night, the main event, and the girls are exercising their lungs again.

Jimmy Cable, the former British and European light-middleweight champion, is on his way to winning the UBO's first title and to becoming the inaugural recipient of the Tom Gribb Belt, a Lonsdale look-alike named after a bare-knuckle champ of the early eighteenth century. Lez Jarvis, his opponent, is putting up a brave show, cheered on by almost as many fans as are screaming for Cable, but as we come towards the close of the sixth and final round, the Swanley man's nose is leaking blood all over the place and the towel flies in right on cue.

A few knowledgeable people suggested to me last week that, at 35, Jimmy Cable is all too typical of unlicensed boxers: a fellow who had his good times, took one pasting too many and should stay retired. His heyday was 1984, when he beat Nick Wilshire and Said Skouma for the British and European titles. A year later he'd lost them both, to Prince Rodney on Hastings Pier and George Steinherr in Munich – 'a bad year for me,' he says. Not long afterwards, he went back to painting and decorating in Orpington.

Eighteen months ago, a friend with whom he plays football took him to one of Reg Parker's promotions. 'I'd been thinking of making a comeback under board rules,' Cable told me afterwards, 'but I was impressed with what I saw and I approached Reg. He told me to have a medical and get myself ready.' Six wins later, Cable is Parker's chief draw.

'To be truthful,' he says, 'I wondered if I still had it in me. But I told Reg I wasn't there to take the mickey, and the guys I've fought haven't been mugs. Anyone who says I shouldn't be in the ring should have seen me on Tuesday. I trained eight weeks for that fight, and I think I'm in just about the best shape of my life. I've never been a big-headed sort, but I think the other night I fought superbly. And I took home more than I got when I fought Nick Wilshire at the Albert Hall.'

So I really don't know. I look at the board's letter heading, with its QCs and MPs and former chief constables and eminent physicians, and I think of Reg Parker telling me that 80 per cent of all the boxers in Britain are black, and I wonder what it means if you put those two things together. Then I think of the people who really run boxing in Britain and of some of the things that have gone on under the board's gaze, and I wonder how much the big managers and promoters really have their fighters' welfare in mind. The one thing I do know is that there are no moral certainties here, just a world of greys, and that the only true high ground is occupied by those who would put a stop to it all. And then, of course, we'd really get some unlicensed boxing.

INDIAN CRICKET
In the Tradition

BOMBAY, 21 FEBRUARY 1993

I WANTED TO FIND the soul of Indian cricket, so I went to Bombay, looking for Ramakant Achrekar. It took two days to find him, but by then I'd seen a lot and learnt some lessons about why the Indian cricketers have been beating Graham Gooch's England.

The only clue I had was this: it had been to Ramakant Achrekar that the 11-year-old Sachin Tendulkar went in search of advice on how to play cricket. Now, eight years later, Tendulkar is the princeling of Indian cricket, a marvellous boy whose name may one day be uttered in the same breath as those of Bradman, Hammond and Worrell.

And it wasn't just Tendulkar, either. The present Indian team also includes two more products of Achrekar's coaching, the 21-year-old left-hander Vinod Kambli and the 24-year-old Pravin Amre. What kind of coach was this? And where could I find him?

I began by walking from Nariman Point, where the high-rise hotels are clustered, down Marine Drive, a boulevard sweeping by the blue waters of Back Bay. Halfway along, I spotted what I was looking for: a row of four cricket grounds, separated by rough fences, facing the sea. These were the communal gymkhanas, the historic headquarters of cricket clubs based on the city's four main religious groupings.

The first ground, with a smart little pavilion resembling a 1930s railway station in a small town in the Tyrol, declared itself to be the Parsee Gymkhana, the home of the descendants of Persian refugees, whose admiration for the British led them, in the early nineteenth century, to become the first of India's ethnic groups to take up cricket. There are still 60,000 Parsees in Bombay, and a game was in progress in the 90-degree heat of this weekday morning.

Further along, several teenage boys were at catching practice in front of the Islamic Gymkhana's pavilion, a 1960s affair of ribbed and finned concrete that could have been a public library in Brasilia. By contrast, the dilapidated and deserted pavilion of the Catholic Gymkhana, a plain, square-sided building that had once been painted dark red, looked like an abandoned movie house somewhere in West Virginia. But in the middle of these, dominating them with a giant edifice of crumbling plaster, six storeys high and as long as a mansion block, was the Hindu Gymkhana, and it was here that I went to enquire after Ramakant Achrekar.

No, I was told by an elderly gentleman who sat with a scorebook at a trestle table while young men in white flannels warmed up on the outfield. No, Achrekar is not here. You will find him in the afternoon, at Shivaji Park in Dadar, on the other side of the city. So, looking to fill the hours before I could take the commuter train to Dadar, I walked back up Marine Drive, past the concrete bowl of Wankhede Stadium, where every Bombay Test has been played since 1974, and turned down the side street leading to its predecessor.

Brabourne Stadium, the home of the Cricket Club of India, was the site of Test cricket in Bombay from 1948 until a schism between the CCI and the Bombay Cricket Association led to the building of the Wankhede. Ten minutes after walking in, I was sitting in a cane chair on the cool veranda of the vast pavilion, taking tea and looking out as sprinklers fanned over a field that once saw centuries by Everton Weekes and Neil Harvey, Hanif Mohammad and Denis Compton.

'If you should see Mr Compton, give him my greetings,' said an old man with the face of an eagle. 'Denis Compton was a naughty, naughty man, on and off the pitch. Just like me!'

Silver-haired Mushtaq Ali, 78 years old, looking like a fashion plate in fresh navy T-shirt, knife-creased tan slacks, argyle socks and brown suede brogues, once scored centuries in both innings of a Ranji Trophy final on this pitch. Now he was visiting from his home in Indore, an hour north by plane, at the invitation of the CCI, which was holding a dinner to celebrate the sixtieth anniversary of the first Test match in India. Just as the Test teams had in the old days, he was staying in the rooms on the second floor of the supreme pavilion, seemingly designed in homage to a Cunard liner, all curving decks and storm rails.

First selected for India in 1934 as a left-arm spinner, Mushtaq became famous as a stylishly aggressive opening bat, good enough to take a century off Gubby Allen, Alf Gover and Hedley Verity at the Old Trafford Test in 1936. 'Plum Warner came to the changing room to congratulate me,' he said. So did Jack Hobbs, who had given him a pair of silver hairbrushes when they played together in India four years earlier. Mushtaq became so popular that his omission from the national side in 1945 caused riots in Calcutta.

'I am a hero to many,' he told me, sipping his tea, 'but I too have my heroes. Denis Compton, Keith Miller, Sir Frank Worrell. I loved their talent, their approach to the game.' And, he added, their *bella figura*. 'In my time, we wore flannel shirts and trousers and blazers. Now …'. And a wave of the hand covered the years between the drop-dead-handsome young Mushtaq, smiling wickedly above his cravat in photographs from the 1930s, and the logo-splattered leisurewear of today's international cricketers.

Mushtaq Ali had been a protégé of the cricket-mad Maharajkumar of Vizianagram, known as 'Vizzy', who captained the 1936 touring team. But Mushtaq's first cricket had been played with an improvised bat and a cork ball on the maidans, the open spaces of rough grass which are the lungs of Indian cities. And, a few hours after saying goodbye to him, still searching for Ramakant Achrekar, I saw the full flowering of maidan cricket.

Shivaji Park is about twice the size of Horseguards' Parade. Within its boundaries, on a hot evening, approximately 500–600 boys, all dressed in whites, were playing cricket. Some were practising in nets. Others were throwing and catching. Most of them, though, were taking part in organized games. Dozens of games, jostling for space on the field, their outfielders often overlapping. What struck me most forcibly was the way these boys – the youngest about five, the oldest perhaps fourteen – were playing. All of them, even the very smallest, bowled overarm, with correct actions. This was not the 'kwik cricket' stuff that is supposed to drag modern children away from their Game Boys, pandering to their short attention span. Here, innings were being built, bats stroked confidently through the ball, the blade angled with an elegant flourish. And tiny fielders made their returns as boys were once taught on the playing fields of England, six inches above the bails.

I asked one of the older players if he knew of Ramakant Achrekar, and was directed to a group of the very smallest boys, a few pitches away. At their centre was a young woman wearing a tracksuit and a cricket cap.

'I am Kalpana Achrekar,' she told me. 'I coach the boys from five to eleven, and my father takes the older ones, up to 22, which is when they go to college. He is not coming tonight, but you can find him tomorrow morning, from seven o'clock, at Azad maidan.' And she broke off to tell a thirsty seven-year-old where to find the water bottle.

Kalpana, who is 27, played cricket for Indian Universities while acquiring a Bachelor of Commerce degree. Now she helps her father to run the Kamath Memorial Cricket Club, to which somewhere around 200 boys and youths belong, paying 75 rupees (about £1.80) a month to attend two hours of coaching every day of the week.

At seven the next morning I walked to Azad maidan, a great field in the middle of the city, cheek by jowl with the picturesquely faded grandeur of Bombay Gymkhana, where the very first Bombay Test was played, against England, in December 1933. Just outside the club's perimeter fence, a middle-aged man of unexceptional appearance sat on a folding metal chair, watching a group of youths bowling in a net supported by bamboo poles. This was Ramakant Achrekar.

I introduced myself and he told one of his boys to fetch me another chair from a tent at the edge of the field, close to a row of lean-tos improvised mostly from sacking stamped 'Indian Post Office', within which families were waking and washing and preparing breakfast. Then I asked Ramakant Achrekar to tell me about himself and what had turned him into a producer of cricketing genius.

'I was born in 1932,' he told me, 'in a village called Malvan, about 500 kilometres from here, near Goa. I came to Bombay with my parents when I was eleven, and eventually I took a job in the State Bank.' There he met and played with Ajit Wadekar, another bank employee, later the first Indian captain to win a Test series in England, and now the manager of the present Test team. Achrekar himself, a batsman–wicketkeeper who had inherited a love of the game from his father, played only one first-class match – 'for All-India State Bank, against Hyderabad, in 1964. I got thirty runs.' Three or four years later, when a schoolboy approached him for advice, he began coaching. That boy later went on to play for Hindustan, the forerunner of two dozen of Achrekar's prodigies to have appeared in the Ranji Trophy.

Ramnath Parkar, an opening batsman who played twice for India in the 1980s, was the first Achrekar product to win a Test cap. Pravin Amre came to Shivaji Park at ten, and Vinod Kambli joined the Azad maidan games at nine. Sachin Tendulkar was brought to Achrekar by his older brother Ajit.

'The first time I saw Sachin,' Achrekar remembered, 'he seemed to be just like the other boys, nothing special. But then I watched him in the nets, and he was middling the ball all the time, hitting it hard, never playing defence. He had good wrist work and wonderful reflexes.' Tendulkar's father, a university professor and a noted poet in the Marathi language of central India, had no great interest in cricket himself, but willingly sent the boy to stay with his uncle, who lived near Shivaji Park.

'Sachin loved to play,' Achrekar said. 'He never wanted to miss a match. Soon he was playing ten, eleven matches a month.' According to the coach, he was so keen that he used to skip lessons at school in Dadar. And, at 13, on Achrekar's recommendation, he made his debut at Brabourne Stadium for CCI. A legend was born.

Watching Tendulkar, Amre and Kambli compiling their innings in the Wankhede Stadium last week, you couldn't miss the wonderful sense of play in their game, alongside the marvellous technique and the confidence to express their gifts. Unlike their nearest English equivalents, they seem notably unoppressed by the business of having to play cricket. Throwing, catching, hitting – whatever they do, thanks to wise old Ramakant Achrekar, they're having fun. Just like the hundreds of little boys on the scrubby lawns of Azad maidan and Shivaji Park, unfurling their cover drives and honing their leg-breaks. Just like the little boys they once were.

DERRY CITY
Border Crossing

IT'S THE HEART of a Sunday night, and we're still almost 200 miles from home. As the coach pulls out of the dim street lighting of Monasterevan, away from the crossroads with a pub on each corner, Claire and Shauna are in the back seat, singing along with Dolly Parton on the country music tape like a pair of honky-tonk angels: 'If I should stay I would only be in your way-ay-ay … So I'll go but I know I'll think of you every step of the way-ay-ay … And I-I-I will always love you-oo-oo ….'.

A few hours earlier, in the flush of victory, the girls had traced a simple message in the road-grime on the white rear panels of the coach: 'Derry City FC Won Today'. Now their words are being carried the length of Ireland, from south to north, on one of the strangest journeys in sport.

Up at the front of the coach, beyond the seats filled with slumped and dozing shapes, there's the hiss of a ring-pull and a sudden surge of laughter in the semi-dark. Somebody's making a speech. Back here, as Claire and Shauna switch along with the tape to 'Just walk on by, wait on the corner, I love you but we're strangers when we meet …', Jim Gallagher is telling me what it means to be a Derry City fan.

'Nobody wants trouble here,' he's saying. 'We're just ordinary people. Nobody cares who you are. We've never had police in the ground. Just our own stewards. And we've never had trouble. Oh yes, the majority of the fans are Catholics. But anybody can come.'

Okay, then: is there a Protestant on this coach tonight?

'Yes.'

Who?

'Mr and Mrs Caldwell,' says Liam Gallagher, chairman of the Creggan Community Supporters Club (and no relation to Jim). 'They're Protestants. They've travelled with us for years. But religion's never mentioned. Only in a wisecrack, maybe.'

That would surprise some people, to whom Derry City is the football club that died in the early days of the Troubles, back in 1972, when a couple of its supporters – 'just young hooligans, not really supporters at all' – set fire to the visiting Ballymena United team coach in the car park at the Brandywell stadium. After that, the Irish League told City that they had to play all their matches away from home. Rather than accept such ignominy, the club left the league, which it had joined in 1929 and whose championship it had won in 1964/65, and shut down its first team altogether.

'It was a ridiculous situation,' Liam Gallagher says. He was watching the match at the Brandywell on the day the Ballymena bus got torched. 'All right, there was a lot of burning and looting going on at the time. But this was just a couple of hooligans. There was no animosity inside the ground towards the visiting team or its supporters. There never had been. And it was a great shame, as a matter of fact.'

Nevertheless, for the next thirteen years Derry City ceased to exist in any real sporting sense. It maintained an active social club at the Brandywell, located on the north bank of the River Foyle, in the Catholic heartland between the Creggan and the Bogside, but the stadium itself became the home of thrice-weekly greyhound meetings, with junior football in the 'D & D' – the Derry and District League – at the weekends.

But in 1985 four of City's former players decided that enough was enough and that the time for a resurrection was at hand. 'It was a sort of committee in exile,' Liam Gallagher says. 'I dare say they could have got back into the Irish League, but with the Troubles and all, it didn't seem worth it. There would always have been a slight danger of clashes. So they just decided to keep away from it.'

Instead, in a remarkable piece of lateral thinking, the newly reconstituted committee of Derry City applied to join the Republic's League of Ireland, to play against the likes of Dundalk, Limerick, Galway United and Dublin's Shamrock Rovers and Bohemians. And, as far south as you can get and still find a League of Ireland club, little Cobh Ramblers, whose ground was where I found the players, officials and supporters of Derry City.

The town of Cobh – the Gaelic spelling of Cove, which is how it was known before a visit from Queen Victoria led to the temporary rechristening as Queenstown between 1849 and 1922 – sits on the rim of Cork Harbour, a magnificent inlet defaced only by a steelworks and a prison. The great grey St Colman's Cathedral looks down on a town that was a tiny village until the British came and garrisoned it during the Napoleonic Wars, building it up into a sort of miniature Brighton, with an elegant waterfront and a little Regency crescent and, now, a population of 10,000. From here, hundreds of thousands left Ireland, first in convict ships for Australia and later, in the mid-nineteenth century, fleeing the potato famine by steamship, bound for America.

At the top of the town, a lung-bursting 130 steps up from the harbour front, a chill November wind whipped last Sunday across St Colman's Park, home of Cobh Ramblers FC, founded in 1922 and now in only their second session in the Premier Division since they joined the League of Ireland six years ago. The sight of the pitch prompts you to count the number of Guinnesses you had for lunch: there's a nine-foot drop from one corner flag to its diagonal opposite, which makes the ground look like a bed with a broken leg.

To most British football fans, Cobh is known, if at all, as the place Roy Keane came from. A local boy, Keane played a season for Ramblers as an 18-year-old before being bought by Brian Clough for Nottingham Forest in 1990. The fee for the powerful young midfield man was £25,000 up front, with an extra £7,000 when he completed his fifth appearance for the Republic of Ireland senior side, plus the takings – about £10,000 – from a friendly match that Forest played at St Colman's Park. Just over £40,000 in all. Three years and 114 league appearances later, Forest received £3.75 million when Alex Ferguson decided to add Keane's talent to his all-star squad at Manchester United. From that jackpot, poor Cobh Ramblers received not a penny.

John Meade, who used to play in Ramblers' defence and is a former chairman of the club, glanced around the humble ground, with its tiny dressing-room building and breeze block walls, and sighed as he thought of the Keane fee. There are no seats at St Colman's Park, except for those in the dugout. Only one side of the ground has cover. He told me about the plan to provide shelter at three sides in all and to install some seating. 'That's the dream, anyway,' he said.

Cobh Ramblers's ground is 320 miles from Londonderry and at least that distance in cultural and financial terms from the world of Derry City. At the Brandywell, where the former Manchester City winger Dennis Tueart masterminded the return to league activity in the mid-1980s with a team including two Brazilians and a Zairean, the present star players may be on £500 a game; last Sunday they included Neil McNab, once of Tottenham Hotspur and Manchester City; Scott McGarvey, a former Manchester United starlet; and Luther Blissett, late of Watford, England and elsewhere. For Cobh's boys, the match fee is more like £50 to £100.

But the presence of Luther Blissett, making his fifth and, as it turned out, final appearance in Derry's red and white last Sunday, gave the match a more obvious note of poignancy. As they kicked off at St Colman's, Britain was watching a live transmission of the San Siro derby on Channel 4's *Football Italia* – a match that Blissett played in exactly ten years ago, when he was a million-pound centre-forward with AC Milan. His Serie A sojourn, of course, was a fiasco – as, a decade later, was his stay in the League of Ireland. On loan from Bury, he scored on his debut at Galway but achieved little else. Against Cobh, with fifteen minutes to go and the score at 1–1, he was pulled off by City's acting manager, Tony O'Doherty, whose judgement appeared to be vindicated when 20-year-old Peter 'Pizza' Hutton and the sub, Barry Ryan, scored two late goals for a 3–1 victory that took City to ninth place in the twelve-team division, one place ahead of the Ramblers.

'Luther will be as disappointed as the fans that he missed so many chances,' said O'Doherty, a 47-year-old former Northern Ireland international who was a member of the club's 'resurrection committee' in 1985. 'He could have made a name for himself.'

'It's a very competitive league,' Blissett remarked a couple of days later, back home in England. 'It's hard and physical, and no one gets the time to put his foot on the ball. The players all seem to feel they have to make contact with the man they're marking, whether he has the ball or not. But I enjoyed it. It's probably as good as our Third Division. And the fans are enthusiastic.'

Eighty thousand in San Siro, 800 at St Colman's. And when Blissett and his colleagues came off the pitch, it took five minutes for someone to find the keeper of the dressing room key. As they stood in the knifing wind, they were knocking the mud off their boots just to keep warm.

'We'll be going through the border at Monaghan tonight,' Jim Gallagher says. 'You'll see, they won't stop us at the checkpoint. They know who we are.'

Eight years ago, when City played Ramblers in the cup, 10,000 followed them to Cobh in a special train and more than a hundred coaches. Now the novelty is gone, and the following is down to a single coach, half-full, and a few cars.

'The logistics of these away trips are horrible,' Tony O'Doherty says. 'But it was the only solution. The other clubs in the North understand that. They'd rather see Derry City playing in the Republic than not playing football at all.'

'Everybody enjoys the craic,' Liam Gallagher says, talking about the long trips every other Sunday. 'It wouldn't be comfortable, as things are, playing the clubs in the North. We'd attract trouble. We're no angels, but we've never gone looking for trouble. As it is, we can just go away and enjoy ourselves.'

It's midnight. At Monaghan the coach slips through the British Army checkpoint and across the border with barely a pause. And in the dark the laughter and the singing and the football talk go on.

THE VIEW FROM THE HIGH BOARD

LANCE ARMSTRONG
Doubt and Pain

MARSEILLE, 16 JULY 1993

IT'S NINE O'CLOCK in the morning, about an hour before the circus is due to arrive in the little valley town of Vizille, but already a small boy outside the gates of the Ecole Nationale Professionelle is using his jacket to practise the technique of the matador's cape. In an hour's time, when the cyclists arrive, he'll jump out into the path of the racers, holding his coat as close to the men and machines as he dares, grinning for the motorcycle cameras while his classmates shout encouragement.

He's probably unaware that another boy a few hundred miles to the north tried a similar stunt three days earlier and felled one of the top riders in this year's Tour de France. Alex Zülle, the 25-year-old half-Swiss, half-Dutch leader of the Spanish ONCE team, was among many experts' picks to put up a challenge to Miguel Indurain, the winner of the last two Tours and the odds-on favourite for this one. On the opening day of the race, Zülle had taken second place behind the majestic Basque in the prologue, a short time trial around le Puy du Fou, a half-ruined château in the Vendée.

In the saddle, bicycle racers look like wonderful machines, exuding rhythm and power and grace. But when they fall, they turn back into small boys: hot tears, dusty grazes, torn shorts, arms reaching out to the motherly embrace of the *soigneur*. At le Puy du Fou, clicking up and down through the electronic gears of his high-tech time trial bike, the pink-shirted Zülle had looked ready to sustain a significant effort. Eight days later, though, his hopes had come crashing down and no one could console him. He got up and carried on, but for him it was already over.

The boy who brought down Alex Zülle and the boy outside the school in Vizille are just two among 6 million. By this time next week, about one in ten of all the population of France will have turned out to watch the eightieth edition of *le Grand Boucle* encircling their country. These are the people who know the greatest free show on earth when they see it.

Last Wednesday, it seemed as though most of those 6 million had camped out overnight in order to watch the riders tackle the first of this year's mountain stages, from Villard-de-Lans, just south of Grenoble, to Serre-Chevalier, a ski resort in the Hautes-Alps. Tens of thousands, at the very least, had found their way by car, bicycle, motorcycle and foot up the slopes of the day's two big climbs: the 1,924-metre Col du Glandon and the notorious 2,645-metre Col du Galibier.

The Tour's first day in the mountains always has a special excitement. Here, the old-timers tell each other, is where the race really begins. This year Indurain had set things up by pulverizing the field in a long time trial around the Lac de Madine in the north-east corner of France, establishing a 95-second lead in the overall classification ahead of his nearest challenger, the Dutchman Erik Breukink, Zülle's number two. Now, having spent most of the first week sitting back and letting the boys play, Indurain had made his statement. The leader's yellow jersey was around his shoulders again, and *L'Equipe* rewarded him with a new title: *le Chrono-Maître*.

A rest after the time trial let the rest of the field absorb the lesson while they flew south to the Alps. What it meant was that on Wednesday and Thursday, when the race entered the mountains, anyone who was still planning a serious challenge had to make his move. Mostly this meant the two Italians, Claudio Chiappucci, last year's runner-up, and Gianni Bugno, the reigning world champion, and a second Swiss, Tony Rominger. Each had made an indifferent start but all are good climbers. Over the next two days, on the Glandon and the Galibier on Wednesday and on the Izoard and the giant Bonette-Restefond on Thursday, they would get the chance to reassert themselves. Otherwise Indurain would probably be wearing yellow all the way to the Champs-Elysées.

None of the significant riders was in the first break, in which nineteen riders participated before an Italian, Stefano Colage, accelerated away to reach the top of the Glandon with a one-minute lead. By the time they approached the Galibier, they had been engulfed.

First included in the Tour in 1911, eight years after the race was invented by Henri Desgrange, the editor of a sports newspaper called *L'Auto*, the Galibier was for a long time the supreme test of a climber. The incorporation of the nearby Alpe d'Huez in 1952 removed its supremacy, but on Wednesday it looked as if it had a mind to take the title back. Up above 6,000 feet the weather was dark and menacing. Only the anoraks and racing vests of the fans added a strip of brightness to the north-facing slopes, the dark grey scree otherwise relieved by patches of leftover snow. It was cold, barely above freezing, as Indurain led a new breakaway of five riders through the narrow chute left by the spectators in the final few hundred metres before the summit. Not even a burly fan in blue salopettes running heedlessly alongside at full tilt could disturb the composure of the Spaniard, who allowed Rominger to lead him over the summit and past the imposing memorial to Desgrange ahead of a Colombian rider, Alvaro Mejia.

At the finish, after a gradual 27-kilometre descent from the grey-faced Galibier into the smiling sunshine of Serre-Chevalier, Rominger and Mejia crossed the line a few yards ahead of Indurain, who seemed perfectly content to let his rivals have the day's glory, secure in the knowledge that he had taken another three minutes out of Breukink, who now dropped behind Mejia and a young Pole, Zenon Jaskula, in the general classification. Rominger had ridden hard and well, but Indurain's gesture was almost certainly prompted by the Swiss rider's ill-fortune in the first week, when he lost two colleagues to injury before the team time trial, was penalized a minute after officials decided that the remaining members had given each other illegal pushes, and then suffered from two punctures and unfavourable weather in the crucial individual race against the watch.

Indurain's serene generosity showed the extent of his dominance. Gianni Bugno certainly seemed to be thinking as much after trailing in almost eight minutes behind. 'It's finished for me, and for everybody else,' said the disillusioned rider in the world champion's rainbow jersey. 'In fact, I think I'm going to find myself a new job. Indurain is a phenomenon.'

Someone, though, was feeling even worse than Bugno. Way back in eighty-sixth place, twenty minutes behind Rominger, Lance Armstrong, the youngest man in the race, had just endured his first day in the Alps, only three days after winning his first Tour stage.

The 21-year-old from Austin, Texas, had not exactly been short of confidence. He greeted his win in the stage from Châlons-sur-Marne to Verdun with a rapid-fire wit that seemed to owe something to the sardonic delivery of John McEnroe. Now, flopped on his bunk in a darkened bedroom of the Motorola team's hotel in Serre-Chevalier, he was facing some new truths.

'I was hurting today,' he said. 'It was a strange feeling. Complete emptiness. I guess I gave a hundred per cent in the stage I won, and a hundred per cent in the time trial. Maybe that's the problem.'

Had the whole experience of a big 200-kilometre Tour stage in the Alps come as a surprise to him? 'Well, it certainly was long. Those climbs today ... it's demoralizing when you see a sign at the bottom that says "21 kilometres to the summit". And they just keep on coming. Boom, boom, boom. I didn't even get the chance to go hard. I was just too wasted. I guess I started the day with my gas-tank light flashing.' A pause. 'Tomorrow may be my last day. I don't want to kill myself.'

The son of a car dealer and a real estate agent, Armstrong swam competitively as a child, took up the triathlon at fourteen and then switched to bikes, becoming a full-time racer three years ago. He turned pro after last year's Olympics and won the US championship in March. Now he is being talked of as the new Greg LeMond.

Sports involving fitness and endurance are his thing. 'I was no good at American football or baseball or soccer, anything you need co-ordination for. I have no co-ordination.' Cycling, which probably makes more demands on a willingness to smash through walls than any other sport, perfectly suits his physique – and his other quality, which is a McEnroe-like intensity. 'I can go to the start-line,' he said, 'and look at the other guys and say, well, there's no way they want to win more than I do. No way. Because I want to win more than anybody.'

It was touching, then, to see him trying to cope with distress. He was thinking about another bad day, in San Sebastian a year ago, straight after the Olympics, when he'd come a hundred and eleventh out of a hundred and eleven in a one-day race. 'I just remember those people laughing,' he said, 'which gives me another reason not to finish this race. I mean, I could finish it, but then I could be bollocksed for the rest of the season. No, I want to be fit to go back to San Sebastian next month, two weeks after the Tour. And get my revenge.'

The next morning, after a leisurely breakfast, the cast of the Tour de France – 3,500 people, from the two women who find cheap hotels for journalists to the president of Crédit Lyonnais, the Tour's official bank – had assembled in the centre of Serre-Chevalier along with their 1,500 vehicles, ranging from a selection of helicopters to a quartet of motor-scooters got up to look like baskets of croissants and baguettes. The motorized breadbaskets were promoting that modern French abomination, a bakery chain, and were part of the *caravane publicitaire* that precedes the race by an hour, giving the spectators something else to look at and incidentally showering the countryside with race maps, sun visors, plastic bags and other promotional detritus. In fresh sunshine the whole deceptively chaotic cavalcade set off to the mournful strains of the 'Marche Marengo', played by the brass band of the local Chasseurs Alpins, neatly turned out in their snow-white uniforms, thick socks and brown mountain boots.

The racing was hard from the start, with Chiappucci trying to redeem himself in the eyes of a disappointed Italy by leading the pack up the moonscape of the 2,360-metre Col d'Izoard and down past the broken tooth of rock to which are affixed twin plaques bearing the likenesses of two great rivals and Tour winners of the immediate post-war era, Fausto Coppi and Louison Bobet, subscribed by the readers of *L'Equipe*.

Not surprisingly, since it was invented and continues to be run by journalists, the Tour takes a sentimental view of history. Thursday's big test, though, didn't have much in the way of form. Opened in 1950, the road over the Col de la Bonette-Restefond had been used in the race only twice before, in the early 1960s. On both occasions the summit was reached first by Federico Bahamontes, the Eagle of Toledo.

When Robert Millar popped over the peak of what the local tourist board calls 'the highest road in Europe' on Thursday, Bahamontes's exploits crossed his mind. The Spaniard was six times crowned King of the Mountains, a title won by Millar in 1984. Until this moment, though, the Swallow of Glasgow had been having a bad race. At 34, Millar was thought to have one more good Tour in him; maybe just one more mountain stage win. But on Wednesday he missed a feeding station between the Glandon and the Galibier, had no energy when he needed it and limped in eighty-seventh, one place behind Lance Armstrong.

He planned to put things right on Thursday, intending to save his effort for the final climb to the ski station at Isola 2000. But events conspired against him and he found himself leading an attack halfway through the 180km stage. Dancing on the pedals as he did in his prime, with a light sway that seemed to impart a frictionless momentum to his machine, his thick brown ponytail bouncing on his shoulders, the little Scot dropped the bunch including the yellow jersey long before the summit of Bonette-Restefond. Then, descending the southern slope, through a bleak national park in which the klaxons and loudspeakers of the *caravane publicitaire* were silenced lest they disturb the protected chamoix and marmots, Millar encountered a headwind that allowed Indurain, Rominger and their pursuing pack to cut his lead from more than a minute to a few seconds by the foot of the last climb.

Remorselessly, moving like a big train, sharing the work, they chased him down before setting themselves for the prodigious ascent to the finish: a forty-five-minute climb of more than a thousand vertical metres in 15 kilometres of road, taking in thirty hairpin bends – each one named and signposted after a former winner of the race.

The road, up the valley of the Guerche, had been closed to traffic for more than thirty-six hours. Nevertheless, every square metre of verge was occupied by a camper van or a tent or a sleeping bag or a picnic table. And every square centimetre of the road was covered with painted exhortations to the favourites. The waiting thousands were not disappointed.

'I didn't have enough time to adapt from riding the big gear in the valley to riding on the hill again,' Millar said afterwards. 'So I took it easy on the first part, the steep bit, and after they caught me, I dropped back and recuperated a bit. Then I rode back up to them and waited for an opportunity.'

With four kilometres to go and the worst of the hill behind him, Millar jumped. Past Pedro Delgado, past Jon Unzaga, past Mejia, past Andy Hampsten and Chiappucci and Jaskula and Bjarne Riis and Rominger, and finally past Indurain himself. In no time the Scot had a lead of a hundred metres. But it didn't work. By the three kilometres sign he was history again. Once more Indurain took Rominger to the line, lifting his head with 10 metres to go and allowing the Swiss to put his wheel in front. Millar crossed the line seventh. 'It was a nice day,' he said. But had it been his swan-song to the Tour? 'I don't know. I suffered a lot yesterday. I only do it for pleasure now. I don't have any real objectives anymore. I just want to finish twelve Tours. And when I've finished twelve, maybe I'll want to finish thirteen.'

Friday was Miguel Indurain's birthday, and he spent it in the peloton, pedalling quietly down from the Alps through the aromatic lushness of Vence and Grasse, through the rustic villages and lavender fields of Peter Mayle's idealized Provence, through the good summer smells of the *arrière pays* and into the scrubby hills of the Massif de la Sainte-Baume, where picnickers hung birthday messages and Spanish flags from the little oak trees. The climbs were the sort of thing that wouldn't have got the yellow jersey out of bed on Wednesday or Thursday, and the pack allowed an obscure Italian, Fabio Roscioli, to sustain a long break through the horrible industrial suburbs of Marseille and over the finishing line at the Plage du Prado.

Now Indurain needs only to avoid accidents to win his third consecutive Tour de France in Paris next Sunday. At 29 he may confidently look forward to equalling the record five victories of Bernard Hinault, Jacques Anquetil and Eddy Merckx. His power, easeful style and strategic maturity seem to be such that he may even surpass them. It would be hard to find anyone in the retinue of 3,500 people following him around France last week who would be remotely inclined to bet against it.

And Lance Armstrong, after Wednesday's trauma, went back into the Alps on Thursday to test himself again. Shepherded by his team-mates Phil Anderson and Sean Yates, he finished just inside the top hundred before announcing, as he had predicted, that his Tour was over. The odds are that he, too, will be back.

LONDON, 23 JULY 1999

SO WHAT MESSAGE would Lance Armstrong, just a couple of days away from victory in the world's most gruelling sporting event, send to those given the news – as he was, not quite three years ago – that they are suffering from cancer? 'I'd tell them not to win the yellow jersey in the Tour de France. It's too much stress, and stress is bad for cancer.'

Those angry words will still be in the air today when Armstrong pulls on the *maillot jaune* to ride the penultimate stage of the Tour, a time trial at the Futuroscope theme park, near Poitiers. He will be guarding the lead established a fortnight ago with a shattering performance in a time trial at Metz and consolidated two days later with an imperious ride through the Alps to Sestriere. Since then he has resisted incessant attacks – some from men in the saddle, others from men with notebooks. Barring accidents, he will arrive in the Champs-Elysées tomorrow afternoon as the winner of the eighty-sixth Tour, and one of its most controversial.

His success will be welcomed in some quarters with profound admiration. 'I'll certainly be cheering,' said Sean Yates, the Englishman who partnered Armstrong in his last race before his illness. 'It's a triumph,' said Dr Jeffery Tobias, a London cancer specialist who happens to be a bike-racing fan and who sees Armstrong's feat as a remarkable endorsement of modern forms of treatment. But elsewhere the 27-year-old Texan has been accused of undermining a race that was supposed to represent the emergence of the Tour from the drugs scandal that came close to destroying it last year.

Coded smears in *L'Equipe* drew resounding denials of drug-taking from Armstrong. But they were followed in *Le Monde* earlier this week by the leaked result of a urine test taken after the race's second stage, which showed a minute trace of a banned substance, a synthetic corticosteroid called triamcinolene. In this case the proportion, 0.2 nanogrammes, was extremely low. Only when the trace is above 10 is a test considered unequivocally positive by the UCI, the international cycling federation. Between 6 and 10, further tests are made. But since triamcinolene is not produced naturally, its very appearance was taken by *Le Monde* as unanswerable evidence that Armstrong had lied about taking drugs.

According to Armstrong, the substance had been part of a skin cream called Cemalyt used to treat the sort of saddle-boil that regularly afflicts all racing cyclists. He had not mentioned it because when he thought of drugs he thought of needles and pills, not skin cream. The UCI believed him and his case was strengthened by the fact that he had also been tested the previous day, after winning the race's prologue, without showing even the tiniest trace. This supported his contention that the substance had been part of a topical treatment rather than the long-term residue of systematic drug abuse.

Some elements of the French press, perhaps smarting from the inability of their riders to win a single stage of the Tour for the first time since 1926, still refused to believe him. Others felt differently. In their view, a victory for Armstrong would represent nothing less than one of the most outstanding athletic feats of the century and a landmark for medical science.

When he encountered Lance Armstrong eight years ago, the first thing Sean Yates noticed was the talent of the teenage amateur who had switched from the triathlon only a couple of years earlier. They met at a Motorola training camp in Santa Rosa, California, and a year later, after Armstrong had turned professional, they were team-mates.

The second thing he noticed was the vigour of the young man's ambition. 'Lance wanted to be successful straightaway,' Yates said.

'When he came to Europe and took a pasting in the classics, like any first-year pro, he started talking about going back home and going to college. We told him that he had to expect that kind of thing – that most of the other guys had been around a long time and that if he showed a bit of patience he'd end up beating them all. But he was very young and confident and brash, and he just wanted to kick everyone's butt into the next century.'

Armstrong had been a swimmer before taking up the triathlon, and the result of the specialized training could be seen in his physique. At 21 he weighed almost thirteen stone and was much more solidly built than the average racing cyclist. 'He was a physical phenomenon,' Yates said. 'He reminded me of Eric Heiden, the speed skater. Both of them only had to look at a barbell and their muscles grew. His build made him a natural for the one-day classics. But he was impatient to become a Tour rider.'

In the first week of his first Tour de France, in 1993, he won a flat stage at Verdun and did so without undue modesty. Three days later he was flat on his back in a dormitory in the ski station of Serre-Chevalier, having learnt a painful lesson as he struggled over the 2,645-foot Col du Galibier to finish in eighty-sixth place. Thirty-six hours later he had abandoned the tour, speaking of saving himself for the one-day race at San Sebastian, where he had been laughed at when coming last the previous year. He wanted to take his revenge. He didn't manage it that year, but a few weeks later he won the world road racing championship, the youngest man since the war to do so, on a wet autumn day in Oslo when his rivals were crashing all over the place and he could demonstrate his sheer guts. But Armstrong is not a man to leave scores unsettled, and in 1995 he went back to San Sebastian and won.

This year he took revenge on the mighty Galibier. 'I love the rain and the cold,' he said after arriving at Sestriere. 'I know that when the weather is bad, half the riders are discouraged. I can tell you that on the Galibier today I didn't feel great, but I looked into the faces of the others and I could tell they were feeling a lot worse.'

His accusers pointed to the fact that he had completed the daunting climbs without lifting himself out of the saddle and without seeming to gasp for breath. 'If you grimace,' he replied, 'although your opponent might not see it, his sporting director, who has a television in his car, will certainly spot that you're in trouble. The cameras are always on us and you have to know how to deal with it.'

Armstrong's relationship with his own sporting director, Johan Bruyneel, is a vital factor in this month's success. His four previous Tours ended in three retirements and just one finish, in thirty-fourth place. To prepare for this year's effort, the two men spent the whole of May reconnoitring the route, riding the Alpine and Pyrenean stages in sequence. Now he talks to Bruyneel during the stages via a radio earpiece and microphone. The US Postal entourage also includes his Swiss chef, Willy Balmat, and a *soigneuse*, Emma O'Reilly, who looks after a physique trimmed down to a stone and a half below its pre-cancer weight – leaving 'just bone and muscle', according to the journalist John Wilcockson, who watched him taking a massage.

Whereas in the old days the triathlete in Armstrong liked the challenge of pushing big gears, this year his pedalling rhythm – the thing the riders call their cadence – is faster but requires less effort. 'Before, he didn't know how to use his power,' Bruyneel said. 'In the end he always cracked. So we watched videos of Indurain's Tours and we talked a lot about suppleness of the legs. Look at the way he went over the Galibier. It was a nice surprise, but I never had the least doubt about his qualities.'

In the autumn of 1996 Armstrong and Yates came second from last in a two-man time trial in Germany, riding together for the US-based Motorola team. 'Lance didn't seem to be going very well,' Yates said this week, 'and the organizers weren't very happy because they'd paid him a packet of money. No more than a month later the phone rang from America and I was told that he'd got cancer.'

After being informed that he had less than a 50 per cent chance of survival, Armstrong underwent two operations. In the first, the cancerous testicle was removed. The second dealt with deposits of secondary cancer in the brain. Then he began a course of high-intensity chemotherapy at St David's Hospital in Indianapolis, eradicating all the residual cancerous cells, some of which had appeared in his lungs, the racing cyclist's engine. And 518 days after his last race, he was competing again. 'In my case,' he said a few days ago, 'the risk of having to face cancer again is less than one per cent. I'm cured, completely.'

'It's totally extraordinary,' Jeffrey Tobias, a consultant cancer specialist at the Middlesex Hospital in London, said this week. 'I happen to think that the Tour is the greatest annual athletic event in the world. You need enormous stamina and grit over an extended period, as well as a variety of skills. If you could describe any class of athletes as supreme, then Tour riders, along with decathletes, would be my nominees. Armstrong had the same type of cancer as Bob Champion, the National Hunt jockey, but in a much more advanced state. It had reached his brain, making it much harder to cure. So his achievement is all the more astonishing.'

Historic, even? 'I would say so, although testicular cancer is one of the forms of cancer that can be completely cured, even if it isn't diagnosed until there has been considerable spreading. The drugs are remarkably effective. And Armstrong is a wonderful advertisement. People who are told they need chemotherapy are still stricken by dread, quite understandably. So this is a triumph.'

But when the dark rumours began to spread, they included a whisper that the cancer treatment might actually have made Armstrong more powerful. 'Oh, I don't think so,' Tobias said. 'Obviously if he's as well now as he was before his illness and if he's training even harder, it might appear to have made him stronger.'

There was also the suggestion that if he were using illegal drugs, he might be running the risk of reawakening his cancer. 'He wouldn't necessarily be in more danger than anyone else who took the risk of using them,' Tobias responded. 'Testicular cancer is so virulent that if it were to come back, it would be within two years of the completion of treatment. He seems to be outside that period. But you have to remember that in medicine, never doesn't mean never, never, never. It means probably never.'

And so Armstrong seems poised to enter history as the second American, after Greg LeMond, to win the greatest bike race of all. His wife, Kristin, is at home in Nice expecting their first baby, conceived with semen stored before the chemotherapy began. According to Sean Yates, Lance Armstrong is now a different, wiser man. 'He knows more about the world and how people are, and he's more at peace with himself. He's settled down, he's got a wife, he's got cats, dogs, a home. He's a changed person.'

In Sestriere ten days ago Armstrong met the parents of Fabio Casertelli, a team-mate who was killed on the descent from Col de Portet-d'Aspet during the Tour in 1996. Two days after the accident, Armstrong had led the rest of the Motorola team into Limoges to win the next stage. 'It was like I had the strength of two men in my body,' he told the team manager, Jim Ochowicz, at the time. As he crossed the line, he raised his arms and pointed the index finger of each hand to the heavens. A few weeks later his cancer was diagnosed.

'I'll tell you this,' he said the other day, 'even if I win this Tour de France, I won't have the same emotion that I had winning that stage at Limoges, two days after Fabio's death.'

There are still those who doubt Lance Armstrong's innocence. To them, he is lying and cheating his way to victory. As we watch him ride up the Champs-Elysées tomorrow, perhaps we can make up our own minds on that.

SAINT AMAND-MONTROND, 27 JULY 2001

LANCE ARMSTRONG IS looking fitter than ever. Lighter and stronger, with his body fat ratio surely as low as a healthy man's can go, he has spent the last three weeks outdoing his own already remarkable achievements and giving cycling fans memories that should live alongside the greatest moments from the long and vivid history of the Tour de France.

There is flame in Armstrong's eyes and an implacable desire in his soul. At the foot of l'Alpe d'Huez last week, having lulled the opposition by feigning exhaustion every time a motorcycle-borne TV cameraman came near, he turned and stared into the face of Jan Ullrich, his principal rival, before accelerating away to produce one of the most prodigious feats of solo climbing the race has seen. Four days later, when Ullrich crashed on the descent from the Col de Peyresourde, Armstrong stopped and waited for him to recover. And as they crossed the finishing line at Luz-Ardiden the following day, Ullrich extended a hand to the American in a gesture filled with meaning and, if you are susceptible to such things, with beauty.

Yesterday afternoon Armstrong got off his bike here in St

Amand-Montrond in the dead centre of France to be told that, at the end of a 61-kilometre time trial, he had won his fourth stage of the Tour and increased his lead over Ullrich by more than a minute and a half. As he has done every day since he took over the yellow jersey a week ago, he mounted the podium to receive kisses, flowers and the acclaim of the spectators, many of them children, crowded behind the barriers at the finish of the day's stage. What he is not receiving, however, is the unanimous admiration of those who have followed the Tour for the past three weeks.

This story of the man who beat cancer to win the world's most gruelling sporting event, which only two years ago seemed to be a feat without parallel in sport, is now being widely seen in a different light. Armstrong is almost certain to win the Tour for the third year in a row in Paris tomorrow, making him only the fifth rider in history to achieve that feat. But he will do so at the centre of a gathering vortex of disbelief concerning his relationship with drugs.

Armstrong has consistently denied taking drugs and there is no direct evidence against him. Yet there were those who, right from the start, refused to believe that he could have made his way back to the top without the help of illegal methods after he had undergone treatment in 1996 for testicular cancer so advanced that it had spread to his brain and his lungs. Two years and five months after his discharge, he did something which, in his pre-cancer years, he had failed to achieve: he won the Tour. Last year he did it again, and now he is on the verge of joining Louison Bobet, Jacques Anquetil, Eddy Merckx, Bernard Hinault and Miguel Indurain in the record books. This could only have happened, according to his accusers, with the aid of a systematic and sophisticated doping programme.

Others, formerly ready to give him the benefit of any doubt, now look at recent circumstantial evidence and feel that Armstrong has abused their trust. A year after French police seized medical refuse, including hypodermic needles and bandages, discarded by Armstrong's US Postal team during the Tour, a judicial inquiry has yet to produce its findings. And three weeks ago, as the 2001 Tour set off from Dunkirk, the *Sunday Times* published information linking Armstrong to Dr Michele Ferrari, an Italian who has worked with many cyclists and who in September will be called into a court in Bologna to answer charges of treating riders with erythropoietin, or EPO, the illegal drug that enhances endurance by increasing the proportion of red corpuscles in the blood.

The evidence against Ferrari includes this month's revelation by an Italian rider, Filippo Simeoni, a member of the Cantina team between 1996 and 1998, that the doctor dispensed EPO and human growth hormone to the riders and advised them on how to mask the presence of these substances. Armstrong, hearing rumours that the *Sunday Times* knew the dates of his meetings with Ferrari at his clinic in Ferrara, going as far back as 1995, pre-empted the revelation by giving an interview to an Italian newspaper in which he admitted the existence of the relationship but denied that doping was a part of it.

This week he held a press conference at which he confronted his chief accuser and again declared his innocence. 'I've lived by the rules,' he said. 'Something like human growth hormone – you think someone with my health history would take something like that? There's no way.'

Of Ferrari, he said: 'I believe he's an honest man, a fair man, an innocent man. Let there be a trial. Let the man prove himself innocent.' He said he had not worked with the doctor during the present Tour, but would have no qualms about resuming the relationship if Ferrari were cleared by the court. 'With what I've seen with my two eyes and my experience, how can I prosecute a man who I've never seen do anything guilty?'

Armstrong talked briefly about his use of a hypobaric chamber, a sort of tent that replicates the effect of training at altitude. Unlike many of the great cyclists of the past, he has an acute awareness of what goes on in his own body. His autobiography, *It's Not About The Bike*, in which he described in detail the surgery and chemotherapy he endured at Indianapolis University's medical centre, made it clear that he is not one of those who lie down on the operating table, close their eyes and ask no questions.

A sharp mind such as his could not be fooled into taking something illegal without knowing it. Neither would he be unaware of the precise boundaries of legality. It would be unrealistic to believe that Armstrong went through his formative years as a junior triathlon and swimming champion in Texas without at least observing the existence of anabolic steroids. During his cancer treatment, EPO was administered. His medical knowledge, at least in a couple of specialized areas, must be well above average. And if it has enabled him to operate up to the very margin of the rules, as may be the case, then he cannot be criticized for that.

He is an extraordinary man in many ways. Brash and arrogant on his arrival in big-time European cycling, he learned his lessons fast. Although there are still those who find him difficult to like, there is no question the surly boy from a featureless Dallas suburb has adapted successfully to an alien culture. He now speaks French, Italian and Spanish well enough to conduct interviews in all three. His illness also gave him new perspectives on human existence. 'When I was sick,' he said, 'I saw more beauty and triumph and truth in a single day then I ever did in a bike race.'

No doubt a psychologist would trace his independence and his motivation back to a difficult childhood. His mother was only 17 when he was born and his father left before their son was two. 'I've never had a single conversation with my mother about him,' Armstrong wrote. 'Not once. In 28 years she's never brought him up, and I've never brought him up.' Her single-handed success in building a life for them, and her devotion to his nascent career, must have left a powerful impression.

But there is a bigger question here than merely one man's guilt or innocence. When it comes to doping, after all, sport is always in denial of one sort or another, whether it is the family of Tom Simpson refusing to accept the presence of amphetamines in his body and in the pocket of his racing shirt as he fell dead on Mont Ventoux in 1967, or Ben Johnson lying and lying and lying until he finally gave way and admitted that he had won the Olympic 100 metres gold medal in 1988 by cheating.

In terms of cycling, history multiplies the resonances. In the old days just about everyone doped and nobody worried about it. The first police raid on the Tour teams, at the end of a stage in Bordeaux in 1966, changed nothing. Nor, it seems, did the raids of 1998, which followed the arrest of the Festina *soigneur* Willy Voet in his drug-packed van, at least if the discoveries on this year's Giro d'Italia are anything to go by.

Guilty or not, Lance Armstrong exists in a climate modified by changed attitudes and values, not least those of the mass media. Will his achievements be allowed to stand alongside of those of, say, Coppi and Anquetil, or is he to be judged by a different set of criteria? 'I cannot prove a negative,' he said this week, 'so it's always going to be a tricky situation. When they find a test for one thing, then somebody stands up and says, "Well, you must be doing the next thing." When they find a test for that, then they say, "Well, you must be using the next thing." It goes on and on.'

As well as the accusers and the recently disillusioned, there is a third group following Armstrong's progress to the podium on the Champs-Elysées. These are people predisposed to believe his expressions of innocence while reserving their right not to be surprised by anything the future may reveal. They are not advocates of cheating, but they acknowledge the fundamental impossibility of imposing a completely drug-free regime on bicycle racing. Their opinion of Armstrong was summed up yesterday by a friend of mine, a German journalist covering his nineteenth Tour. 'My admiration,' he said, 'is bigger than my suspicion.'

PAULA RADCLIFFE
The Good Girl

SOMETIMES YOU CAN catch them before their look changes, before they start staring over your shoulder into the middle distance or letting their eyes slide away from a question, before they get into the habit of referring to themselves in the third person.

'It's still a bit of fun, really,' Paula Radcliffe says, looking the questioner straight in the eyes. 'I'm not looking to make a living out of it. Obviously it's nice that there's a bit of money coming in, but that's not my goal. I just want to do my best and still enjoy it.'

Fame tapped Paula Radcliffe on the shoulder this month, on a frosty Saturday afternoon at Aykley Heads. In the fog and ice she finished the Durham International Cross Challenge a few yards behind Derartu Tulu, the Ethiopian who won the 10,000 metres gold medal at the Olympic Games last summer. More to the point, she was in front of Elana Meyer, the South African who shared Tulu's lap of honour in Barcelona and now went slipping and sliding into third place. Suddenly the *Grandstand* cameras were on the runner-up, transmitting the image of a pretty, charming, highly excited 19-year-old English girl live to the nation. Something about the way she handled the interview combined with the significance of her performance – this, it turned out, had been her first race as a senior – to suggest that it wasn't going to be the last we'd be seeing of her.

Waiting in a cold wind outside the bookshop at Loughborough University one day last week, Paula Radcliffe looked exactly like all the other students milling around the campus: jeans, boots, shirt, parka, winter pallor. And with a direct look not yet blunted by the need to deflect others' importuning. Nothing, as yet, to show on the surface that here is anything more than a very bright girl attending the lectures – French, German, economics – that make up a Modern European Studies course, let alone an athlete of such potential that one day we may know her name as well as we do those of Liz McColgan and Yvonne Murray.

She'd just been to see *The Bodyguard* on the special students' night at the local cinema, and had liked it so much that, back in her twelve-by-six room, the soundtrack lay on top of a small pile of CDs on her desk, not far from an open Virago paperback – something by Mary Webb, the pre-war Shropshire novelist. There were messages from friends scribbled on a sheet of paper stuck to the door; a postcard of a cat; a mosaic of family snaps; one of those posters of a couple of young nouveaux-bohos embracing. Only the second pair of muddied running shoes and the 1993 calendar of international athletics meetings pinned about the narrow bed gave clues to the true nature of the occupant.

Paula Radcliffe is the world junior cross-country champion, a title she won in Boston last March, on a day when Liz McColgan was favourite in the senior event. Radcliffe had just recovered from a lengthy bout of anaemia; she was not expected to beat the Kenyans. But she made a shrewd choice of spikes to suit the icy conditions, and ran in five seconds ahead of the field. McColgan was offered a spare pair of Radcliffe's spikes by one of the coaches but declined. She finished forty-first.

Today, Paula Radcliffe will be pointing her green VW Polo back to where she feels most at home: among the junior middle-distance girls of the Bedford and County Athletics Club, cheering on their representatives in the southern area cross-country championship.

Alec and Rosemary Stanton, who run the thirty-strong group, are her coaches; it was they who took her on as an 11-year-old and gradually encouraged her to develop her talent.

'In my first year with them,' she recalled, 'I came 299th in the national championship. I'd only been with them a couple of months. Mind you, I was happy with that, because I was in the top half of the field. But a year later I came fourth. That's what their work had done for me. After that I was always second or third – until I won it for the first time, as an under-17.'

High-pressure training is not the Stantons' style, perhaps because they came into athletics almost by accident – when, fifteen years ago, their daughter Kim took an interest and joined Bedford. When Kim dropped out, they stayed. Now their group is so popular that three boys – including Paula's 17-year-old brother Martin – recently wangled their way into it.

'You can't tell how anyone's going to turn out,' Alec Stanton, a 57-year-old group leader on a motor-factory production line, said last week. 'At 11 years of age, they're all ordinary little girls. And that's how they are until they're 16 – some are going forward, some are going back. Paula was never a southern champion at under-13 level, for instance. But it's often the good runners who make great runners, if you see what I mean. When they get to 15 or so, really, that's the nitty-gritty. Of course, if you've got the right mum and dad, it's a big help. Sometimes you see ones who aren't satisfied with their daughter's performance. They can't stop pushing. Paula's lucky there.'

Her parents both participate in the life of the club. Peter Radcliffe, aged 46, the director of marketing and human resources at a division of the Whitbread brewery, is a vice-president, while Pat, a deputy headmistress, manages the cross-country team. Paula's first run came when, as a six-year-old, she ran alongside Peter while he jogged in order to lose weight after giving up smoking. Pat, too, became a fun-runner, but neither had a background in athletics.

'Paula always ran well, even when she was jogging with me,' Peter Radcliffe said. 'But it was quite a surprise to us all when she came fourth in the nationals. That was splendid for her coaches. There's a lot of loving care there, and attention to detail. Teaching motivation is part of my job, and I know how good they are. They're naturals.'

So what motivates Paula? 'I've always motivated myself to work hard,' she said, 'because it's the way I am. I have to do the best I can possibly do, to try and get the most out of life.'

'She just likes to do well with everything she does,' her father said. 'She's a perfectionist, which can be a frustrating existence.'

For Alec Stanton, motivating Paula has never been a problem. Her special quality, he said, is 'her ability to get five or ten per cent more out of herself in a race than in training. That's very rare. In fact it's usually the other way round: they leave five per cent on the starting line. She likes a challenge, too, and she's got a terrific amount of fight. But I don't fill her mind with what she should or shouldn't do. It's up to her. She's got a quick enough brain that she can turn things round during a race. She's an intelligent lass. And if one of the other girls has had a bad race, she'll be on the phone from Loughborough to talk to her.'

She does most of her training in the parks around Loughborough, running with fellow students ('usually lads – most of the women don't want to run that hard'), but drives down to Bedford on Wednesdays for an evening session with her coaches, who often come up to her at the weekends. 'They've had me since I was 11,' she said, 'and they know exactly how much work to give me. They know that if I'm working hard and getting uptight, they can ease back on the training – although they know I don't want to stop altogether, because I need it to relax me and get rid of whatever is making me uptight – if I've been doing a lot of studying, say. And they know that the way I push myself in training, I can do a lower mileage, because it's a lot more intense. A lot of senior women runners will be doing 80 miles a week now, running steadily. But I can do 35 miles a week, because I push myself hard.'

Not surprisingly for such an assertive character, she likes to run from the front: 'That's my natural way.' In Durham she felt confident enough to take the race to Tulu and Meyer. 'I didn't have anything to lose, so I went out to go as hard as I could and just hang on. It felt fast but I didn't feel out of my depth. I knew I'd have to break, because I'd seen Tulu's sprint finishes. I didn't really think much of my chances, but I thought I'd give it a go and try to break her on the downhill stretch. When she went, with about a thousand metres to go, she was too strong. Everyone said I was closing on her at the end, but really she was just easing down because she knew she had me covered. She makes it look easy.'

It was the first time that she'd raced as a senior in such a field. 'It didn't feel any different, really. When the gun goes, it's a race the same as any other, and you've just got to try to get up to the sharp end as quickly as you can.'

Her future involves a concentration on the 3,000 metres, the distance at which she is most comfortable. 'I've got a difficult decision coming up, because the World Student Games clashes with the British trials for the world championships in Stuttgart. I'm ranked fifth in Britain in the 3,000, behind Yvonne Murray, Alison Wyeth, Lisa York and Liz McColgan. We send a team of three – and since Liz will be doing the 10,000 metres, that puts me up to fourth. So, realistically, I'll have to improve another five seconds to knock one of the others out. And I've got to decide whether the risk is worth staying at home for.'

Further ahead, the Olympics are, for now, merely something her coaches tease her about. But when Atlanta comes around in 1996, she'll just have completed her studies. 'Running is a big part of my life,' she said, 'but there's no way it's going to stop me getting my qualifications.' ('She's always had quite an old head on her shoulders,' her father said. 'And in athletics, you're only one injury or one illness away from it all being gone.')

'I'd like to get to Atlanta,' Paula continued, 'for the experience as much as anything.' Four years later, at 27, she should be in her prime as a 3,000 metres runner. 'But she's still got a lot of work to do,' the cautious Alec Stanton observed. 'She's capable of winning big races later on, but what those races will be, I don't know.'

Thinking about the claim made last week by Prince Alexandre de Merode of the International Olympic Committee that one in ten athletes now take performance-enhancing drugs, and wondering whether that direct look in Paula Radcliffe's eyes would ever be dulled by the self-absorption success can bring, I asked her father whether he had any reservations about his daughter pursuing a career in athletics.

'No,' he said. 'Not at all. You have to encourage people to succeed in what they do. There are pressures in what she's doing. We can only help her.'

As I watched her gliding over the rough parkland hills above Loughborough on an afternoon training run, I thought of something Alec Stanton had said: 'She's a great girl, you know, never mind about athletics.' Later on, I told someone else about her. 'Wait 'til the marketing men get at her,' he replied. Well, maybe. And maybe not.

TIGER WOODS
Crushing

ST ANDREWS, 24 JULY 2000

I N A WAY, the greatest compliment to Tiger Woods as he toured St Andrews yesterday was the sound of the cheering for his opponent. The crowd thronging the Old Course had paid their money to bear witness to Woods' genius, but they wanted to see somebody give him a game. David Duval is not the most charismatic of golfers, even though he is ranked second best in the world, and he will seldom receive the sort of encouragement that came his way during the final round of the 129th Open championship.

Once the issue had been decided – around about the 12th hole, on which Woods made his third birdie of the day while Duval was recording his second bogey in succession – the mood changed. Now it was time to give Tiger his due, to enjoy the presence of one of the great champions and to salute the lessons in technique, strategy and dignity that he had dispensed throughout the four days of the tournament. Only when he turned the corner at the Road hole and entered the final straight ending under the grandstands at the 18th green did the round turn into a lap of honour.

'The game is very fickle,' he had said earlier in the week. 'You can go out there and have it one day, not have it the next, and wonder why.' Every golfer of any level of competence knows just what he means. But the most impressive aspect of Woods' play at St Andrews was the way in which he cut down the element of variation. His play was solid from beginning to end, with only three dropped shots and no visits to bunkers in the entire 72 holes.

If he did not provide the kind of flamboyance that some might expect from a 24-year-old, then that is another measure of his maturity. Here he played in a tournament alongside Gary Player, Jack Nicklaus, Bob Charles and Lee Trevino, all former champions now in their sixties. It is unlikely that any of them would claim to know more about the game than Woods, who seems to have crammed forty years of experience into his four years as a professional.

His crushing of Duval in yesterday's head-to-head between the world's number one and number two golfers was chilling in its inexorability. He began the round as he often does, without fireworks. For a while it even looked as though he was not quite on song. But a glance at the scoreboard was always enough to correct the impression. Woods' length off the tee allows him to get so close to making birdie on just about every hole that a par is almost a disappointment, which is why he is sometimes surrounded by a slight air of anticlimax when in fact he is playing superlative golf.

Imagine the challenge facing poor Duval – to play Tiger Woods over eighteen holes and to give him six shots' start. He had made brave noises about looking his friend in the eye and putting some pressure on him, and with four birdies in an outward half of 32 he attempted to give substance to the threat. But Tiger was making his pars with the sort of metronomic regularity that suggests he is laying a platform, and a burst of four birdies between the 10th and the 14th holes destroyed Duval's hopes of matching his achievement on the front nine, when the lead was cut from six to three strokes.

Woods' rivals, if you can call them that, are usually ready to concede the existence of a divide between their golf and his. 'He's on a different wavelength,' Nick Faldo said on Friday night. Thomas Björn, the Dane who was only a stroke away from playing the final round with Woods and ended up tied for second place, remarked: 'Someone out there is playing golf on a different planet from the rest of us.' Faldo went on to say that Woods' mental strength was the factor that gave him the edge, and no one who heard the champion analyzing his performance a few minutes after the end of a round would be likely to dispute the claim. Woods is the best not just because he hits the ball so hard and so far and so straight, but also because he loves his job and is willing to put an enormous amount of thought into it. To such a man, no factor is too small to be unworthy of attention.

They say he makes the game look simple, but what he really does is show us how complicated it is, how delicate its internal mechanisms. To the outsider, this level of concentration on detail can sometimes seem almost comic. There were stifled giggles in the press tent last week when a reporter asked Woods about his success in achieving 'end-on-end rotation' with his putting. What he means is hitting the ball in such a way as to ensure that it rolls rather than slides towards the hole, enabling it to travel more smoothly and securely over the minute obstructions that may be in its path even on a well-tended green. This requires a subtle modification of his technique, to do with striking the ball when the clubhead is already past the lowest point of its travel, thereby imparting a measure of overspin. Such refinements are the signature of this particular champion and the guarantee that he will continue to develop his art.

All that was missing was the sort of weather that might have provided the test of his composure that no human opponent was able to supply. The wind is the fourth dimension of links golf, setting up problems of abstract dynamics that he would welcome – particularly after last year's experience in the gales and wild rough of Carnoustie. But there will be plenty of opportunities in the future for him to face that particular contest.

When Jack Nicklaus ended his thirty-seven-year career at the Open on Friday night, those who examined his record and noted the astonishing consistency of his high placing as a young man might have put it down to the lack of depth of competition in his heyday, before golf became a global game with vast rewards even for journeymen. That depth is certainly there now, but it is the measure of Tiger Woods' talent that here he made it look like an optical illusion.

LINFORD CHRISTIE
The Superstar of Block 3815

WHEN HE WALKED into the self-service restaurant in the athletes' village late on Sunday night, he was starving. He hadn't eaten all day. So, as he went through the restaurant door with a little group of team-mates and officials, all he was thinking about was a big plate of food to replace the energy he'd burnt up.

The place was less than half full. Most of the village's temporary inhabitants were back in their rooms, dreaming about what destiny would have in store for them in the days to come. Within seconds, however, the late diners had registered his presence. And the applause began. The applause of his peers this time, a precious sound to add to the tumultuous ovation from the stadium crowd earlier that evening and to the unheard cheers of the millions back home who watched on television as he ran himself into immortality.

The athletes who broke off from their late-night bowls of noodles and salad in the village were recognizing him as someone special in a world of special achievers. The winner of the men's 100 metres race is somewhere above and beyond the rest. Last Sunday, Linford Christie became their victor ludorum. The winner of the games.

Watching him in Stuttgart last week as he lived out the second half of his great double triumph, seeing how he received his laurels with grace and dignity and a proper measure of humility, observing the aura created by his now formidable presence in the backstage areas of the world athletics championships, it certainly didn't look as though Linford Christie has a problem, even though that's what people say.

For the past week Christie's home has been Block 3815, a rectangular concrete edifice thrown up in the late 1950s for the men of the US Army, successive generations of them posted to the barracks at Nellingen, a small town on a hilltop a few miles outside Stuttgart.

There are two dozen of the big whitewashed blocks dotted around the grassy slopes; between them, willow and ash and birch trees were planted in an attempt to make the place feel more like the ideal American suburb. But two years ago, when the cold war ended, the soldiers and their families went home. Now the sandpits are overgrown, the swings and slides broken, and there's a competition among local architecture students to devise a future use for this monument to old certainties.

Briefly, these last few days, the life has returned to the barracks at Nellingen, its pathways crowded with beautiful young bodies in bright sports clothes, its windows and doorways hung with the banners of 180-odd nations, its sports fields marked out for the rehearsals of the world's greatest athletes.

Christie's status within this world is such that no one would have raised an eyebrow had the British team captain chosen to base himself in a suite in one of Stuttgart's luxury hotels. That was the option taken by Carl Lewis, Christie's great rival, and his colleagues from the Santa Monica Track Club, the elite corps of the US track team, who have been spraying what one member of the British squad described as 'essence of superstar' around the lobby of a five star palace.

The morning after his 100 metres triumph over Lewis and the other Americans, Christie made plain his disapproval of such divisions. 'I don't believe I'm a superstar,' he said. 'I'm just a normal athlete. So I stay in the village, eating the same grubby food as everybody else.' He didn't realize the significance of it, he said, until athletes from other countries started coming up and telling him how much they respected him for it. 'Anyway, in hotels you get bored. There's no one to talk to. Some of the guys I race against don't even know their own team-mates. And how can I encourage the others if I'm not sharing the same life? I wouldn't swap the atmosphere of the village for anything.'

Christie's willingness to put up with plain food and a narrow bed that made his back ache all week is consistent with the way he has accepted the responsibility of team leadership. Not that he was an obvious choice when, one day in 1989, the British suddenly found themselves in need of a captain. At first, being given the job didn't mean much. In fact, the team hadn't had a captain at all since the hurdler Alan Pascoe almost two decades earlier; during the era of Ovett and Coe and Thompson, nobody had felt the need of a titular figurehead. Then, one weekend in Gateshead, the British team discovered, greatly to their surprise, that they were about to win the Europa Cup. And two officials, Tony Ward and Les Jones, realized that someone would have to go up and accept the trophy. 'Les and I looked at each other,' Ward remembers, 'and there was really only one man we could ask.'

That's not quite right. Many people thought that if the team needed a captain, the more mature and articulate Kriss Akabusi would have been a better choice than the occasionally aloof and volatile Christie. But Ward and Jones chose perhaps more wisely than they knew. Automatically respected by team-mates for his achievements on the track, Christie has won their affection and loyalty for his refusal to play the superstar game.

That's how Darren Campbell feels, anyway. When Christie arrived at his morning-after press conference last week in a Mercedes saloon, he was accompanied by his coach, Ron Roddan, and by Campbell, the 19-year-old silver medallist at 100 metres and 200 metres in the 1992 world junior championships, who has been sharing a dormitory in Block 3815 with Christie and Colin Jackson.

Now, as Christie was engulfed by reporters, Campbell spoke with enthusiasm of the help and encouragement the Olympic champion had given him over the last couple of years. In turn, Christie was telling his listeners that if British sprinting was to have a future after his own retirement, then it had better start looking to the needs of young athletes such as Darren Campbell.

Christie's commitment to the welfare of his team has been proved in a variety of situations. In Barcelona last year it was his task to calm the disgraced Jason Livingston and get him on a flight home with the minimum of fuss and damage to the collective morale. In Stuttgart last week, only a few minutes after his 100 metres final, he physically put himself between the young 800 metres runner Curtis Robb and Johnny Gray, the veteran American. Gray, expressing his belief that Robb had barged him out of the semi-final, was hurling shoes, hitting furniture, pointing fingers and waving fists in the changing area. 'Leave my boy alone,' Christie told the near-hysterical American. 'Lay a finger on him and you'll answer to me.' And then on Wednesday, at supper with Sally Gunnell, the captain of the women's team, on the eve of her final, he responded to the uncertainty of his fellow Barcelona gold medallist by saying a wonderful thing. Just think, he told her, what'll happen if you don't win tomorrow. Just imagine arriving back at Heathrow after the weekend. I'm walking out first, showing my gold medal to the photographers. And you're standing at the back, in the shadows, watching me. Is that what you want? So simple, so wise, and it worked.

More rewards came on Friday night, when Christie led the celebrations for Jackson's world record and the silver medals of Tony Jarrett and John Regis. His friend Colin's run, he told reporters, had given him twice as much pleasure as his own.

A hero, yes, but also a human being, with flaws and blemishes. There have been the semi-public rows with Frank Dick, the national coach. There is the payment of maintenance to the mother of twins (although he has been in a steady relationship with his girlfriend, Mandy Miller, for several years). There is the matter of his close association with Andy Norman, the paymaster-general of British athletics, and his membership of Chafford Hundred, the controversial elite athletes' club run by Norman's girlfriend, the former javelin champion Fatima Whitbread, which is thought by some to cream off money that ought to be more widely distributed. And then there are his confrontations with the press.

This other side of Linford Christie had come out less than an hour after his final in Stuttgart, when he sat alongside André Cason and Dennis Mitchell at the medallists' press conference.

He'd said most of what he had to say when a German reporter phrased a question in good but not quite perfectly idiomatic English.

'Did you get a personal reaction from Carl Lewis?' he asked. Christie looked blank. Seeing his puzzlement, the reporter attempted a clarification. 'Do you have a personal relationship with him?'

A flicker of scorn crossed Christie's face.

'Yeah,' he said. 'He's kissing me on the lips every night.'

There was a sort of gasp and a bit of a titter, and the faces of Cason and Mitchell quickly turned into masks. The reporters from the British papers looked at one another and winced. Just like Daley Thompson, they were thinking, and his loose-lipped line about Princess Anne having his babies. Some people never learn when to keep their mouths shut.

The source of Christie's remark was to be found neither in his view of Carl Lewis's sexuality, nor in a desire to become known as a stand-up comedian, but in his general contempt for the people who ask him questions: newspaper people. That attitude is not constructive, but it can be understood.

Look at it this way. Born thirty-three years ago in Jamaica, Christie was brought to England at the age of seven. He grew through adolescence to manhood at a time when young black men in districts like his adopted West London were thought to be characterized by fecklessness and a disregard of the law – by their fondness for taking drugs, for playing loud reggae records at unsociable hours, for fathering children out of wedlock and stealing car radios. Christie himself was subjected to the sort of police surveillance known to many young blacks, who classify it as harrassment. Yet, while never cutting himself off from his roots in the West Indian community, he has consistently expressed pride in his British nationality. 'When I win,' he has said, 'I win for my country.'

Here, then, is a man whose achievements could make him an invaluable model for a section of the population that had been given little incentive to aim high, and which has reacted by creating serious problems for the rest of society. So how did we respond a day or two after this fellow won the gold medal in the most important event at the 1992 Olympic Games? We filled the pages of the country's most popular newspaper with speculation about the size of his genitals.

Luckily, his response has been to despise journalists as a class rather than the society that produces them, just as he chooses not to take the attitude of the policemen who wrongfully arrested him in 1988 for that of the nation as a whole.

Whenever Christie wins a big title nowadays, his first instinct is to pay tribute to the grey-haired 61-year-old who spotted his potential at a stadium in Wormwood Scrubs in 1979. Last Sunday night, Christie was hardly off the track before he was describing Ron Roddan as 'the real world champion'.

He couldn't tell Roddan that to his face because the coach was a few miles away, in a Stuttgart hotel room, watching the 100 metres final on television, since that way he'd get a clearer view and the benefit of replays. Over the phone a few minutes later, though, Roddan scolded the new world champion for 'a bit of slackness' that he had detected in the middle section of the race. Reflected glory and easy praise are not Ron Roddan's style, not the way of a man whose rigorous approach has transformed Christie from a lazy, domino-playing youth into a proud figure on the world stage.

What had Roddan seen in the 19-year-old? 'A tall, gangling lad, nice looking, no muscles on him at all. Most sprint coaches look for someone fairly tall, with a good build, the right proportions, a full range of movement. He had all that, but I never thought he'd turn out the way he has. It took me a couple of years to begin to see it.' A turning point seems to have been the first time Christie pulled on the Great Britain vest, at an indoor international in the mid-1980s. 'He came back,' Roddan remembered last week, 'and he said, "I like this!"'

Nowadays Christie pays Roddan's expenses on trips to warm places such as Monaco, where they made their final preparations for Stuttgart, but the coach declines a fee for his work with a man whose tariff, even before last week, was £25,000 a race. 'I wouldn't feel comfortable taking part of someone's earnings,' he said. 'If I did, I'd feel responsible for ensuring that they made money. And then maybe there'd be the temptation to get them to do things that might not be the best for them. Anyway, I'm not in coaching for money. And although Linford's making money now, he isn't in it for that either. He's in it because he loves it.'

Roddan's view of Christie's character is that 'he enjoys himself, he enjoys having people around him and he's a very bright person. I know other people have had trouble with him, but I think that if you treat someone in the right way, that's what you get back. If you treat them wrong, you get the other thing. That's how Linford responds.'

In the build-up to his 100 metres final in Stuttgart it was obvious that whereas his main rivals – Lewis, Cason, Mitchell – would each settle into the blocks suspecting that he might be the fastest man in the world, only Linford Christie knew for sure that he was. The way he carried himself excluded any other possibility. So, now that he is indisputably one of the greatest sporting performers Britain has ever produced, how will Britain treat him in the years to come?

'Linford isn't the type to wait around for someone to do something for him,' Roddan said. 'I think he'll do some coaching, but only with good young runners. He hasn't got the patience to work with big groups of mixed ability.'

Roddan also sees in Christie a man whose qualities could have an application beyond sport. 'I've got a feeling, though, that in this country at this particular time, it doesn't work like that. It's not just the government. It's everything. It's the way people like Linford are so often used just to give someone else a boost. He could do a good job in any number of different ways, if he thought he was being asked for the right reasons.'

Maybe in thirty or forty years' time people will still be applauding when Linford Christie enters a room. And perhaps not just for what he did last year in Barcelona and last week in Stuttgart.

It's certainly nice to have his medals in the nation's trophy cabinet. But the use we make of Linford Christie in the years after he quits the track may turn out to say less about the man himself than about the country he has been proud to represent.

MICHAEL SCHUMACHER
One Step Away

SILVERSTONE, 15 MARCH 1994

WHEN THEY'RE SQUIRTING champagne over each other, he's the one who looks genuinely pleased to be there. Pleased to have finished in the top three. Pleased to be getting yet another absurdly grand trophy to clutter the mantelpiece back in the apartment he shares with his fiancée, Corinna, in Monaco. Pleased to be in the gaze of a billion-strong worldwide television audience. Pleased to be earning a few hundred thousand pounds for his weekend's work. No, the more tiresome little niggles of early success haven't managed to spoil Michael Schumacher's fun.

For the rest of them, it's all fear and politics and little stratagems designed to undermine other egos. Not Schumacher, though. His raised-arms salute and openly joyful smile haven't changed since he exploded on the grand prix scene three years ago, a talent seemingly already matured at 22 years of age and one of only half a dozen men since the war who have looked absolute certainties for the world championship from the moment they stepped into a Formula One car.

Nobody as successful as Schumacher in such a specialized and demanding sphere of human activity can possibly be described as uncomplicated, but the young German at least gives the impression of straightforwardness. Even when his astonishing debut at the 1991 Belgian Grand Prix – seventh place in the unregarded Jordan-Ford – led to an unseemly struggle for his services and to angry charges of contract-breaking, somehow the brown stuff has never adhered to his racing overalls.

For now, Michael Schumacher's life looks gloriously simple. Next week the 1994 grand prix season starts in São Paulo. The clear favourite – the clearest favourite in many years – is Ayrton Senna, at the wheel of a new version of the Williams-Renault, the car that took Nigel Mansell and Alain Prost to the last two titles. The best driver in the best car. The only man with a real chance of challenging him, people are saying, is Schumacher, third in the rankings in 1992 and 1993, and now ready to prove what many observers suggest: that he might be even faster than Senna.

'It's nice to know that people have that trust in me,' Schumacher said, sitting in the bright green Benetton motorhome in the infield of Silverstone's South Loop and pondering his response to the question of whether he is ready to take on the Brazilian for the title of undisputed number one. 'But I think it's not possible to answer the question in that way. The only thing I can say is that I've got another year more experience. That's now the third year of experience I have. But there's no way for me to say, "Okay, I'm behind this driver or in front of that driver." You can never really say that unless you have all the drivers in the same team, with the same car.'

Outside the windows of the motorhome, it was what generations of English motor racing fans have come to think of as a real Silverstone day: bright blue sky, angry black clouds, frequent downpours, brilliant sunshine, a sudden hailstorm. Small groups of men in co-ordinated anoraks and radio headsets stood in clumps between the trucks and the temporary marquees, listening to a solitary car wailing at full throttle down the distant Hangar Straight.

Schumacher was hanging around, waiting for something to happen, which is what usually happens at Silverstone testing sessions. In the Benetton marquee the dozen members of the full-time test team were fussing over the new car, the B194, some of them working to rectify a fault in its gearbox. If the rain and the hail permitted, they were planning the car's first test over a full race distance: an hour and a half's flat-out running.

Testing had been going on at various warm weather circuits around southern Europe – Barcelona, Estoril, Imola – for five or six weeks. The previous week, during the last day of formal testing at Imola, Schumacher had established a considerable psychological advantage by ending up almost a fifth of a second faster than Senna. During what was reported to be a furious final assault, neither Senna nor his team-mate, Damon Hill, could match the pace of the Benetton – a result that would have been impossible last year.

'It was a good week,' Schumacher said. 'We improved the car. It's already quite good, basically – we saw this from the first test we did here at Silverstone. We've continued, looking for reliability, so that everything is right for the beginning of the season. Which is good. You have to do this. But now we have to look at developing the car.'

To the layman's eye, the B194 appears to differ from last year's car only in its paintwork, which now shows a change of allegiance from an American to a Japanese brand of cigarettes. The truth is very different: designed to a completely new set of technical regulations, this is a brand-new vehicle, all of its systems requiring practical proof of the qualities they showed on the computer-simulation screens in the team's flat white factory block, 20 miles away.

No active suspension, no ABS, no traction control. Even Benetton's unique innovation, four-wheel steering, has gone. Of the computer-controlled systems – which Schumacher refers to collectively as the *technik* – only the semi-automatic gearbox remains, operated by two little black fingertip paddles under the steering wheel. Yet, astonishingly, at Imola the B194 was three whole seconds faster than Schumacher's qualifying time for last year's race at Imola, set in a car bristling with driver-aids. Weren't we expecting to see the cars going slower?

'Ah,' Schumacher said, 'but the point is that with the *technik* I believe we would have gone another one or two seconds quicker still! I'm sure of that. I'm happy that we're running with the technical situation as it is now, because it's going to make the competition more even. Hopefully, anyway. With the *technik*, for a lot of teams it meant new things – and with new things you have to experiment. Sometimes that was difficult, and it was more difficult for teams that didn't have the money to make it work as well as we did.'

When he first drove the new car, had he missed all the automatic bits and pieces which presumably made his life easier?

'As a driver,' he said, 'you have two things in mind. One is to drive as quick as possible and to enjoy it and to make a gap between yourself and your team-mate or the other drivers. You have to prove yourself. The other is to make the car as quick as possible, to set it up in the best way without compromises. With all the *technik*, it was a lot easier to do this. You didn't have to make too many compromises. Now, without *technik*, there are things on which you have to compromise – and maybe driver potential counts for more.'

Schumacher is one of the few drivers – like Jean Alesi and Johnny Herbert – who makes it obvious to the paying customers in the grandstand that he actually enjoys the real business of racing, the white-knuckle ride of outbraking and overtaking. Do the new non- *technik* cars put that sort of thing higher on the agenda?

'I think we won't see a different overtaking situation. The aerodynamics are still so important, and the point is that if you drive up close behind somebody, you lose the downforce. So you have to let the gap open, and you don't get the overtaking situation. That could still happen, like last year. I enjoyed go-karts … I enjoyed them because you drive wheel-on-wheel, you drive bumper-to-bumper, and this is real racing, which I enjoy very much. Some of this we do miss in Formula One. I don't know if it's possible on that level. It might not be.'

Nevertheless, his feeling is that the rule changes will compress the field and that this will bring back a measure of excitement. 'I can't say the racing between the first team and the second team will be more fun, but I think the whole field, from the first to the last, will be closer than in the years before.'

His father and mother run a go-karting centre in Kerpen, near Cologne, which was where the boy Michael first sat behind the wheel of a racing machine. At 15 he was the national junior karting champion; at 18 he had the German and European senior titles. Right from the beginning he wanted to race wherever and whenever he could, whatever the conditions – which was how he acquired his phenomenal speed in the wet, a talent that brought him his first grand prix victory, in a rain-affected race at Spa two years ago.

'When I was something like 10 or 12 years old, I couldn't do serious racing, because I was too young. And the point was then over the weekend when other people were there and it was raining and nobody wanted to drive, I always said, 'Come on, let me drive, let me drive.' I always enjoyed driving in those conditions, playing with the car, making 360-degree turns. That's the best way of getting the feeling for a go-kart or a car. Racing in the rain is difficult, that's true, but you just have to be careful and handle the situation. If you can't see, you have to back off. I'm not a driver who still goes flat out when you can't see anything. I don't want to risk my life or even other lives.'

That first win, with its carefully planned tyre stops, also emphasized his strategic flair. Back at Spa a year later, a botched start called on other qualities: a combination of aggression and patience that saw him climb through the field from last place to second, only a few seconds behind Hill's Williams, at the finish. In terms of raw heroism, it was a drive to mention in the same breath as Fangio at the Nürburgring in 1957 or Clark at Monza in 1967.

'There's some characters you really can fight with. They don't play games, they don't drive with … How can I say this? I have to be careful … With some people, if you have the feeling that there's the chance to pass them, you really go for it – you brake late, you dive to the inside. And the next lap he might do it with you. But with some people you can't do that, because you don't know what they're like, they're unpredictable … You have to be more clever than them and overtake them in a different way, where they don't expect it.'

Which does he prefer to race against – the predictable or the unpredictable?

'Certainly the predictable. But I've found there's always a way to run around the unpredictable. In fact, sometimes I like to drive against the unpredictable, because they're more difficult to handle, and when you find a way around them it's even more of a pleasure.'

The sky was clearing and the test beckoned. As he prepared to go, Schumacher expressed his confidence that, having overcome Ferrari to take third place among the constructors over the last two years, this was the season Benetton could push past McLaren into second position. 'Number one would be too ambitious,' he said. 'It's not realistic at the moment. Hopefully we can push the Williams, sometimes stay close, sometimes win a race, but as for the championship, I think we're still one more step away from that.'

So is it inevitable that Senna will win his fourth title this year?

'I think he's the main contender, together with Damon Hill. They have the best package for this season. But that doesn't mean that in some races where they don't find the right set-up, we might find a very good set-up – and we'll be very close, we'll fight together, and then by strategies or stuff we're going to win races. But too many bad things would need to happen to other teams for us really to have the chance to win the championship. Drivers like Senna or Hill, a team like Williams … they don't make mistakes.'

MELBOURNE, 1 MARCH 2002

AS HE APPROACHES tomorrow's start of the grand prix season, there are already two names that Michael Schumacher is tired of hearing. One, that of Juan Manuel Fangio, is from the past. The other, Juan Pablo Montoya, belongs to the future.

When the cars leave the grid in Melbourne, the Formula One circus expects to see the opening chapter of an epic battle between the world champion and Montoya. With a series of spirited displays last year, the Colombian presented himself as the long-awaited challenger to Schumacher's dominance.

'If that is going to be a good battle,' Schumacher said, 'I'm looking forward to it. I've had many good fighters close to me in my eleven years in Formula One. I'm sure Montoya is one of them, but there's still a question mark against him.' He will have known that Frank Williams, for whose team Montoya drives, recently suggested that if the Colombian wants to be a world champion, he would be well advised to emulate Schumacher's total dedication to his team's cause.

Fangio's challenge is not quite so easily handled. Can a man who drives a computer from inside a carbon-fibre survival cell possibly deserve comparison with the sort of hero who stepped out of a racing car with hot oil covering his face and raw blisters on the palms of his hands? In other words, if Schumacher wins tomorrow's race in Albert Park and goes on to match Fangio's record of five world championships at the end of the season, will that make him as great as the greatest racing driver who ever lived?

Whatever drives Schumacher, it is not a sense of his place in history. 'Statistics do mean something,' he said this week, 'but for me it's really about the love for Formula One, the love of racing with four wheels around me and the challenge to go fast. What motivates me is winning races and doing the best job I can. That's more important than any numbers I might have in my head.'

If he achieves the record, however, history will certainly claim him, and rightly so. Whatever blemishes may been have placed on his record by the notorious collisions with Damon Hill in 1994 and Jacques Villeneuve three years later, Schumacher's 53 wins from 161 starts entitle him to a place alongside the handful of all-time greats. Exactly where he ranks among them is a harder question.

'It's a matter of completely different eras,' Rubens Barrichello, his Ferrari team-mate, says, 'so it's hard to know how good Michael is. We saw him driving against Ayrton for a year or so, and it was very difficult to know if he was better or not. For sure in the modern era he can beat everybody who's there to beat. But I will never know if he is the best there has ever been.'

As for the nature of the task Schumacher is required to perform, it can only be said that different times require different approaches. Fangio's skills were those of a Spitfire pilot. Schumacher's Ferrari belongs to the age of the Stealth fighter, as do his techniques.

Just turned 33, and the unquestioned *patron* of the grid, the world champion arrived in Melbourne this week in a relaxed and genial mood. Three weeks with his wife and their two small children in Mauritius, where he swam, cycled and played beach football, were followed by a spell of fitness training in Norway. 'The season is so long and so hard that you really have to absorb the maximum time you can to recharge yourself and store up the energy you'll need later in the year,' he said.

As soon as the Ferrari team returned to activity after the long winter break, however, they had proof of his continued enthusiasm. 'Early in January we were doing some systems testing,' Ross Brawn, Ferrari's technical director, said this week. 'We don't ask the race drivers to do it because it's tedious and they get fidgety. But Michael rang me up and said, "I haven't driven for two months – I want to drive." He came down and afterwards he said, "That was fantastic – I just wanted to make sure I could still do it." He loves racing and everything that goes with it.'

No one knows more about Michael Schumacher the racing driver than Brawn, the technical director behind all four of his world championships, first at Benetton and then at Ferrari. He is the one who sits on the pit wall during the race, discussing strategy with the driver over the radio. Scanning the readouts from on-car telemetry, Brawn is the first and sometimes the only witness to the minute variations in Schumacher's performance. If anyone knows where the world champion's extra quantum of speed comes from, he is the man.

'What really makes the difference,' he said, sitting at a table behind the Ferrari garage in the Albert Park paddock, 'is the way Michael enters medium and high-speed corners with such commitment and confidence. Lots of people can come through the middle of a corner and make their exit well, particularly with the traction control systems we have now. You just put your foot on the throttle and the electronics will take care of it. But in the bravery of getting into a fast corner, there's no substitute for driver ability.'

It is, he explained, a question of touch. 'When you're doing 300kph and you're going into a corner that's 250kph, you've got to kill that 50kph somehow. Michael uses a combination of throttle and brake to minimize the disturbance of the car and to enter the corner at exactly 250. He doesn't go down to 240 and back up to 250. He goes straight to the margin, keeping the car at the limit of its performance.'

Consistency is another factor. 'He can drive fifteen or twenty laps of a race and everything is within a few centimetres on each lap,' Brawn said. 'Sometimes people get close to him in qualifying, but in a race he just builds and builds and that small gap becomes greater because he hits the limit all the time – every corner, every time.'

There is also his ability to make the most of the possibilities offered by the array of coloured buttons in the centre of his steering wheel, governing such matters as engine tuning, traction control, brake balance and differential adjustment. New rules mean that certain adjustments can now be made from the pits, by remote control, but most of the significant variables will remain within Schumacher's sphere, and this is where he is able to demonstrate a new range of skills, perhaps just as extraordinary as Fangio's.

'Michael is a great enthusiast for making adjustments during the race,' Brawn said. 'He likes to tune the car as he's driving it. And this is where he's very strong.'

In the areas he continues to control, Schumacher can adjust settings programmed to recognize which corner the car is entering and to behave accordingly. He can alter the way the engine reacts as he lifts off the throttle into a certain corner, for example. He can alter the characteristics of the traction control to give him better stability at certain points, or adjust the behaviour of the differential to take account of wearing tyres.

All these require swift mental calculations based on a number of parameters. 'It's a bit of a complex operation,' Brawn said, 'and we can help him find the ideal solution to any problem, because we're studying the data. Our discussions during the race are just like the one you and I are having now. You'd never imagine he was driving a racing car.'

But as well as speed, precision and coolness, Schumacher also possesses a more fundamental quality, which is the gift of suppressing his ego and blending into the team. When he was asked, at the launch of Ferrari's 2002 car, how he felt about matching Fangio's record, the phrasing of his answer was significant. 'No doubt it would be great to achieve number five,' he said, 'because all the effort that we as a team have put into the new car is tremendous.'

The team, he said, is like an extra family. 'Nothing is better than to win with Ferrari and for Ferrari's fans. The human relationships that have been built up since I arrived here in 1996 is something I never believed that I would experience within a team. To have so many friendships makes it worth a lot more.'

No one who has watched him at work, and observed his

closeness to mechanics earning barely a thousandth of his £25 million annual retainer, would see this as an empty claim. 'He's a team person,' Brawn said. 'One or two drivers you don't feel like that about. Eddie Irvine, to me, is not a team person. He works hard at trying to create a team, but inherently he's not a team player. He's more interested in his individual needs. Michael is the other way round. He respects everybody in the team for what they do.'

One thing Schumacher is not is pretentious. For all his mansion in Switzerland and his private jet, in many ways he remains recognizably a son of Kerpen, a small and superficially unattractive town a dozen kilometres west of Cologne, on the way to the Belgian border. Sindorf, a neighbouring industrial zone, is where his father's old kart track has mushroomed into the vast Michael Schumacher Kart-Center, located on Michael Schumacher-Strasse, with indoor and outdoor tracks and a 'fan shop' selling the merchandise that has contributed to doubling the income he receives from racing.

'He has no airs or graces,' Brawn said. 'He loves his family and he has a close group of friends. He's quite a private person in that respect. He obviously has some nice toys, but he's not part of the jet set. And with the team, too, he's working with a group of people who are thinking the same way. I don't think he likes to change teams. He likes to be part of a group, and he accepts their strengths and weaknesses.'

Schumacher's work ethic certainly helped drag the team out of a long barren period. Ten years ago, the Scuderia Ferrari was a mess. Now, with an annual budget believed to be in excess of £300 million and a payroll of more than 600, the racing department has regained its pride and its pre-eminence.

'What we learned today was something we knew already,' Frank Williams said ruefully after watching Schumacher and Barrichello top the list of times in yesterday's practice sessions, 'which is that Ferrari are in a class of their own.'

The world champion played a big part in that improvement, and this week's bad news for every other team was the quiet announcement of his intention to start thinking about negotiating an extension to his current Ferrari contract, which expires at the end of 2004. 'It will be with nobody else but Ferrari, that's pretty clear,' he said when asked about his future. 'I don't see any other team that would interest me at all.'

'People say Michael Schumacher runs the Ferrari team,' Ross Brawn said, 'but that's not true. What he does is set an example to the Ferrari team. If you need any extra incentive to get up in the morning and go to work, you only have to look at the job he's doing.'

In the fifty-two years of the world championship, only a handful of drivers – Fangio, Clark, Stewart, Senna – have been held in unquestioned awe by their rivals. At the end of yesterday's session, Schumacher appeared to have joined their number. And there is a chance that, by the end of tomorrow, we shall know whether he has it in him to reach the most exalted level of all. If so, this controversial and often reviled figure will have permitted us that rarest of sensations: the feeling that we are living through a golden age of our very own.

SERENA WILLIAMS
Doing It for Herself

6 JANUARY 2003

IT WAS ON her 20th birthday that Serena Williams told herself to shape up and make the most of her talent. The decision she made that day – 26 September 2001 – was to reshape the hierarchy of women's tennis.

'Things took a turn in my life,' she mused the other day. 'I said, "I'm going to get serious about my tennis. I can be the best. I can be No.1." I had been on that route but I got misguided somewhere along the line.'

Had there been a specific catalyst for her decision?

'Yes, there was something, but I won't let you in on it. It's personal.'

There is no secret, however, about the steps she took in order to unlock the potential that her father had seen half a dozen years earlier, when he predicted that she would one day take over from her older sister Venus at the top of the world rankings.

'I had to become more serious, to stop making so many

mistakes on the court and to study a little harder off the court,' she said. 'Just small changes can make the world of a difference.'

At 17 Serena had won the US Open, beating the former champion and world No.1, Martina Hingis, in the final. Fifteen months younger than Venus, she became the first of the sisters to win a grand slam tournament. But then followed almost two years without another major success, while Venus won Wimbledon twice and ascended to the top of the world rankings.

Nick Bolletieri watched the change occur during Serena's frequent visits to his tennis centre in Bradenton, Florida, a 150-mile drive from the house the sisters then shared in Palm Beach Gardens.

'Something clicked,' the coach said this week. 'She told herself, "I'm tired of finishing second, third, fourth. It's time I stepped up to the plate and became a champion." And no matter what anyone says, when you have two siblings who are that good, it's tough for one of them to focus on herself individually. I think that was somewhat of a hindrance to her in the past.'

More solid and compact than her long-limbed sister, and three inches shorter, Serena worked not just on technique but also on her strength and power as she prepared for the 2002 season. After an ankle injury forced her to miss the Australian Open, she re-emerged as an altogether more formidable competitor.

In February she beat Hingis, the world No.5, and then Jennifer Capriati, the No.2, to win a tournament in Scottsdale, Arizona. 'For me it was a big win because I was really, really ill,' she remembered. 'I get the flu every year right around that time and I was still able to win it. I hadn't played all year and I was still able to beat the top players. Then I went on to win Miami.'

There she vanquished Hingis and Capriati again, those quarter-final and final victories sandwiching the first of the season's four victories over her sister. The other three matches in which she beat Venus were the finals of the remaining grand slam tournaments, the French, Wimbledon and the US, in which she did not concede a single set. Halfway through Wimbledon she was promoted to the No.1 ranking for the first time.

'The difference is that she's concentrating on her shot selection and on cutting down on the unforced errors,' Bolletieri said, reflecting on the technical changes she made last winter. 'She'd be playing unbelievably well but then all of a sudden she'd make an unnecessary error. Her shot selection has improved unbelievably.'

But whatever her critics may say, glancing in mingled envy and disapproval at the muscle definition in her calves and the power of her torso as it strains against the shiny, clinging fabric of the startling black dress she wore at Flushing Meadow last year, she is not a machine. As she prepares to serve, she might bounce the ball once. Or twice. Or sometimes four, five, even six times. Serena has a groove, but it was not cut by the computerized lathe of modern tennis coaching. Like her sister, she invents her own rhythms; but while Venus swoops and dives around the court like a huge exotic bird, Serena hurtles to meet the ball with a primal force that can make a stadium shudder.

Last year the groove was deep enough to take her to the brink of what golfers call the 'Tiger Slam', and which she, without undue modesty, refers to as the 'Serena Slam' – in other words, all four major tournaments in a row. On Monday in Melbourne she will begin her attempt to collect the set.

'It's going to be tough,' she said, 'specially going down under and playing in that heat. Plus I think that Venus is really going to try to win that event, so we'll see.'

Her rivals take comfort from her unexpected defeat by Kim Clijsters in the WTA championships in California at the end of last season. 'Everybody's human, and out there anything can happen,' Elena Bovina, the promising Russian player, said last month. 'We saw that she's not out of reach. Kim proved to everybody that you can do it. She's the first girl, after Martina [Hingis] did it two years ago, that beat the two sisters in a row. You do that and you win the championship. Definitely Serena is going to Australia as the favourite, but, you know, nothing's impossible.'

Serena bristled at a suggestion that defeat at Clijsters' hands had constituted a reality check. 'No, it didn't. I'd played so much tennis by then that I was gone. Physically I felt like a 98-year-old woman with a hip replacement. I don't even know how I was able to play that tournament. I was just happy to have even gotten that far. It's going to go against my permanent record, and that's kind of sad for me because I had a good record against her before. But she's a good player. I'm always having to look out for her, most definitely.'

In Melbourne last week she met Clijsters again and delivered what she no doubt considered a correction to the historical record. The score, an exact reversal of the original 7–5, 6–3 result, looked almost as if it had been devised for its symbolic value.

Yet even as she glances down on the world from the No.1's vantage point, Serena remains the little sister. When they played doubles together at a tournament in Dublin before Christmas, Venus could be seen adjusting Serena's headband and straightening the shoulder of her T-shirt. Every now and then Serena glanced at her, as if for guidance.

Accustomed to being 'family', they find old habits hard to break. Venus looks out for Serena, as she has done since they went on the tour together. And that, as their father noticed before any of us had heard their names, is what gives Serena a competitive advantage when they face each other.

She demonstrated her growing independence by buying an apartment in Los Angeles before Christmas, paying $1.4m for a two-bedroom pad in a high-rise condo with a pool, a gym, a concierge, valet parking and extensive security systems. She will use it as a base from which to pursue her acting career, having made an appearance last year playing a school teacher in a television series called *My Wife and Kids*.

Venus, meanwhile, has launched her own interior decoration company in Florida and continues to study fashion design at the Art Institute of Fort Lauderdale. Many feel that she will be the first to quit professional tennis, although when she protested in Dublin that 'I'm only 22 – I have a few years left', it was tempting to recall that her father, who has not got many things wrong, said in the mid-1990s that he wanted his daughters out of tennis and moving on to other areas of endeavour by the time they were 23.

By that measure, Serena has a couple of seasons in which to confirm her dominance. 'I haven't reached a peak yet,' she told me. 'Not at all. There's a lot of stuff I can do better and that I hope to do better.'

Bolletieri was more precise. 'We've worked on her serve,' he said. 'That's been a big thing. We spent a lot of time on that before she left for Australia. Mechanically, she has a much better serve than her sister. Venus opens up and serves with her arms. Serena serves with her lower body and her legs. And she's developed a good slice and a drop shot.

'She's also going to be spending a lot more time up at the net. The reason she's been overhitting from the baseline is because when someone has retrieved one of her shots, she'd just try to hit it back even harder. But she's more comfortable at the net now.

'She's very confident and she's become a real perfectionist. She spent two or three days here, but she wasn't satisfied, so she came back and spent another two or three days with me. She becomes very angry when she makes a mistake. Right now, she feels that she shouldn't be missing anything. This year I believe she's going to be competing against herself.'

THE VIEW FROM THE HIGH BOARD

MICHAEL ATHERTON
Standing Up

SABINA PARK, 26 FEBRUARY 1994

I T WAS THE FACT that he stood still that made you worry for him, even from a hundred yards away. Stillness was somehow the more frightening reaction, after a moment of such naked violence. But he didn't fall. He didn't even recoil. He just stood there, upright, motionless, like a photograph of the moment when the five-and-a-half ounce leather ball hit him at 80 or 90 miles an hour, smashing the grille of his helmet and banging the metal into his cheek.

Through field-glasses, you could see that his eyes were unfocused, looking somewhere inside, fighting for control. When Graeme Hick, his fellow batsman, arrived, closely followed by the team physiotherapist, they got no response. He wouldn't move, wouldn't speak.

If he moved, perhaps his head would fall off. If he opened his mouth to speak, maybe a jawful of teeth would clatter to the ground.

This was the moment, after weeks of pleasant formalities, when

England's Caribbean tour got real. And no one knew it, and understood its implications, better than Michael Atherton. He wasn't going to hop around or sit down or make any kind of a fuss. He was damned if he was going to show them that it hurt.

As displays of foolish but rather wonderful courage under fire go, the sight of the young England captain coping with the experience of Winston Benjamin's best bouncer detonating against his jaw looked like a VC job. And, of course, it is an English tradition that such displays must be accompanied by a degree of self-deprecation. Three days later, when the first Test was lost, Michael Atherton was disinclined to make any more of the incident.

So, how badly had it hurt?

'It didn't. Not really. No, seriously. It's the shock, because as a batsman you don't expect to get hit. You think your reflexes are good enough. But on that pitch, the ball was occasionally coming through low and I'd decided to stand up and play the short balls rather than ducking under them. So when the occasional ball got big on me, I was in trouble.'

You can believe the stuff about it not hurting if you want. But you shouldn't underestimate the significance of the accident.

Atherton had scored 19 runs when it happened. He had lost his opening partner and vice-captain, Alec Stewart, and his troubled senior batsman, Robin Smith. With an hour or so to play, he was looking to drop anchor for the night. But now, as he and we knew they would, the West Indian bowlers decided to put him to the test.

Three years ago, at the age of 22, Atherton played nine Test innings against the West Indian touring team and scored a total of 79 runs, for an average of 8.77. Coupled with a long-term back injury that was to lead to surgery, the failure cost him his England place and his confidence – the quality he has called his 'invincibility'. For the first time, a seed of doubt was sowed in his young mind. At about four o'clock last Monday afternoon on a humid afternoon at Sabina Park, the West Indies bowlers remembered that seed, and wondered if they could make it flower.

After Winston Benjamin's efforts, Courtney Walsh took over the assault. Bowling with sustained venom, he hit Atherton on the arm-guard and had him somersaulting away from a steepler in a rag-doll tangle of limbs. And then, halfway through the 12th over of what was, in its own terms, a majestic spell, Walsh went round the wicket, bowling short and directing his fire at Atherton's body. Two balls later the England captain was gone, caught off his glove at short leg. The bowlers' job was done. England's novice captain had been softened up.

'Oh, that's what people will think,' Atherton said over lunch after defeat had been sealed. 'I don't know. Hick got the treatment, too. It would have happened to whoever had been batting. I felt, actually, quite confident of surviving. I thought I was seeing the ball and playing well. And you need a bit of luck sometimes when they're bowling like that. One more ball and Kenny Benjamin would have been on – and I'd have seen it through, no problem. That's the way it goes.'

Walsh's hostile spell on Monday night was the third of three episodes that Atherton was later to identify as the decisive passages of the match. They began with England's batting collapse in the first innings and continued with the West Indian batsmen's recovery from a start which saw them stumble to 23 for three before the left-handed trio of Brian Lara (83), Keith Arthurton (126) and Jimmy Adams (95 not out) counter-attacked to build a winning position.

England's failure lay in the inability of their seam bowlers to maintain the pressure. 'Yes,' Atherton said with his best lopsided, rueful grin, 'we were bubbling then, and on top. The ball swung for Caddick early on, Desmond Haynes played a poor shot and Richie Richardson fell nicely into a trap. But we need the killer instinct. To be fair, the West Indians played positively and dug themselves out. But we also bowled poorly at them. I can accept Devon Malcolm going for four or five an over, because he's an attacking bowler who's likely to get wickets. But when I see some of our other seamers, and I see their left-handers virtually getting on to the front foot before the ball is bowled and stroking it through the covers, it begins to look like a Sunday league outing. We gave them an easy ride.'

His fast bowlers, he said, had been slow to realize that unlike most left-handers, these West Indians would punish anything aimed across them, slanting towards off. 'Give them a little bit of width around the off stump,' he said, 'and they'll smash it away. But you can tuck them up either by bowling straight or by coming round the wicket at them. Look at the way Lara was bowled in the second innings, behind his legs. Look how far across he was. These are things to look at and learn by, and maybe we'll get it right next time.'

The need for patience, for time to let his England team grow and mature, has been a keynote of Atherton's public pronouncements since he assumed the mantle of captaincy last summer and opted for a selection policy based on youth, promptly putting a stop to the losing sequence in the final match of an Ashes series. Last week's result in Kingston began the harsh process of scrutiny that some of his predecessors have found intolerable.

'I came on this tour firmly believing that we could win and would win,' he told me. 'And I'm not saying now that we can't win. But it's also a period of finding out about players. It's a question sometimes of taking two steps forward and one step back. That's how it will be for a while. People must be patient with that. We've got to get a Test side together, and it won't happen overnight.'

Had he nevertheless already found himself regretting the absence of one or two seasoned campaigners?

'Um. There are obviously moments of self-doubt, when you wonder if you've done the right thing. I'm convinced we have. To me, if you look at the way England played against the Australians in the early part of last summer, it was obvious to everybody that English cricket needed a shot in the arm. It did. If people say it didn't, they're wrong. And for me, this was the best way to provide it. The side was losing with experienced players in it. If it loses now, at least we might be getting closer to having something worthwhile in a year's time.'

The business of 'finding out about players' can be harsh. On the one hand, Atherton feels that Hick 'marked his arrival as a Test-class batsman' with the knock of 96 that lent respectability to England's second innings. On the other hand, there is Chris Lewis, whose loose bowling – a combination of short leg-side deliveries and off-stump half-volleys – was largely responsible for letting the home batting off the hook in the first innings. When I asked him about the perpetually enigmatic all-rounder, Atherton clutched his forehead and grimaced.

'Well,' he said, 'when Louie came out here he must have realized that he'd been close to not getting selected. He needed a good start to the tour to get into the frame. So I was disappointed when he missed the first game in Antigua with sunstroke. Then he didn't perform especially well against the Leewards. People may criticize us for selecting him for the Test, but it was his performance in the one-day international that got him into the side. He showed there that he could get reverse swing, which would have been useful in the Test match. Now I'm willing to stick by people provided that when I ask them for something, I get it, and they show the right attitude and application. What I'm less willing to do is stick by people if you ask for something and they don't give it you.'

Robin Smith, so unexpectedly vulnerable in both innings at Sabina Park, where he was dismissed for nought and two, is another matter. 'He's looked uncomfortable,' Atherton said, 'but he always does. He looks nervous and edgy even when he's getting runs against pace bowling. We certainly need him to perform. We can't afford him having a bad series. We felt that we came with three experienced Test-class batsmen in myself, Alec Stewart and Robin, and to my mind Hick's now joined us as the fourth. We need a fifth to come through, because a good Test side needs five experienced batsmen all playing well, so that your sixth batsman can be a young lad whom you're bringing along.'

Atherton believes in picking players and then letting them get on with it. So how does he help Smith to sort himself out?

'It's a difficult one. I mentioned to him something I'd seen in his batting. I'm not going to say what. It's a technical thing. But of course when you say something it may sound like jumping on the bandwagon just because he's had a bad game. So it's up to him whether he bears it in mind or not.'

The captaincy of a touring side is about group dynamics and individual welfare. Isolated during England's last tour, left to take taxis back to the hotel from solitary net practice, Atherton understands the pastoral role and the need to share himself around.

'The way this party was selected,' he said, 'it was without superstars, and if we were going to be successful, we needed to have a very strong sense of togetherness. So while cliques do develop and certain people go off on their own, I'm trying to be a bit of a binding force.'

How do you do that? Just by being nice to everybody?

'No! Well, you choose who you go out with at night. I try not to go out with the same people all the time. On this tour, Hussain, Ramprakash, Thorpe and Stewart mingle around. Maynard, Smith and Tufnell mingle around. Then there's Watkin, Caddick, Hick and Salisbury. I try to flit between all three. Lewis stays out on a limb a little bit. But there's a pretty good spirit.'

Atherton knows how it feels to be left out. 'There are a couple of guys on this tour who haven't played very much yet, and I know what they're going through. But sometimes there's no obvious reason for picking someone or leaving someone else out. Mark Ramprakash was very unlucky not to play in the first Test. He was desperate to play. He's a very intense cricketer. And he was massively disappointed, particularly since I hadn't had a chance to tell him before the team was announced. So I talked to him during the match and he argued his case, and in the end he was very good about it. But all I could tell him was that the decision had been based on an instinctive gut reaction, which really doesn't help anybody.'

He's finding out, he says, which players need pushing and which are self-motivating. At team meetings he tried to encourage others to talk – 'although I've found it difficult to get a response because of what's gone on in the past, when it all came from the top down and the players just sat and listened. I don't want people sitting there like sheep, particularly players like Ramprakash and Nasser Hussain, who both have reputations for being fiery characters, but they have good cricket brains, very sharp, and it's my job to bring that out.'

He inherited from his predecessor, Graham Gooch, the services of Peter Terry, a sports psychologist who was brought in midway through the last Ashes series and returned to take part in the preparations for the Caribbean tour. 'Goochie's quite a big believer in it,' the new captain said. 'I'm not so sure.'

'Visualization' is the chief technique of this pseudo-science. 'If you can visualize success, you've more chance of getting it. I do it as a matter of course when I'm preparing for an innings. You remember a time when you did well against these particular bowlers. You remember your career average and tell yourself you're a decent player. So you build up your expectation. Just common sense, really. If I'm about to face a barrage ... well, now I can remember last Monday night, and I can think, I was good enough then ...'. He caught himself and laughed. 'Or almost good enough again ...'

The common sense is probably invincible. The sense of humour, on the other hand, may take a damaging blow or two in the coming weeks. Just don't bet on seeing their owner flinch.

OLD TRAFFORD, 29 JULY 1994

'AS FAR AS I'm concerned,' Ray Illingworth said through clenched teeth, 'this matter has been dealt with and is now closed.' On the word 'closed', he brought his right hand down and slapped the table in a gesture of exasperated finality. That was at a quarter to eleven last Sunday evening in a room on the top floor of the Lord's pavilion, and far from being closed, the whole business was about to explode.

The Atherton affair lasted all week, and the echoes will reverberate far longer. When the captain of the England cricket team was accused of being a cheat and a liar, and the evidence was available for television replay, suddenly everybody had an opinion. And, for a while, they seemed unanimous.

'Go!' said a *Times* leader.

'Go!' said the BBC's cricket correspondent, with the authority expected of a former Test player.

'Go!' said an intense young publisher in a fashionable London restaurant.

'Go!' said an elderly lady in West Yorkshire, to whom cricket was a matter of blood and honour.

'Go!' was what Michael Atherton was being told by young and old, rich man and poor man, black, brown and beige, aficionado and ignoramus alike. In England hundreds of thousands of words were written and probably millions of conversations held, fuelled by the national appetite for instant aggro, instant villains – 'Gotcha!' 'Up Yours, Delors!' 'Turnip!' For Radio 5 Live it justified the new Babel of sports phone-ins. In other cricketing corners of the world, notably Pakistan, interest was just as keen – for here, perhaps, was the final humiliation, the payback for generations of colonial arrogance.

And it couldn't have happened to a nicer fellow.

Of course, people said with a nod and a wink, he's no choirboy. But they didn't really mean it.

A year ago this weekend, England entered the Atherton era. That was how it seemed when he turned up for his first selection committee meeting, succeeding the defeated and dispirited Graham Gooch. Atherton, then a fresh-faced 25 to Gooch's careworn 40, stood for old values and new thinking. England – who as recently as 1988 had employed four captains in a single calamitous series – gave the impression of having made, for once, an imaginative appointment with the long-term future in mind.

And for a year it worked. The results improved almost immediately. Atherton won a consolation Test match against the Australians at the Oval, and then another, against the West Indies at Bridgetown, albeit with the rubber already lost. And he managed to win a series against New Zealand – not entirely convincingly, perhaps, but the curve was certainly pointing upward. Morale was higher, to the extent that it could survive incidents like the dismissal of the entire team for a total of 46 runs in Port of Spain. The captain established sound working relationships with his team manager, Keith Fletcher, and his chairman of selectors, Ray Illingworth. Together they brought back some old faithfuls for reconsideration, but in general their choices pointed to the future, as Atherton promised they would. His own batting gained in strength and conviction; now he could lead by example, never more than when, at Sabina Park, he faced a barrage with conspicuous courage.

On tour in the Caribbean, Atherton could be seen at his best. Touring parties inevitably divide into cliques, and Atherton's skill was to permit this to happen, to allow his men the right to self-expression, while binding the whole group together by ensuring that no section or individual became marginalized, as he himself had been on Gooch's trip to India. He shared himself around, drinking with the roisterers one night and with the quiet bunch the next. A Cambridge graduate with a Lancashire accent, he could mix with the blazers and the lads alike. He knew when to join in, and how to remove himself without seeming aloof. This, at last, was the captain for whom England had been searching.

Then, last Sunday, he seemed to come undone. In the course of an agonizing twenty-three-minute press conference at Lord's, cornered on the subject of whether or not he had tampered with the ball during the afternoon session of the third day's play against South Africa, Atherton – still half-traumatized by the most savage defeat of his stewardship to date – veered from openness to evasion, from mild contrition to a barely suppressed petulance, from ill-judged attempts at humour to the occasional transparent pretence that nothing unusual was happening.

After seeing the television replays of what Peter Burge, the match referee, indelibly referred to as 'unfamiliar actions', Atherton had realized that he owed the world an explanation. But somewhere along the way he lost the courage that had enabled him to confront Benjamin and Walsh in Kingston. What we heard was a defence that dealt with some questions but left others screaming to be answered.

He may have been telling the truth when he claimed not to have been using dirt in his pocket to tamper with the ball, and in that he was certainly supported by the judgement of the referee and the umpires that the ball's condition had not been unduly altered during Saturday's afternoon session. But the first of his damning evasions came in this exchange:

Q: 'Michael, the footage seemed to show that when your hand came out of your pocket, presumably now dry, you then started to work on the ball.'

A: 'Absolutely not. I did not alter the condition of the ball at all. The dirt was there solely to keep the sweat off my fingers and my hands off the ball.'

Q: 'But your fingers were on the ball. What were they doing?'

A: 'Well, of course they were. That's the whole point of having the dirt on the fingers, so that the sweat doesn't get on the ball.'

Q: 'So what were you doing when you were rubbing the ball?'

A: 'I wasn't rubbing the ball. I polished the shiny side and kept the sweat off the dry side.'

The TV pictures showed him removing his right hand from his pocket, putting his fingertips to the ball, and rubbing one side of it with a purposeful action which seemed to leave no doubt that he had carried something from the pocket to the ball. The fact that he rubbed the ball on its rough side – we knew this because we could see him turning it in his hand before polishing the smooth side on his flannels – was beyond challenge. But he chose to dispute the evidence of our eyes, merely adding to the impression that something was not quite straight.

The technical minutiae of ball-tampering preoccupied the sports pages, but the question of the England cricket captain's truthfulness rang a more general alarm. The key moment came when he tetchily deflected questions about his conversation with the referee.

Q: 'Did Mr Burge at any stage ask you if you had something in your pocket?'

A: 'The conversations between myself and Mr Burge shall remain that way.'

Q: 'It's a pretty straightforward question, though.'

A: 'And I've just given you a pretty straightforward answer.'

Even his admirers found it hard to stomach that transparent attempt to use a quasi-legal formality – the pretence that a conversation between a cricketer and a match official enjoyed some kind of privileged status – to avoid incriminating himself.

The referee's own statement, released on Monday, did nothing to clarify the matter. Pakistanis in particular, still smarting from the various ball-tampering accusations of recent years, were outraged by his refusal to impose a separate punishment. Burge's acceptance of Illingworth's pre-emptive £2,000 fine on the captain as sufficient sanction appeared to them an endorsement of post-colonial justice, of one law for the brown and another for the white. Not at all the kind of thing, in fact, that one had expected from the Atherton era.

It had taken him twenty minutes on Sunday to work himself deeper into the hole; five days later it took him almost exactly twice as long to dig himself most of the way out, when he convened another press conference at his home ground of Old Trafford, hoping to clear the air before the second Test.

Clearly in a more settled frame of mind after a few days on the run in the Lake District with his girlfriend, he began by issuing a new and slightly fuller written statement. Then, as he knew it would, came the real inquisition, and so forensic was the mood that there were times during the forty-five minutes when Perry Mason and George Carman QC would have come in useful as Atherton and his chief accuser, Jonathan Agnew of the BBC, tied themselves in knots over the question of whether the dirt had come out of the pocket on the fingers, whether some of it had been transferred to the surface of the ball, and what degree of intent, if any, had been involved in those actions.

He stumbled a few times, over little things that loomed large.

Q: 'On Sunday you denied rubbing the ball in any way.'

A: 'I didn't deny it.'

Q: 'You did.'

A: 'I didn't.'

Q: 'I have a clear recollection that you denied rubbing the ball in any way.'

A: 'The TV evidence clearly shows that my hand came out of my pocket, and my hand was on the rough side of the ball. The TV evidence is clear on that. It's clear that dust falls off the ball. I'm hardly going to deny something that's totally clear …'

Q: 'But on Sunday you were specifically asked that question and you denied it.'

A: 'Well, all I can say is that I've not denied it.'

But, as we knew, he had denied it, perhaps in the heat and confusion of the worst moment of his young life. Now ostensibly calmer but still in some kind of deep torment, he was denying the denial.

Yet if this was not to be an entirely satisfactory recantation, then at least one of the big questions was dismissed early on.

Q: 'Why didn't you tell the truth straight away?'

A: 'That's been my biggest regret all week. I should have come clean and told Peter Burge straight away about the dirt in my pocket. I didn't take my trousers in – they were open to inspection the whole time. He asked me if I had resin in my pocket, and I said no. Then he asked me did I have any other substance in my pocket. I replied no. That's where I made my mistake. I was thinking of other substances such as Vaseline, Lipsyl, iron filings ... I confirmed that there was absolutely no artificial substance in there.'

In his written statement, he added this significant sentence: 'Thinking back to that meeting, I gave my response without considering the consequences and believing that I had done nothing improper, but not wishing to raise any suspicions about my actions.' In other words, he crossed his fingers behind his back when he said no. A sort of an off-white lie, now exposed and admitted. And, perhaps, to be forgiven – at least by those who are still capable of taking into account such factors as character, previous behaviour and extenuating circumstances.

A week ago, one reporter suggested to him, he had enjoyed universal support. Did he think he could ever regain that position? 'It's an enviable position to have,' he replied. 'It's not many times that an England captain could say he had full official and public support, with no threat to his job. That's certainly not the case now, and it's my fault.'

When asked if he thought that the stigma of the affair would last for the rest of his career, his reply was unhesitating. 'I think there are going to be suspicions that linger on,' he said, very quietly. 'People will either believe me or they won't. I'm totally clear as to what my intentions were. Hopefully, if we can put together some good performances, this kind of thing may die down. But everybody's got to be remembered for something, and I suppose this will be my epitaph.'

Cricket is the hardest of games to legislate, since its meaning, its beauty and its claim to uniqueness are to be found in its infinite variety. Unlike baseball, in which the ball is changed literally dozens of times during a game in order to ensure that each delivery is projected according to the same ballistic parameters, cricket demands from its players an ability to act according to variables: how will this ball deviate in these atmospheric conditions, on this strip of grass, at this time of day? How will it change when all those factors have changed? These decisions can take micro-seconds, or days, in conditions that change hour by hour. All this enriches the game by putting a premium on knowledge, experience, nerve and cunning. And it makes cricket a tough proposition for rule-makers, since any two apparently similar actions are seldom identical.

No wonder, then, that Law 42.5 is so hard to pin down: ' …or take any other action to alter the condition of the ball …'. Now what exactly does 'alter' mean when you really try to test it? If you were to take action to maintain the condition of the ball in a steady state, would you not in effect be 'altering' the natural course of events, i.e. the ball's deterioration over time? And what is an 'artificial substance' anyway? Vaseline, obviously. But is dust artificial? If it isn't (as seems likely) and if 42.5 doesn't allow you to rub the ball in the dust on the ground, may you rub it with dust kept in your pocket? Last week two centuries of custom and practice and law-making in the world's most cerebral outdoor game were called into question and found to be of little help.

My own judgement is that Atherton used the earth from his pocket not just to dry his fingers but to dust one side of the ball, drying the sweat marks and maintaining the matt finish rather than abrading the leather (which would have required far more emphatic and persistent rubbing, perhaps with something more like those mysterious 'iron filings' to which he referred). In so far as that seems to have been the primary function of the dust, at least on the two occasions the camera caught him, I continue to doubt the detail of his explanation. But I also believe – and here is the crux of the trial of Michael Atherton – that the captain of England was not seeking to gain an unfair advantage, and that his offence was a misdemeanour rather than a felony.

Beneath all this lies the true reason why the affair occupied so many people's thoughts last week. Cricket, wherever it is played, presents a lesson on social behaviour and a constant test of integrity, its imprecise laws demanding honesty and goodwill from its players. Children who learn its codes are the better for their knowledge, even if they never play the game again. So when people suggest, as they do, that we should start treating cricketers like tennis players or footballers, and stop burdening them with unreasonable moral demands, we know that such an apparently realistic and logical change would cost us something worth preserving.

Anyone can have moral principles; it is the ability to act on them that constitutes integrity. When Michael Atherton appeared to run short of that ability last week, he did so under the harshest scrutiny. As the captain of England, that is his burden and his privilege. Now perhaps those in authority will see a chance to extend cricket's moral range by testing the proposition that one mistake can be the making, rather than the breaking, of a man.

THE OVAL, 27 AUGUST 2001

As MICHAEL ATHERTON approached the boundary rope bareheaded, he lifted his bat and raised it briefly to each corner of the ground. All around him the spectators were on their feet, applauding not the nine runs he had just scored off 20 balls, nor even the 7,728 he had scored in 115 Test matches since his debut in 1989, but something that went beyond the moment and the statistics into questions of pride and honour and the way a sporting career can compress a lifetime of glory and humiliation into a few short years.

Then he trotted quickly up the pavilion steps, leaving behind a crowd convinced it had seen him lay down England's standard for the last time. Or so the rumour went. For evidence they had only the untypical wave of the bat. But the Australians seemed to share the belief, since they too had applauded him from the field, in recognition of a singularly durable opponent whose dismissal – as Shane Warne confirmed on Saturday – has always carried a special bounty. 'It's the big wicket,' Warne had said, 24 hours after knocking back Atherton's off and middle stumps, 'because he's a great player.'

If yesterday's salute did indeed represent a farewell, it was one wholly in character. Neither in word nor deed has Atherton ever demonstrated a liking for anything that hinted at showiness. Given his choice of an exit line, he would probably appropriate the one with which Sinatra signed off his classic version of the ballad 'Angel Eyes': 'Excuse me while I disappear …'

As a result, the emotion in yesterday's response was entirely genuine. At this stage England might be better without Atherton or they might be worse, but the very fact of his departure changes the scenery of international cricket.

In his newspaper column last week he wrote that he would make up his mind on retirement at the end of the season, and there is no reason to disbelieve him. But the tenor of his words, which dwelt on the extent of the commitment involved in making himself available for this winter's tours of India and New Zealand, appeared to suggest the way his thoughts have been tending.

How sad it seems, then, that the dominant response to the prospect should be one of regret. In conversations on the subject there are sighs and sad little shakes of the head. The career of a man who scored sixteen Test centuries and captained his country on a record fifty-four occasions is somehow seen as characterized by the disappointment too often reflected in his own rueful grimace.

No doubt the weight of early expectations was largely to blame for shaping the perception of his achievements. His emergence at Manchester Grammar School and Cambridge created the myth of an anointed one, a man destined to lift English cricket out of the doldrums. To outsiders his ascent seemed to have an air of inevitability. To himself, by contrast, his early career felt like a series of peaks and troughs from which he emerged with a resolute belief that he should never allow himself to be lifted too high or cast too low.

His arrival in the England team, aged 21, brought him a duck against Australia at Trent Bridge. Two caps later, in the first match of a series against New Zealand, he registered his maiden Test century. By 1991 he had been appointed Graham Gooch's vice-captain, but that turned out to be the year his back broke down. An inherited condition called ankylosing spondylitis began to cause excruciating pain and to affect his performances. The remark in his recent column that 'the time for cortisone injections is almost past' was freighted with more pathos and remembered agony than he would be happy to acknowledge.

Surgery cost him a tour and a World Cup without eradicating the problem. But he had fought his way back by 1993, and for the fifth Test of the disastrous six-match series against Australia he was presented with the captaincy. He lost his first match in charge but won his second and went off to the Caribbean that winter at the head of a rejuvenated team, only to run into a West Indies squad better equipped in every respect. His personal heroism in the face of Courtney Walsh's barrage at Sabina Park helped establish his reputation for almost suicidal obduracy, a display reproduced in his equally torrid battle with Allan Donald at Trent Bridge in 1998.

In the meantime the dirt-in-the-pocket affair at Lord's in 1994 had left the first stain on his escutcheon. All it proved was that he was a professional sportsman, but the combination of cricket's special claim to a sense of moral rectitude and his own middle-class background led him to be judged by other standards. He survived but thereafter his tendency to public dourness was subject to a different and less charitable interpretation.

As captain he was arguably unlucky with his team managers and chief coaches. In the early months of his captaincy he said that at team meetings he liked to 'take a back seat and get other people thinking about the game', mentioning Nasser Hussain and Mark Ramprakash as people with 'good cricket brains' who needed to be encouraged, a judgment that looks pretty sound seven years later. An impeccably democratic impulse with an admirable eye on long-term development, it resulted from his own unhappy experience as a junior member of the squad. Some would say, however, that it was not necessarily the attitude most urgently required by England in recent years.

He was never the ideal man to make the Agincourt speech, and his insistence on behaving with moderation ran against the grain of the times. But when he said, at the height of the dirt-in-the-pocket affair, that 'everyone will be remembered for something, and this will be my epitaph', he was wrong.

MANCHESTER UNITED
Birth of a Dynasty

ALEX FERGUSON WON'T let me talk to Ryan Giggs. That's nothing new. He's never let anyone with a pencil or a microphone talk to the 19-year-old who made his first-team debut for Manchester United two seasons ago and is now the most exciting footballer in Britain. As far as the media are concerned, there's an exclusion zone around Ryan Giggs.

It isn't just Giggs, though. Here are some of the other footballers Alex Ferguson won't let me, or anyone else, talk to: Simon Davies, George Switzer, Ben Thornley, Keith Gillespie, Nicky Butt, Robert Savage, Paul Scholes, Craig Lawton, David Beckham, Gary Neville.

Mark those names well. Some of them you may never hear again, at least in the context of Manchester United. The odds are, though, that among them will be one of those rare footballers whose appeal transcends normal loyalties, whose gifts are enough to persuade the disaffected to check in their cynicism for a season or two, who can show us dreams and give us memories.

'I'd be really hard pressed,' Ferguson is telling me, 'to say where we'd go to get better than the young players we've got coming through now. That can be a dangerous thing to say, but …'.

Last season, while his first team was falling at the final hurdle in the race for the league championship, Ferguson's young players won the FA Youth Cup. More than a quarter of a century after their last league title, United's hunger for it is all-devouring – to the point, some would say, of neurotic obsession. But many, including the managers of other clubs, also think that the youth team's success was more significant than the failure of the seniors. They look at the growing power vacuum in English football, at the implosion on Merseyside and the damp squibs in north London, and suspect that Ferguson has laid the foundation for a dominance that could last a generation. Manchester United, it is felt, might be on the way to achieving the kind of national hegemony currently enjoyed in Italy by AC Milan.

The burden of such expectations can lie heavy on young shoulders, and Ferguson's fierce protectiveness stems from bitter personal experience. Some years ago, when he was managing Aberdeen, he found himself having to thrust a batch of youngsters into his first team, all at one go. It didn't work, either for the club or the boys concerned. Is that still in his mind?

'You wonder,' he says, and pauses. 'I don't know. I'm still conscious of it. I brought about six of them in, and none of them, I think, are playing now … they never became the players they should have been, anyway. Maybe it catches up with them when you get the best out of them so early.'

Then it happened again, in his third season at Old Trafford, 1988–89, when he found himself in trouble with injuries to his senior players. Again he reached for the starlets, and for a few weeks the back pages were full of the new names. People talked about a new generation coming through to match the legend of the Busby Babes. And again the promise was unfulfilled. Now, four years later, Mark Robins, Tony Gill, David Wilson and Deiniol Graham have gone elsewhere. Russell Beardsmore, whose midfield talent flickered excitingly during those early days, went on the transfer list a couple of weeks ago. Lee Martin is skippering the reserves. Giuliano Maiorana, an explosive left-winger, suffered a bad knee injury and has not played a game in three years, although he is still on the staff.

Of them all, only Lee Sharpe – who was not, as it happens, a product of United's apprenticeship scheme, but was bought at 18 from Torquay – is now in the first-team squad.

Did Ferguson learn a lesson from these misfortunes? 'I'm very aware of it, put it that way. It's why last year we rested Giggs quite a lot, left him out of games. Andrei Kanchelskis, too, in his first season in English football.'

But no one, he says, gives you any credit for that. 'Resting' isn't in the English fan's vocabulary. If a lad's doing well, how can you leave him out? So he plays and he plays and he plays. And one day he's gone. Unless, perhaps, you're Alex Ferguson and you've learnt a few hard lessons.

It's a rainy Tuesday night in Bury, and the groundsman is going spare. He's got four games here this week, including a first-team match on Saturday, and his precious surface is starting to look like a half-eaten shepherd's pie: islands of dark brown mud rise between sheets of water that reflect the yellow floodlights. Sliding tackles are covering the length of a cricket pitch. Passes are stopping yards short. Not a night for young thoroughbreds.

'This won't suit us,' says Alex Ferguson, wrapped up warm in the main stand while United's reserves struggle through the early stages of their match against Leicester City's second team. 'What you need when it's like this is strength. Look at them.' He gestures in the direction of the visiting blue shirts. 'Big lads.' From his point of view, there's nothing to be learnt here.

Ferguson began renting Bury's little ground for United's reserve matches last August, at the beginning of a season in which the fans expect him to repair the shattered dreams of the previous campaign. Among Ferguson's long list of reasons for United's calamitous last-ditch failure to win the league last year, alongside the fixture pile-up and a crop of injuries, was the state of the Old Trafford pitch. Now the grass in the theatre of dreams is being maintained in pristine condition for the present championship leaders.

Meanwhile, on the rapidly deteriorating surface of Gigg Lane, some of the red-shirted figures are familiar from more elevated surroundings – notably Lee Martin and Les Sealey, heroes of the

1990 FA Cup-winning side. But also in the starting line-up are a couple of last year's Youth Cup winners, the tall, composed midfield player Simon Davies and the left-back George Switzer, and a pair of this season's juniors, the midfielder Paul Scholes and the forward Robert Savage. Two more trainees come on in the second half: Gary Neville and David Beckham. But Leicester's experienced team hang on to a 2–0 lead, and by the time the referee blows the final whistle, Alex Ferguson is already on the M62 in his Mercedes, radio tuned to the League Cup quarter-final between Ipswich and Sheffield Wednesday.

He's talking about a Wednesday striker whom United's fans, disappointed by Ferguson's failure to sign Alan Shearer last summer, would love to see in their colours. 'He's got a lot of skill,' he's saying as Wednesday attack, 'but he gets a lot of injuries. Shearer's so strong. He just knocks people out of the way.'

The words are still in his throat when there's a sudden shout from the radio. The striker is through, the goal at his mercy. But in the act of shooting he pulls a thigh muscle, and is carried from the field. Alex Ferguson sighs and shakes his head.

The next morning, United's young hopefuls are pulling on their boots at the Cliff, the club's training ground, three or four miles across Salford from Old Trafford. Amid the banter and the ball-juggling, the 17-year-old Gary Neville is being quizzed about last night's game.

'What was the score, Gaz?'

'Two-nil to them.'

'Did you get on?'

'Yeah, in the second half.'

'When it was nil-nil?'

'Nah. Two-nil down. I take no responsibility for the score.'

Mark Hughes, an older pro, walks stiffly by, a heavy bandage on his calf covering a wound closed by nine stitches, the legacy of a controversial tackle by the Queen's Park Rangers defender Alan McDonald in London two nights earlier. That, in an overheated match, was one of several incidents that led to a confrontation between Ferguson and QPR's manager, Gerry Francis. The echoes are still filling the back pages of the tabloids as, in his upstairs office at the Cliff, Alex Ferguson talks about what he found when he arrived at Manchester United at the end of 1986.

'The first vibe I got,' he says, 'was that Manchester City were getting the young players. So that was a challenge, right there. We set about it in quite a vigorous way. We increased the scouting throughout the city and we brought in Brian Kidd, who'd been the local Football in the Community representative. Right from the start we were giving trials, and it was at one of those that we got Ryan Giggs. He was at City's school of excellence at the time, and fortunately he was only 13 and they couldn't sign him until he was 14. So maybe I came in at the right time.'

Ferguson is a notable believer in fate, but he tries not to leave too much to chance. So he started United's own schools of excellence, in the fertile ground of Durham and Belfast, one night a week for about thirty recommended boys aged 10 to 14. The idea was to let people know that United's youth scheme was back in business. 'It's really important to this club, to the supporters, to see young players coming through. The longer you're here, the better you understand that.' He added twenty-odd scouts to the staff, promoted Brian Kidd – the scorer of a goal in United's 1968 European Cup final triumph over Benfica – to assistant manager with special responsibility for local talent, and hired Paul McGuinness – son of Wilf McGuinness, the 'favourite son' who briefly succeeded Matt Busby as manager in 1969 – as youth education officer. In charge of their accommodation, diet and entertainment, McGuinness also gives them training in handling everything from media to money. Now, Ferguson says, the club is spending £80,000 on doing up a building at another training ground, 'so that they'll have a place for the evenings'.

He wants parents to see that this is a place where their boys will not only be looked after, but will also get a real chance to make it to the top. 'You've got to do that. You've got a responsibility to any young player's parents, if they're going to sign for you. They're not all going to be top. That's asking for a miracle. But at least you want to be able to say, "We've given you a career in football."'

Paradoxically, in one sense, the life of a young star at Old Trafford is comparatively easy. 'There's a special pressure here on anyone who's in the first team,' Ferguson says, 'but it's easier for the young players because the crowd love them so much. It's harder here if you've been bought. The crowd are waiting in judgement: is he a Manchester United player or not?'

Still, though, only two members of the present first team, Hughes and Giggs, are youth-scheme products – six years after Ferguson took over. Isn't that disappointing? 'Not really. It takes time. And the first group of players to get the benefit are the ones who're starting to emerge now. The whole thing can take five or six years to get in place – which is maybe why some clubs don't go down that road.'

Whatever happens with the youngsters, though, Ferguson will still play the transfer market. 'I think we should buy a player every year,' he says, 'to keep that edge on everyone, to make it obvious that we want to win things.'

I tell him what Fabio Capello, the Milan coach, had said to me a few weeks earlier, that the era of the big squad at the big club means that everyone – manager as well as players – has to change his way of thinking. Capello, who is in charge of twenty-four first-team players, feels that the 'settled side' is an obsolete concept, given the accelerating pace of the game, the growing demands on the players' athleticism and the increasing number of injuries.

'Well, a settled side has helped us this season,' Ferguson replies. 'But I can see what he's getting at, especially if you want to maintain your success on all fronts. Getting a big squad together isn't the hardest thing. The job is to handle it. But it's a bit different in Italy, where they normally play only one game a week. When we come to the end of our season, we can find ourselves playing four games in six days, which is what happened last year. That's crazy. So it's usually based on simple mathematics – how many players you've got fit on a Saturday morning. And, in the main, our players understand that you've got a hard job picking the team, because they all want to play.'

When he behaves as he did at QPR on Monday night, when frustration suddenly overwhelms him and rage reddens his face, Alex Ferguson seems like a 51-year-old man with a problem. Then you wouldn't say he was any more likely than his five predecessors – McGuinness, O'Farrell, Docherty, Sexton and Atkinson – to step out of the shadow of the great Matt Busby.

In his own environment, though, he can show a warm and generous side, very different from the fretful, defensive creature whose anxiety last year seemed to put extra pressure on his players when the crunch arrived. The difference now may be the arrival of Eric Cantona – who, Ferguson often says, has brought something to the club that hadn't been there before. What, exactly?

'Vision. All the best players in the world have imagination. They can see a picture that no one else can quite make out. Eric can see those things. His head's up, you know? The point is that anyone who comes to this club must cope with the expectation. Some players haven't done it, unfortunately – good players at their last club, who couldn't quite handle it because the stage can be a bit frightening. Eric's attitude is, "This is where I should be!" It's more a question of us having to tailor the expectation to suit him.'

If Ferguson's players succeed in reaching their target this spring, then perhaps Cantona's insouciance, his lack of nerves, will turn out to have made the difference – infecting colleagues, dispelling the shadows of the past, enabling the talent to flow.

SVEN-GÖRAN ERIKSSON
In a Strange Land

JANUARY 2001

I F SVEN-GÖRAN ERIKSSON has stopped to consider what sort of a welcome awaits him in England, he may be feeling somewhat confused. 'Sven Can You Start, Boss?' the *Daily Star* asked on its front page yesterday, managing to convey in a single headline the absurd inflation of football's importance, the cringing desperation of the English game and the broader culture of inane jokiness in which it is embedded – and which is ready to turn, as Eriksson may discover, to poisonous rancour at the slightest pretext.

Eriksson is a serious man and has no doubt taken the trouble to acquaint himself with these phenomena. But in his attempt to understand the scale of the problems confronting English football in these feverish times, he would not have been comforted by the words of Gordon Taylor, the chairman of the Professional Footballers' Association. Speaking on Radio Four, Taylor offered the sourest of welcomes to the first foreigner to become the head coach of the national team.

'I wish him well,' the leader of the players' union said, 'but I think there will be tears at the end of the day. I just can't see it working out. It is a very sad day for English football and a terrible indictment of our national association when they are responsible for coaching and can't select a product of that coaching system to manage the national team.'

Marvellous. So the cream of England's young footballers are being encouraged, by the man most directly responsible for their general welfare, to view a coach with whom they will be working for the next five years as a failure even before he starts, simply because his very appointment is a consequence of failure. Far from illuminating the problem, Taylor's words encapsulated the dim-witted insularity that got us to this state in the first place.

Like John Barnwell of the League Managers' Association, who described the decision as 'almost insulting', Taylor is still fighting yesterday's battles. Theirs is the view of the traditionalists: that to choose Eriksson is to betray the heritage and traditions of the English game.

But even those who disagree with them would endorse Taylor's description of the decision to appoint a foreign coach as 'a terrible indictment' of English football's failure to nurture its own generation of coaches and managers. Principally this means an indictment of the Football Association, the governing body. But surely it must also constitute an indictment of the officers of the PFA, who share in the responsibility to ensure that those of their members who wish to continue in the game after their playing days are over have been properly prepared for the opportunities and challenges they will face.

Under Taylor's leadership, the PFA's record in that respect is hardly glorious – even though the enrichment of their members in recent years has enabled the chairman to indulge a sentimental whim by paying over a million quid for an L.S. Lowry painting of a football crowd at Burnden Park, where Taylor himself served his apprenticeship. Although he must know, from observing today's players as they roll up to contract negotiations in their Ferraris, that things have changed, his opinion comes with an unmistakeable coating of dubbin and embrocation.

And yet there are other, deeper reasons for the appointment of a foreigner than the failure of people inside football to do their jobs with imagination. The biggest indictment of all must be directed at the English education system, divisively structured and carelessly administered. All the necessary evidence is to be found in the styles of the candidates to whom the FA looked when it concluded that there was no suitable English-born applicant.

Arsène Wenger, probably the only candidate the FA would have preferred to Eriksson, shares with the Swede an interest in other cultures, a subtle intellect, a strong will and a gift for irony. You would need to go a very long way before you found a home-bred football manager answering that description, thanks to a willingness in England to encourage a mindset that is inward-looking, distrustful of innovation, inclined to take the easy option and the short cut, reluctant to take responsibility or to commit itself to a vision, respectful only of the quick profit.

That is why we have no managers like Wenger and Eriksson. That is also why we have no clubs like Barcelona, which is owned by its 100,000-plus members and whose representatives this week attended the auction of the fixtures and fittings of Wembley stadium and were astonished to find themselves taking home the tunnel, one of the steps up to the royal box and various other bits and pieces of the place where they won their first European Cup in 1992, all at a cost of barely £7,000. Did the game's heritage, they asked, really come so cheap?

But there is hope. Eriksson is not a Bora Milutinovic, a Red Adair in reverse who arrives at a trouble spot in the hope of starting a fire. The fact that the Swede was attracted to the job is the proof that England can still think of itself as potentially a major football power. He must have done his homework and concluded that among the likes of Owen, Heskey, Woodgate, Dyer, Robinson and the Coles – Joe and Ashley – there is the basis of a team capable of mounting a World Cup challenge. And, in Peter Taylor and Steve McClaren, coaches capable of rising to the challenge when his time is up.

'We mustn't kid ourselves,' Adam Crozier said at yesterday's press conference, giving his most convincing performance to date as the FA's chief executive. 'If we've learnt one thing, it's that we have to work for the future. This is a big step into that future.' Or perhaps a belated step into the lesson of the last ten years, which is that

English institutions – from sports clubs to the Royal Opera House, the Dome and Tate Modern – sometimes benefit from a foreign influence.

And sometimes, of course, they do not. So will he be a Wenger or a Christian Gross? A Jürgen Grobler or a Michael Kaiser? A Duncan Fletcher or a Pierre-Yves Gerbeau? A Lars Nittve or an Egil Olsen? Appointing a Swede to coach the English football team is not like appointing a Swede as the director of Tate Modern, where most of the exhibits, like those of the Premier League, are foreign.

Questioning the new man's suitability, Gordon Taylor said: 'He needs to know the players in England.' But the chances are that Eriksson and his talent-spotter, Tord Grip, will not find it too difficult to identify the real young talents within the English game. Whether they can persuade the Wengers and Ranieris to give them a consistent run in their respective first teams is another matter, and it would be no great surprise if, in the not too distant future, the man whose Lazio XI regularly contains seven non-Italians is heard campaigning on behalf of a quota system.

Taylor was not entirely wrong to call it a sad day. The inability to find an English coach of sufficient quality speaks poorly of the country in a much wider sense. But at least football has finally faced up to reality and has come to the logical conclusion. Eriksson's appointment is the consequence of the recognition of a defeat. It is not the defeat itself. That defeat, at least, is history. Now only the future awaits.

TED DEXTER
Lampoon and Harpoon

LONDON, 27 JUNE 1993

C OME IN, TED DEXTER said, standing in the hall of his mock-Georgian town house in a leafy North Ealing street. Inside, on the living-room television, Chris Bailey was two games away from defeat at the hands of Goran Ivanisevic. We sat down and watched as the Brit did his best to fend off the inevitable.

As Bailey accepted defeat and saluted his supporters, I asked Dexter if he was going to Wimbledon this year.

'Well, we were going tomorrow,' he said, indicating to his wife, Sue, who had also been watching. 'The LTA invited us. But the way the cricket's been going, the sight of the chairman of the selectors at Wimbledon might be more than the *Sun* could bear. So we aren't.'

Dexter poured a couple of glasses of red wine and led the way into a small walled garden, where we sat on a wooden bench. How did it feel, I asked him, to be a member of that select group, including the Prime Minister and the manager of the England football team, whose efforts on behalf of the nation have attracted universal derision?

'If I am,' he replied, 'I don't feel it. Within the England squad we have totally outlawed the tabloid stuff.'

Reading it?

'Yes. It doesn't do us any good.'

But you can't be unaware of it.

'I am unaware of it.'

You must be aware of it.

'Very mildly.'

And it's not just the tabloids. Last week even the broadsheets joined in.

'Not the *Telegraph*. I read the *Telegraph*.'

But only the other day the *Sunday Telegraph* referred to …

'Don't read it to me. Please don't read it to me.'

…to 'the buffoons and scoundrels of the TCCB'.

'I don't read it.'

And after your press conference at Lord's on Monday, when you said something about England losing because of the planetary aspect, fun was poked at you from every quarter.

'Lampoon. Lampoon and harpoon.'

How does that affect you?

'It seems to me to have nothing to do with the job that I'm supposed to do. It's absolutely incidental.'

But you're not a man without pride.

'I'm sure if I read it, it would hurt me. But I don't read it. What I will listen to is reasoned comment from within the game, with no axe to grind, whoever that may be, whether it's a county captain or a chairman or secretary or ex-England captain. But the fact is that everybody, all the rest, have an axe to grind, and it has to be said that of the ex-cricketers who are in that mould, you could look at almost every one and say that they are disaffected personally in one way or another. And if you look at the list of, let's say, ex-England captains who might actually know what the situation is, they are not party to that chorus.'

So whom do you take seriously?

'Who're the people I talk to about the game? Oh, among the administrators I see quite a bit of Doug Insole, Peter May, Colin Cowdrey. We all talk about the game. Who else? Our advisers – the Bob Taylors and the Alan Knotts, those type of people.'

Have you had, in your career, a guru? Somebody whose views you felt shaped your own?

'Gubby [Sir G.O.B. Allen, the grand old man of the English cricket establishment, who died in 1989, aged 87]. Yup, very much so.'

Do you miss him?

'Not now. But I'm a great believer that people you've known and who've influenced you, they live on in you. I quite often tune in to Gubby, as it were. I didn't always agree with the things he had to say, but some of his principles are sound and live on, and live on in the way I think about the game. He was a major influence on me and he undoubtedly sort of helped my career because he believed in me and he told me that he believed in me.'

But who believes in today's English cricketers? Why have they lost seven in a row? Is the rest of the world getting better or are we getting worse?

'In the long term,' Dexter said, 'there's no question that the other countries have come up. I don't think we've got worse, but we haven't changed with the times. Until this year, when we've at least got a four-day championship, basically we've been doing the same old thing. In fact, not even the same old thing. The same old thing with many variations and distractions in terms of one-day cricket and three-day-covered-wickets-declaration-game-seven-days-a-week cricket.'

Which single factor, then, would you blame for our failure to improve at the same rate as the other countries?

'Ten years of hit-and-giggle cricket. Absolute soft options on the cricket field, all the time, particularly for the bowlers. Just turn up, bowl, doesn't matter whether you get a wicket or whether you don't. If you're potentially a quick bowler, slow down a bit to be more accurate. If you're a slow bowler, speed up to keep the runs tight.'

Graham Gooch has been talking about a lack of 'mental fibre' in the team. What did he mean?

'Exactly what I've been talking about. In county cricket, results have been there for the taking without anybody taking any decisions.'

But what people don't understand is why these chaps, when they get picked for the Test team, can't seem to gear themselves up. The supporters look to the captain to set an example and they don't see him giving it.

'They didn't see him give an example at Old Trafford?'

In his batting, but not in the field.

'When Richie Richardson was losing, where was he in the field? He was all vague and hopeless. Now he's winning, he's a star. When Allan Border was losing every match, he was a complete down-and-out and an idiot. But he's still the same person. He hasn't learnt so many tricks that he's suddenly turned these players into world-beaters. If you keep saying, "Right we're going to set this field," and people keep bowling in the wrong place, the captain's made to look a mug.'

So the captain is powerless in those circumstances?

'Absolutely powerless. If somebody bowls five dreadful overs, you say thanks very much and bring someone else on, and if they bowl rubbish, too, where do you go? In fact, in this series I've watched Allan Border bring on a bowler and he's bowled absolutely tripe and he's let him bowl. Hasn't gone and talked to him or done anything. But somebody else has performed and got him out of the muck … or we've made a nonsense of it. So I think it's subjective when you start taking views like that from the ringside.'

But that's how people feel.

'Of course, if you're losing.'

The Aussies do show an aggression and a zest that we haven't got.

'There's a certain amount of the aggression that's certainly over the top. It wouldn't be tolerated in our team, and that's a fact.'

With respect, I think people would like to see it there, being not tolerated, if you see what I mean.

'Well, that may be. That may be. But … our players are as they are, and they have had success being as they are. Currently, what are we? We're not a year into a bad spell.'

That's quite a long time.

'D'you mind? Do-you-mind? Australia won one game in fifteen years against us. We're talking about months here.'

In 1989 you said, 'You can't do anything if the opposition is better than you. What you can do is influence the mood of the players.' But we aren't seeing the mood we'd like to see.

'No, they're lacking in confidence. There's no question about that. And everything we have done has been towards improving their confidence.'

In what respect?

'In every respect. Everybody who's got anything to do with running the side has been involved in trying to improve the confidence of the players.'

In what ways?

'I am normally not involved with the players. Why? Because we have a captain and a team manager who are involved with the players. But because I thought some of the batting was frankly wet behind the ears at Old Trafford, I told the team so. Not in a negative way. I said I have certain views about the way things went and I'd just like to point out some principles and this is surely what's expected, et cetera, and I know you can do it, and tried to boil them up. Fletcher's been doing the same, Graham's been doing the same, so … The captain introduced a sports psychologist to the side because he felt things were really not right at Old Trafford and he'd met this guy, he thought he was good, so that was another area which was involved.'

Do you talk to the players about whether they benefit from that?

'I don't have regular relationships with individual players. I'm an administrator. I'm not a team manager. We employ a very highly paid team manager and we have a team captain, and it is their bailiwick. If I and the England committee feel that they're not doing what they should, then it's up to us to remove them or admonish them or whatever. In the case of the captain, at Old Trafford to me he was head and shoulders above everybody in terms of the way he went about playing his game. So I didn't feel that was any time to be dispensing with him. In fact, the England committee took the view that it showed fairly conclusively that he was the man who should lead England, and continue to do so.'

The big question: do we choose too many young players or too few? And when we select them, are they given enough time to establish themselves? Dexter is proud of the success of his under-19 and A-team schemes, but is adamant that timing is vital to the introduction of a Test cricketer.

'You want to put them in when they're having a run of good

form,' he said. 'With a bowler, you want to bring him in if he's copping a few wickets. Because then you start to expect to get wickets. But, by golly, we've brought them in. The number of guys who've played is legion.'

Does that deter you from trying more in the current crisis?

'No, no. In the England committee Graham Gooch said, "Look, our job is to replace people. If they're not doing it up to a high level, our job is to replace them." And there has been a big turnover. People say we're sticking with the same players, but in the last X months we've played five spinners, we've played thirteen quick bowlers …'.

But there is a feeling that old hands are sometimes brought back without good reason – Larkins, Emburey, Gatting. Is that constructive?

'It's simply a question of trying to get a bit of each, to give the newcomers a background to play against. Which the Australians have got now, for instance. They've got two or three young batters, but they're within a framework of the established players.'

Is it the captain's influence that brings back the older players?

'I think every case is different. But Gooch's attitude is, by and large, "If they've got talent and they're young, get them in." The idea that he says, "Oh, I'll have my old pals back in the side" …. not true at all.'

Why wasn't Mark Lathwell given a go in the last of the one-day games?

'Because we'd lost two and we desperately wanted to win one. Winning would have been a huge fillip. We wanted to play our best side. The Australians had the luxury of, "Oh, you stand down and give him a game." We didn't have that luxury. And Lathwell's got the world in front of him.'

It's been said to me that it was the captain's influence that kept him out, that Gooch doesn't rate him. True?

'It's not the way it works. We have a committee and we pick the team.'

But can one man exercise a veto?

'Not at all. Doesn't work like that.'

But it can't just work on consensus.

'Most of the time. Since I've been chairman, I haven't taken anything to a vote. The job of the chairman is to feel the mood of the meeting and to bring it to a conclusion without having votes.'

But assuming that Lathwell continues to make runs at his present rate, when will be the right time for him?

'Look, he's the only player that I've written sort of a couple of pages of my impressions about his innings. That was in Tasmania, when he got 170. That's the first time I've ever actually written it down on paper, because it was extremely impressive. I was there and I watched every ball. Brilliant. Absolutely brilliant. I'm certain he has a future and we showed that because we popped him into the one-days. He was reserve batsman, he got a taste of what it's like to be in the England dressing room, et cetera. He's done incredibly well, he's way up there, making runs all the time. The opportunity will come.'

Will it come this summer?

'No idea.'

Will it be a setback for him if it doesn't come this summer?

'Ha! You don't know! Until you sit down in a selection meeting ... there are four people and they all bring all their knowledge and their feelings with them, and out of that arises a team. Now ... you also have a policy to follow through. Our A-team policy is real, and we've shown it by the way these guys have been selected. If we've shown logic, people will come through. When it is, maybe this game, maybe the next, or it may be the winter, but he's talented and he'll get a chance.'

Supposing the third and fourth Tests go the way of the first two, will you think, right, the series has gone, now we have to make a fresh start?

'You can never begin afresh. Are you going to leave out all our current players? No. If you bring people in, it's got to be within a framework where they can expect to succeed.'

Perhaps we need a new framework.

'It's a matter of judgement. Always is. You want to bring people through, you want to be replacing people as you go, you don't want them to get to their absolute last knockings before the next person is in there. But I'd rather think more positively about what's happening now and go on to the next game.'

Is it true you've been in favour of the inclusion of Jack Russell all the time – of the inclusion of a specialist wicketkeeper, and of Russell as the best specialist wicketkeeper?

'I don't really want to comment on that. As I say, it's a matter of consensus. The trouble is, in three separate series we've started with a specialist wicketkeeper and each time we were going down the tube, and the only way out appeared to be to strengthen the batting by giving Alec [Stewart] the gloves. Now, against West Indies it worked. We won at the Oval, largely because he was there and made two important innings. Australia didn't work. But three times Russell had lost his place because we were going down the tube. And there are people who don't think he can keep anyway.'

Are there?

'Plenty. Plenty who tell me so.'

What do you think?

'I listen to the experts.'

Oh, come on.

'I do! What do I know about wicketkeeping? Zilch.'

Who do you listen to?

'I listen to Knott and to Taylor. They tell me Russell's the best, and that's good enough for me.'

So you don't pay attention to people who say he can't keep wicket.

'No. But that's what they say.'

People say all sorts of things.

'They bloody well do.'

Night had fallen over the little garden. Ragtime piano music issued from an upstairs window. Slowly, painfully, Dexter was explaining that the squad's emphasis on physical fitness didn't contribute to Igglesden's pre-match breakdown at Old Trafford, justifying the decision not to replace Igglesden with Ilott, and bemoaning the inability of Tufnell and Such to spin the ball as much as Warne and May ('England bowlers of that generation, that's typical … I can't find an England spinner who has a callus on his fingers'). Since he took it on, four years ago, it's been a hell of a job. Has he endured many dark nights of the soul?

'No. The only time I get browned off is on two counts. One, when the media gets silly. Like that thing in India. It was the fourth day at Calcutta. We were obviously going to get beaten but we weren't going to get beaten until the next day, so they'd got nothing to write about. "Ted, could you possibly come and talk to us? Please?" So I go and sit down with them for an hour. Within a whole lot of discussion, I mention that, incidentally, we've got this chest specialist here – our blokes have been desperately ill and I've asked him to just actually let us have some chapter and verse on what the effect of this level of pollution is when it comes to exerting yourself, bowling thirty overs. Because I haven't a clue. If a player says to me, "How can I play in this sort of thing?", I haven't got an answer. I've given them an hour of my time, made quite a lot of comment on the cricket, and two blokes who weren't even at the press conference pick it up and lampoon it. And that's become Dexter's contribution to the Indian tour. And similarly the other day, at Lord's. They say, "We want to see Ted." Half an hour. Every question is a when-did-you-stop-beating-your-wife question, and then they pick up some little titbit and agree that they're going to lampoon me. Well. And the next day the BBC beg me, "Could you please come on our morning programme, Mr Dexter? Oh, we'd count it such an honour." And then they introduce the news item – this is a news item – what is the news? Dexter is sitting in his garden, that's the news. They get the two key words into the introduction: "humiliation" and "resignation". And when I question the guy and I say, "By the way, who's calling for my resignation?", he says, well it's in the *Mirror* and the *Sun*. This is the BBC! It's at those moments you think, is this the country that we thought we cherished and loved? So those are the low points.'

How do you react?

'Laugh about it. Talk to my friends about it. Think of it as an innings where there's some nasty shitty fast bowlers whanging it round your ears. I want to survive because I want to do the right thing. I want to win. I want to do a decent job.'

And what's the other thing that upsets you?

'The other is when the underlying commercialism of the game just keeps crawling through. Micky [Stewart] and I, often we'll be in conclave, we've been working away together on England affairs, we've spent three hours on something and we say, do you know, we haven't said a word about cricket? Not a single bloody word. We've been talking about sponsors and clothing and rates of pay and accommodation and expenses and everything under the sun that surrounds the England team, which has to be done, and at those times I've thought, what's going on?'

Have you thought of resigning?

'No. No.'

What do you think you'll do next year, when your contract expires?

'I haven't come round to that yet.'

It seems a lot of full-time grief for a part-time £20,000 a year.

'Well, money's always nice, but the twenty grand isn't essential. There's one point I really have to make, which is that the board actually put me in place as an administrator. I'm not a team manager. My responsibilities are pretty wide. The whole idea is that somebody has to fight England's corner in all the cricketing decisions, and those decisions are made at a broad spectrum of committee meetings. That, I think, is very important if England is to go forward in the long term. Because some very, very funny things can jump out of the woodwork in committee meetings. It may all seem very peripheral and unimportant, but it isn't.'

It's not what the man in the street sees, though. He sees the bloke who picks the team that has lost seven Test matches in a row.

'Yes. Well. What can you do? You do your best.'

Would you do it any differently if you were getting £120,000 a year?

'Phewff. No. I can't see what I would do differently. Extra money would suggest that one could give it more time and more thought. If that was productive, it would be good, but I don't know ….'.

Ever since 1989 you've spoken of working towards the long term. You must feel you've been doing the right things. Wouldn't it seem a shame to go before the effort bears fruit?

'No, I don't think that would bother me. I can be involved. It's rather like becoming a backbencher again. You can still be involved, which I would very much expect to do, if and when I'm kicked into touch, or kick myself into touch. I've learned a lot about how it all works. I'm an experienced administrator now, which I wasn't when I started, and I hope I could bring it all to bear somewhere along the line.'

Meanwhile, there's nothing for the health of the game like a successful England team, is there?

'Absolutely.'

So what's to be done in the short term? Like this week at Trent Bridge?

'Ha. Somehow conjure more than half a good day or one good day. Sustain one good day into two good days and three good days, and lift the confidence level. That's what's to be done. It'll come out of two or three quality individual performances.'

So all you can do is pick the team, pat them on the back and hope?

'Well, that's the lowest form of putting it. But to an extent that is true. It's an individual game within a team game, and individual responsibility is paramount. You've just got to pick people and say, "We believe in you." And "England expects." All those things. They all get said. And you just hope that two or three people get a gleam in their eye and can take it with them on to the field. It's quite difficult, sometimes. Some people take the game on to the field better than others. That's the phrase I use. I've used it about Mike Atherton. Perhaps he's not the best player in the world, but what he's got, he takes it with him on to the field. Ian Botham certainly did that. One or two of them, sadly, leave it behind in the dressing room.'

So you have to find eleven men who can take it with them.

'Exactly. The trouble is that you never know whether they can do it until they've tried.'

THE VIEW FROM THE HIGH BOARD

IV

FRANCE 98
Coupe d'Etat

B Y DAY, THE Stade de France looms over the northern suburbs of Paris like a low-flying platinum Frisbee. But at night, when it becomes a majestic white-gold temple of light and pleasure, you see the real point of it. *Lumière*, but also *son*. Driving back into Paris on the elevated section of the A1 on a Sunday evening, halfway through the World Cup, after France had beaten Paraguay in an excruciating match in Lens, it was possible to roll down the car window while passing above the suburban streets and overhear, through the swish and roar of the traffic, the noises of despair and elation leaking out of the glittering edifice as Denmark proceeded towards their unexpected elimination of Nigeria.

Erected close by the basilica of Saint-Denis, where the relics of monarchs and martyrs repose, the £250 million stadium is the World Cup's most obvious symbol, a magnificent and properly equivocal monument to ambition. And we all want one like it. How long, we wonder enviously, will it take before Wembley is rebuilt into a fitting cathedral for the English and their new religion? But the comparison doesn't work. Wembley is a remote place, invisible to people going about their daily lives in London. To equal the impact of the Stade de France, the British would need to pick up the Millennium Dome and put it down next to the Westway, perhaps where the White City stadium once stood. Saint-Denis, an unprepossessing place, has been given new life by the French sense of theatre.

But the symbol and the soul are not always to be found in the same location. To those who wondered why several World Cup matches were being staged in Lens, a town with one street and two slag heaps, it was pointed out by the tournament's co-president, the former football idol Michel Platini, that here the real heartbeat of the French game could be felt, in a stadium whose capacity outnumbers the town's population, yet whose gritty, unfashionable team sometimes wins championships. Lens is a place of beer and burgers. When a football match is taking place there, only the sight of Emmanuelle Béart and Romane Bohringer in the grandstand cheering on *les Bleus* reminds you that this isn't the era of wooden rattles and the maximum wage.

In France the World Cup has many forms and many registers. In the south, empty CS gas canisters littered the streets of Marseille's Old Port, and there were days when the sound of a door slamming in the breeze in a side-street off the Canabière would make lunchtime shoppers flinch. But 50 miles away, in the town of Arles, yet another kind of World Cup was taking place. In the ancient Place du Forum, under spreading plane trees and canvas parasols, in a sun-dappled setting of wrought-iron balconies and faded wooden shutters which practically defines the Conran ideal of Provençal life, someone had set up a large television outside the Café Vincent Van Gogh, its screen visible not only to that restaurant's clients, but also to those of the half-dozen other establishments whose tables crowd the square. Here, where public executions took place in the Middle Ages, locals and tourists were able to keep an eye on the games. And when the referee blew the whistle to end Croatia's 3–0 defeat of Germany, the sound of applause rippled from one end of the square to the other, rising above the babble of conversation, as though a string quartet, say, had just finished an al fresco recital.

Here, and elsewhere throughout France, it was possible to believe that the French people had kept the World Cup, the quadrennial festival of the most popular sport on earth, in decent, civilized proportion. They were able to support their national team and enjoy the tournament while getting on with the rest of their lives. In the immediate vicinity of the stadiums, drycleaners and driving schools dressed their windows with flags and favours. When France reached the semi-finals, revellers jammed the Champs-Elysées. But elsewhere there were few signs of the sort of emotional hysteria and commercial exploitation that might be expected were the tournament ever to return to Britain. No *coupes Mondiales* on the dessert menu; no *coups Mondials* at the hairdresser.

Although a Frenchman, Jules Rimet, invented the World Cup in 1930, and the national team twice reached the semi-finals before this year's campaign, in 1982 and 1986 (to be beaten on both occasions by Germany), football is not an absolute obsession with the French. Their league teams, even the most fashionable, are indifferently supported and rarely do well in European competition. Monaco, heavily subsidized by Prince Rainier, won the French championship last year, but the crowds in their lavish ground, which looks out on to the Mediterranean, are often dismally small. Even the future of the Stade de France itself is uncertain, because Paris Saint-Germain, the most consistently successful French side in recent years, cannot be persuaded to move there from their old home, the Parc des Princes, near the Bois de Boulogne; they are fearful that their average crowd would be lost amid the 80,000 seats of the new stadium. No French city has two major clubs, and attempts to solve the Stade de France problem by establishing a second big outfit in the capital are meeting with no response. France is a sports-mad country, but it also has cycling, rugby, tennis and other disciplines on its mind, and football is not allowed to swamp them.

Yet their system of finding and training young players is currently second to none, which means that some of the best teams in other European countries have a French spine – Arsenal and Juventus, the current champions of England and Italy, being the best examples. French players have been happy to leave their native land in order to escape high taxes and to take advantage of the greater prosperity of foreign leagues. But for the World Cup, of course, they return to the colours, creating a team full of style and technique.

L'Equipe, the daily sports paper, has been full of lovely rhetorical stuff about the team fulfilling its destiny and entering into legend, but you could tell that they wouldn't be very surprised if it didn't happen. Failure would provoke a lot of expressive gestures, but no one would be demanding the return of the guillotine to deal with Aimé Jacquet, the national coach. Tricolour flags fly above the front doors of French schools and other municipal buildings at all times, but pride in Frenchness is a less obviously empathic thing than, say, English or Argentinian patriotism. It seems more securely based, however reasonable that may be, seldom requiring proof of its existence on the field of battle. The French are very keen for their team to win, but the world wouldn't end if it didn't happen. Optimistic support is the thing, not the immoderate expectation that characterizes some of their rivals.

There was a good example of this early in the tournament, when France's best and most influential player, Zinedine Zidane, got himself sent off in the team's second match for raking his studs across the back of a Saudi opponent: there was regret but no outcry. Zidane, the son of Algerian immigrants from a tough quarter of Marseille, received a two-match suspension, which seriously imperilled his team's chances of making progress into the later rounds, but he was not made to share the fate of David Beckham, whose dismissal during England's defeat against Argentina turned him into a national pariah. Across France the debate was not how Zidane should be further humiliated, but how the team might be rearranged to compensate for his temporary absence. In the end they held on, but only just. Zidane's return, in time for the quarter-final, was greeted with relief.

For France, their football team became a positive example, as did the tournament in general, although one of the editors of *Libération* may have been going over the top when he wrote: 'This World Cup has shown a double elegance in the attitude of the protagonists and the game. Fair play on the field, purity of action, sophistication of tactics. Football has achieved a choreographic dimension which has charmed a reticent public.' But he had pertinent things to say about the national team, which contains men whose origins are in Algeria, New Caledonia, the Basque country, Argentina, Guadeloupe and Armenia. 'It's a formidable poke in the eye for the National Front,' he observed. 'The team behaves as a family, whose members live in the modern world. They're far from being caricatures of footballers with brains in their feet. They breathe the joy of playing, and they offer a redoubtable antidote to a sceptical country.'

Thierry Henry, a 20-year-old from the housing projects in Ulis, a Paris suburb, and France's most expressive attacker, mentioned during the tournament that he wouldn't be interested in a transfer from Monaco, his present club, to Paris Saint-Germain, because his father had once been attacked by skinheads wearing PSG colours. He also recounted a bittersweet memory of boyhood street games, when they played at being Brazil versus Germany. The white kids, he remembered, always had to be the Germans.

Another member of the French squad offered perhaps the most unexpected and original perspective on the event, at least from inside. Frank Leboeuf, the shaven-headed defender who plays for Chelsea, mentioned that he was avoiding watching any of France's matches on television. 'I want to hang on to the images I've seen with my own eyes,' he said. 'I want to keep them inside myself. In that way, the memories of the World Cup that stay with me won't be distorted by what I've seen on television.'

Goodness knows what memories, if any, the Croatian fans will have of their team's successful progress; the French were horrified to discover that they like to celebrate their victories with a mixture of wine and Coca-Cola. And when people behaved extravagantly during the World Cup, they were usually foreigners. In Paris a Nigerian student of ethnography and international relations founded and trained a troupe of pom-pom cheerleaders in order to support the Super Eagles more effectively. In Marseille, Oyvind Eckland from Norway and Rosangela de Souza from Brazil were married in front of tens of thousands of spectators half an hour before their two teams kicked off in the Stade Vélodrome. A week earlier, the city had endured the rioting between English fans and local youths of North African descent. 'After careful consideration,' the football authorities announced, 'it has been decided that this wedding could be an occasion for demonstrating that football brings people together in love and peace.' Fortunately, the result – a surprise win for Norway – eliminated neither team, and precipitated no riots.

But football's governors did not always act with such good sense. In the land where a baguette and a lump of cheese can taste of heaven, they accepted sponsorship from McDonald's, whose establishments were allowed to style themselves 'the official restaurant of the World Cup'. Most absurdly, after Daniel Passarella, the intense coach of Argentina, a man who had himself lifted the trophy twenty years earlier as his country's captain, came off the bench before extra time in the match against England with a cigarette burning between his fingers, the ruling body tried to ban coaches from smoking during the matches. In France, for heaven's sake. It didn't work. And it was far too late anyway for a man like Cesar Luis Menotti, who coached the side skippered by Passarella in 1978, and who could be seen this year in the media stands, analyzing the games for Argentinian television, still looking as louche and mysterious as a character out of a Borges story and still smoking more thoroughly than any man alive.

Carlos Gardel, a compatriot of Passarella and Menotti, smokes even in death. A tango singer whose standing in Latin countries resembles that of Sinatra, Elvis and Valentino combined, the French-born Gardel was killed in a plane crash in the 1930s but his legend lives on. Like Sinatra, Gardel smoked while on stage. In Buenos Aires' Chacarita cemetery, a life-size bronze statue stands above his grave, gesturing as if in mid-song. And at weekends, local people visiting their family tombs are in the habit of lighting a cigarette and wedging it between the first and second fingers of his right hand. When Argentina played their first game in Toulouse, Gardel's birthplace nearby was opened up for the benefit of the many fans who had crossed the Atlantic to follow their team, and who took the opportunity to pay homage to another national idol.

And in response to such hospitality, the leaders of the *barras bravas*, the gangs of travelling supporters attached to clubs such as River Plate, Boca Juniors and Estudiantes de la Plata, ordered their followers to maintain peace both with the representatives of other nations and between themselves. 'We're here to support our team, inside and outside the stadium, and we intend to behave properly,' they announced. But when Argentina went out to Holland in the semi-final, European photographers were spat on and pelted with coins as they left the pitch.

Such ugliness was the exception, at least after the English had gone home, taking with them their explicitly mimed requests for toilet facilities in family restaurants. Elsewhere, win or lose, supporters from around the world entered into the spirit of the fête that had begun on the eve of the competition, with that extraordinary and widely criticized event in which four separate processions made their way towards the Place de la Concorde. Each had at its head a gigantic animated figure, as tall as an office block, representing the peoples of the four corners of the world. Converging from different points of the compass on one of the world's most spectacular public spaces, they moved with such agonizing slowness that French television found it necessary to enliven its blanket coverage by inviting the actress Juliette Binoche to read a selection of poems over the images. Dealing with matters of sport, art and life, the poems seemed to have been inspired by the advertising copy for a particularly pretentious perfume. Some time towards midnight, when it had begun to drizzle, the gargantuan figures arrived at their destination and performed a robot-ballet around the giant obelisk – which had been converted, for the purpose of the festivities, into a replica of the World Cup trophy itself. Just up the street, various dissidents began a series of minor skirmishes with the police.

To those who remembered the spectacular show created by Jean-Paul Goude for the bicentenary of the French Revolution in 1989, it was a disappointment, a mini-festival of bathos. And the impression was confirmed the next afternoon, when the Stade de France was filled for the opening ceremony. The need to hand out thousands of tickets to blazered administrators and sponsors' guests at the expense of the fans from Brazil and Scotland, whose teams were about to stage the first match, created a lukewarm atmosphere. But even the freeloaders didn't deserve the show that they were about to see.

These highly-wrought galas are playing an ever more prominent part in major sporting events. Sometimes, as with the

1992 Olympics in Barcelona, they throw up an impressive, although still unnecessary, spectacle. On other occasions they provide a bit of light farce. At the opening ceremony of the 1994 World Cup in Chicago, someone had the idea of borrowing the way baseball starts its season, when the President throws the first pitch. Diana Ross, no less, was invited to take the inaugural penalty but missed the goal entirely. Perhaps she'd never seen one before. Nor are the British much good at these events. To kick off Euro 96, someone created a pageant that had all the panache of a primary-school country dance competition.

The characteristics these ceremonies share is an obsession with childishness, and the event in the Stade de France widened the frontiers of juvenility. In the name of illustrating the notion of *le jardin du foot*, hundreds of people dressed as fruit and vegetables careered across the pitch in kaleidoscopic patterns, kicking beach balls, while others abseiled off the overhang of the stadium's roof in order to wave flags above the heads of the crowd in a nightmarish meeting of Busby Berkeley, Albert Speer and the Teletubbies. Like the dance of the giant robots in the Place de la Concorde the night before, the whole affair seemed predicated on the sentimental idea that football is a game, and that games are what children play, and that being like children – innocent and unreflective – is therefore the condition to which all grown-ups should aspire. This worldwide epidemic of infantilism is surely what persuaded seven Italian footballers out of the squad of twenty-two to use their day off in Paris for a visit to EuroDisney (while one, Roberto Baggio, paid a call on the city's Buddhist centre and the rest went shopping).

Once the games had begun, however, the World Cup found in France a setting and an audience to justify its claim on our attention. And by mixing joy with gentle irony – from Saint-Etienne, where a conical heap of slag with giant coloured ribbons wound round it was the first sight greeting supporters arriving by train, to Saint-Denis, where the burial vault of Louis XVI and Marie-Antoinette rang to the sound of the 'Marseillaise', sung by French fans marching from the town square towards the stadium – it discovered ways, sometimes unconsciously, to keep that claim in perspective. It's an idea the rest of us might find useful.

THE RYDER CUP
Two Ways to Win at Golf

I F THAT'S THE way they want it, they should do the thing properly. They should line the fairways and greens with chain-link fences. Sell air-horns along with the commemorative golf bags and gold-plated ball-markers at the pro shop. Let the people make as much intimidatory noise as they want, whenever they want. Teach golfers to approach a putt for the match just like a professional footballer has to treat a penalty kick in injury time at a cup final, tuning out the cat-calls of the opposing fans.

Nobody is perfect, and Europe – England in particular – has nothing to teach the United States in the matter of fan misbehaviour at major sporting events. But on the 17th green of the Country Club in Brookline on Sunday, when Justin Leonard sank a 45-footer and began a dance of joy that ended with virtually the entire US Ryder Cup team and their immediate families cavorting on the green while José-Maria Olazábal waited to play his own putt to halve the hole, the game of golf appeared to be taking a big step into a different dimension.

When Leonard stroked his 45-footer – the putt heard around the world, according to the *Boston Globe* – up the ledge towards the cup at the 17th, he was flying on the wings of a recovery that had taken him from four strokes down at the 11th to all square at the 15th. This was the ninth of the day's twelve singles matches, and as the putt rolled up a ledge and across the green, the US had already won eight of them, giving the team a total of fourteen points. When Leonard's ball dropped, it meant that Olazábal had to sink his own putt in order for Europe to go to the final hole on level terms. If he missed, Leonard would be one stroke up with one to play, and certain to earn the half-point that would win the cup for his team, providing the climax to an extraordinary day-long crescendo.

Many of the US team were gathered behind the green, clustered around the captain, Ben Crenshaw, and his assistants, the former Ryder Cup players Bill Rogers and Bruce Lietzke, along with various caddies, wives and girlfriends. There was Tom Lehman, a captain's pick who had been sent out at 10.30 that morning as the team's point man, patiently and methodically destroying Lee Westwood to register the first kill for the US. There was Davis Love III, whose swift destruction of poor, disillusioned Jean Van de Velde had given him the time to walk the preceding six holes with Leonard. There was Tiger Woods, conqueror of the admirable Andrew Coltart. There was David Duval, the silent man who finally understood what the Ryder Cup was about and used his new-found motivation as a weapon with which to obliterate Jesper Parnevik. There was Phil Mickelson, who had gained his yearned-for revenge over Jarmo Sandelin. And there was Hal Sutton, Hal the Horse, whose dogged contribution in the early phases of the tournament was credited by the team with keeping their hopes alive.

There had been a bit of a dress rehearsal a few minutes earlier when Mark O'Meara was mobbed at the same hole after sinking a downhill six-footer while Padraig Harrington still had a putt to make. But O'Meara gave Harrington his putt, so the euphoric incursion had no significance. When Leonard's putt dropped, the full performance took place. The American exploded with delight and raced along the green with arms raised to embrace his team colleagues, and within seconds the area was awash with people.

Meanwhile, Olazábal waited for the furore to subside,

wondering how he was ever going to manage to concentrate on a putt following roughly the same line.

'It was an ugly picture to see,' the Spaniard said afterwards. 'It's not the kind of behaviour anyone expects. I don't want to make a whole thing out of this, but it shouldn't have happened. We're playing a match and we're trying to show respect for each other. I understand there were a lot of emotions going on, but I don't think it was the right thing to do.'

More than 300 yards back, Colin Montgomerie was watching from the 17th tee, waiting to play his drive. 'I couldn't believe what I was seeing,' he said. 'I thought they'd all just walk off to the 18th tee. I couldn't believe it when the green cleared and he was left on his own to have a putt. Very, very difficult for everyone concerned.'

Olazábal missed the putt, of course, his ball sliding by on the low side. And the US celebrated all over again, Crenshaw falling to the ground to kiss the turf. It didn't matter to anyone but Olazábal himself that he went on to win the 18th with a birdie three and thereby halve the match. 'You try to hold on the best you can,' he said. 'We are all professionals and I think I proved it on 18, even though it was too late.'

Later, even in their triumph, the Americans were mostly embarrassed by what they had done. 'We do know what happened,' Crenshaw said. 'We do apologize sincerely. There really wasn't any call for that. The celebration started spilling over and it really was not something that we need to be proud of and we've apologized.'

'What happened was unfortunate,' Lehman said. 'There never was any ill intent on anybody's part. We were very excited. And obviously in retrospect we probably wish we all would have jumped up and down in place instead of running down the side of the green. But I'm not going to apologize for being excited.'

'I'll take the blame,' Leonard interjected. 'I shouldn't have run off the green. I should have just calmly walked over to my team-mates, which would have been very hard to do. So if you're looking to point a finger, please point it at me. And I do apologize for that.'

'I'd like to stick in my two cents' worth,' Steve Pate said. 'It was a little bit out of line, and we're sorry it happened, but it had absolutely nothing to do with the outcome.'

No European thought it had, but that was not the point.

Leonard went to some lengths to explain that he had run off the green to the side, and that he and his colleagues had not committed the cardinal sin of crossing the line of Olazábal's putt. But they had crossed their opponent's line of thought in such a way that they might have done less damage had they dug a trench between his ball and the cup.

They were showing emotion, which is what the mass media require of today's sportsmen and women. Golfers are coming under the same pressures as anyone else, and they are beginning to oblige. Tiger Woods, who pumps his fists at every small success, is worth tens of millions more than David Duval, who hides his emotions. And Woods' excessive gestures – excessive, that is, by the game's traditional standards – are catching on. Just watch the way young Sergio Garcia celebrates. This is what the sponsors want, because it creates an image that sells shoes and shirts. And it will slowly change the game at every level, for better or worse, just as Jimmy Connors and John McEnroe changed tennis, from the top down.

When the golfers were back in the clubhouse and the celebrations were in full swing, Ben Crenshaw took Justin Leonard aside in the locker room and told him the history of the 17th hole at the Country Club. About how Francis Ouimet, the 20-year-old local amateur, had finally caught Harry Vardon and Ted Ray, the English professionals, with a 20-foot putt on the 17th at the US Open in 1913, and how Ouimet, accompanied by a 10-year-old caddie, had sunk another putt of similar length at the same hole in the playoff to earn himself a historic victory and a parade back to the clubhouse on the shoulders of the crowd.

The emotion of the thought had Crenshaw in tears, not for the first time over the weekend. He was also thinking about his own father, who died earlier this year and who had followed him around the Country Club in 1968, when Crenshaw competed in the US junior championships as a 16-year-old. He could still see his father, he said, walking the 1st and the 18th, where the old trotting track had stood.

Great memories. The stuff of the most beautiful sporting legends. And now Crenshaw, who sent his men out in shirts bearing sepia-tinted photographs of their predecessors, has bought himself a new place in the game's history. Sadly, however, posterity's verdict on the legacy of the 1999 Ryder Cup may involve more than just the oft-told tale of a heroic American comeback.

THE BELFRY, 29 SEPTEMBER 2002

ESTINY DOES NOT come alike to all men. For most of the world's best golfers, the four major tournaments provide the measurement of their greatness. For Colin Montgomerie, something happened yesterday to suggest that his stature may one day be assessed by a different yardstick.

As Montgomerie marched up the short 14th fairway to finish off Scott Hoch a few minutes before two o'clock in the afternoon, the noise of the crowd jamming the banks around the raised green should have confirmed a belief that the Ryder Cup is the tournament for which he was made. He cannot fail to have noticed that the cheers contained not just admiration for his achievement on the day, but also a genuine affection built up over the fifteen years of his professional career.

Monty has some history with this competition. He has said that addressing the opening tee shot at Oak Hill in 1995 was the most petrifying moment of his career. At Valderrama two years later he hit the drive of his life at the 18th to halve the final match with the very same Hoch and win the half-point that enabled Europe to retain the trophy. At Brookline three years ago he showed great dignity in rising above the disgraceful taunts that so upset his watching father.

The knowledge of all this was contained in the warmth of the cheers that washed over him as he strode towards the 14th green at the Belfry, struggling to suppress a dirty great grin until the job had been completed. His stride was long, his shoulders set, his chin up. This was Monty at his most confident and determined, at ease with himself and his task.

No golfer over the whole weekend rose to the challenge as he did or accepted as much responsibility for establishing his team's mood. He had spoken last week, in the build-up to the event, of his acceptance of the role, with Bernhard Langer, of the team's on-course leader, available to dispense advice to the younger players. 'It's a position that I like and thrive on,' he said.

Yesterday Sam Torrance called on a different aspect of his

leadership qualities when he invited him to go out first and lead Europe into the round of twelve singles matches, the element of the competition in which history said they had most to fear. Torrance saw Montgomerie as a figurehead, and the 39-year-old Scot responded magnificently.

Two months ago Torrance feared that he was going to lose Montgomerie altogether, thanks to a recurrent back complaint. More recently Monty mentioned that, while being treated for the problem, his heart had been given a precautionary checkover. This gave cynics all the material they needed. When he screwed up in the Ryder Cup, they said, he wouldn't know whether to clutch at his back or his chest. But he came to the Belfry in sound heart and good humour, relaxed and affable enough during the preliminaries to offer his club to a spectator when he found himself facing a chip from an unfriendly lie. On the practice range yesterday, preparing himself to face Hoch, he invited another bystander to have a go and supervised his efforts with previously unsuspected comic gifts.

A few minutes later he was delivering the first blow of the day with an arrow-straight three wood off the first tee, a wedge to 15 feet and a solid birdie putt to give himself an immediate lead. After Hoch played himself out of a bunker to restore parity at the par-five 3rd, Montgomerie re-established his advantage at the 5th and increased it with a 20-foot putt at the 6th. A difficult downhill chip from 40 feet put him in position to take another hole at the 9th, and at the 10th tee he was joined by Torrance, who watched him lay up and put his second shot 12 feet from the pin. As Montgomerie crossed the bridge, he walked into a wall of applause from the spectators clustered around the tight green, the Belfry's own little Amen Corner. The gentlest birdie putt of the day rolled down into the cup, giving him a four-stroke lead over an opponent who, whatever he could muster in terms of tenacity, was never able to locate significant gaps in Montgomerie's armour.

Hoch did pull back to three under at the 12th, but Montomerie's beautiful wedge shot spinning back to 18 inches at the 13th had the American veteran picking it up and pretending to hurl it to the gallery before smiling and handing it back to its owner.

Four up with five to play, Montgomerie saw no reason to be merciful. At the 14th he watched Hoch miss with a chip of 20 feet from the rough before curling his 9-foot putt into the dead centre of the hole. He dropped his putter, looked at the heavens and knew that he had delivered his part of the bargain.

'I've played six of these singles matches now and this was the best I've ever played,' he said as he came off the green. 'This is what we were hoping would happen. Sam put his strength at the top of the order because he remembered what happened at Brookline, when we had six defeats in a row. He's a courageous man, like most Scots.'

He was, he said, 'officially tired' now. 'I didn't really expect to play five straight games. My game wasn't great coming into the Ryder Cup. I don't know what it is, but it seems to fire me up.'

Eight times he has finished in the top ten in the four major tournaments, without managing to win one. Rising 40, his chance has probably gone. But what happened yesterday renders that irrelevant. And what he learned from Sam Torrance about the art of captaincy will stand him in good stead when his turn comes, as it surely will, to ask a younger man to take the lead in a cause whose rewards stretch far beyond the glory of the individual.

MICHAEL JORDAN
Taking Off

CHICAGO, 20 JANUARY 1999

A S WINTER BRIEFLY relaxed its grip on Chicago this week, the shivering citizens raised their fearful eyes above the downtown skyscrapers and waited for a new silhouette to emerge from the morning mists: that of the reshaped Bulls, following perhaps the swiftest and most thorough demolition of a great team in the history of sport.

One man's disappearance has taken most of the limelight in this extraordinary affair. Literally so in the 44-storey headquarters of an insurance company on South Wabash Avenue, where lights have been left on at night in an arrangement that spells 'THX MJ' in giant letters down one wall and '23' down another. This is corporate America's grateful farewell to a man whose skills and leadership of the Bulls brought championships to Chicago, dreams to the hearts of children from Manchester to Manila, and a warm glow to the balance sheets of a number of multinational companies. But Michael Jordan has retired before. This time the rest of them have gone with him.

The recent collective bargaining agreement between owners and players which ended the six-month shutdown of that unique combination of sport and showbiz known as the National Basketball Association prefaced anything but an immediate return to business as usual at the United Center, the Bulls' home stadium. Jordan's decision to turn down almost £25 million for one last season was swiftly followed by the announcement of the retirement of Dennis Rodman, the outrageous rebound king, and of the departure of another three senior players: Scottie Pippen, Luc Longley and Steve Kerr. The coach, Phil Jackson, also confirmed that he would be taking a year off, and might resume his career elsewhere. Of the household names, only Toni Kukoc, the 6ft 11in Croatian forward, remains.

The fans in this sports-mad town are bemused and disappointed. 'It's shaken the city up,' said Jeff Wallenfeldt, a publisher's editor. 'The Bulls' success over the years had locked the city into an expectation of an annual ritual, if not a championship.' And each capture of the NBA's O'Brien Trophy was greeted with a mass expression of joy. 'The next day, people would just pour into the city from the suburbs,' Wallenfield continued, 'hundreds of thousands of them heading for Grant Park, wearing Bulls shirts and carrying pennants. The atmosphere was like a championship game itself.' Others are rueful but realistic, in the way of Chicagoans. 'All good things come to an end,' John Castelli, who drives a limousine, said. 'And we got six world championships out of this team.'

How do we measure the true dimension of this phenomenon? Let's imagine that when Eric Cantona called it a day after winning a second league-and-cup double with Manchester United, he took Ryan Giggs, David Beckham, Roy Keane, Paul Scholes and Peter Schmeichel with him. Oh, and Alex Ferguson. Actually, it's worse than that, since an NBA team only has five players on court at any one time, and the big five have gone. And, well, United aren't the Bulls.

The collective identity of this team reached out far beyond their own universe. These were the men who completed the transformation of basketball into a global marketing phenomenon, a process begun at the end of the 1970s by the appearance of such talents as Larry Bird and Magic Johnson. Before them, as the

Pulitzer Prize-winning author David Halberstam writes in *Playing For Keeps*, his book about Jordan, basketball was 'considered to be badly tainted ... it was seen as far too black, and the majority of its players, it was somehow believed, were on drugs and willing to play hard only in the last two minutes of each game.' After Jordan, the NBA's logo was up there with McDonald's and Coca-Cola.

Chicago is currently staring at the retreating backs of players who, under Jackson's wise stewardship, won six titles in eight years (missing out only in the two years when Jordan took a leave of absence to try his hand at pro baseball), who set an NBA record of seventy-two victories in a single regular season in 1996, and who sold enough merchandise to put half the male youth of the world in shiny red singlets, most of them with the number 23 on front and back.

And now they're gone. All gone. Leaving the Bulls with only three players under contract. Leaving their owner, Jerry Reinsdorf, and his widely abused general manager, Jerry Krause, furiously negotiating with prospective arrivals from clubs across the nation. Leaving the sponsors and merchandisers scratching their hands. Leaving the fans – or however many of them turn up at the 19,000-seater United Center when the abbreviated season begins in two weeks' time – to peruse their programmes and try to sort out the identities of a bunch of understudies and newcomers.

Some of those unfamiliar silhouettes were visible this week at the Berto Center, the Bulls' training facility, an unsignposted and outwardly unremarkable building set amidst a park of corporate headquarters in Deerfield, a rural enclave in Chicago's opulent northern suburbs. This is close by the place where Jordan and Pippen made their homes, in a planned village called Bannockburn, amid the variegated architecture preferred by commodity dealers and corporate lawyers: mansions ranging from Hollywood Tudor to blank-faced concrete bunkers, surrounded by groves of ash, fir and silver birch. These dream-palaces lie off Half Day Road, so called because it once took half a day to get there from Chicago by horse and cart ('Takes a million dollars now,' my cabdriver muttered).

Locked out for half a year, the younger players had been allowed back into the Berto Center to go through individual exercise and practice routines, but were having to wait for the NBA and the players' union to sort out the last details of their deal before getting clearance to return to full, supervised training. And, incidentally, learning the names of their new team-mates. For the first time since Jordan's arrival from the University of North Carolina in 1985, the parking lot behind the building contained not one superstar's supercar.

Jordan's departure was not the reason for the simultaneous exits of Rodman, Pippen, Longley and Kerr. Although his colleagues respected his unique ability and the finishing touch he brought to the team, he was not as popular as that in the locker room. The reasons were mostly to do with the complex salary rules under which the NBA clubs operate and with the desire of Chicago's management to look ahead and build a new generation of Bulls for the post-Jordan era.

Pippen, Longley and Kerr were out of contract and had become free agents. But the NBA's curious rules on maximum salaries mean that a club can re-sign their own players for a higher salary than another club could offer, and then, in this case, trade them to those other clubs, where they are then paid the salary agreed with the original club. This benefits the players, obviously, and might be seen as a reward for their loyal service. 'One of the things we felt was that the players had given a lot to the city,' Jerry Krause said this week. 'We felt we had some situations where we could help them.'

But such apparent generosity also works greatly to the Bulls' advantage. By replacing their departing stars with a bunch of decent players – such as forwards Martin Muursepp from Phoenix and Roy Rogers from Houston, and a man sarcastically described by the *Chicago Tribune* as 'the immortal Bubba Wells' – whose contracts end at the close of the forthcoming season, the club will be giving itself greater room for financial manoeuvre in preparation for the first season of the new millennium, when they will have approximately $25 million in the war-chest with which to attract free agents for the new coach, Tim Floyd from Iowa State, to mould into title contenders.

Many fans blame Krause for starting the fall of the dominoes by alienating the much-admired Phil Jackson, whose book, *Sacred Hoops*, a philosophical disquisition on teamwork, became a national bookseller. Krause's own philosophy is more Damon Runyon than Black Elk. 'When we're winning in the play-offs,' he has said, 'it's amazing how good-looking I get. People come up and compliment me on my diet. But if we lose, I'm a little fat slob again.'

Even Krause has his defenders. 'What happened is not Jerry Krause's fault,' said John Castelli, the limo driver, who can remember a time before there were Bulls at all, when Chicago's basketball team was the Zephyrs, who played through the 1940s and 1950s before going under. 'It's always the same with general managers. When they win, he's a hero. When they lose, the guy's a goat. Chicago was lucky to get Michael in the first place. When he arrived, he made it clear that he wasn't just in it to do tricks but to win championships. And Krause went out and bought the players to help him do it.'

The Jordan-led Bulls eventually outgrew the Old Barn, their original arena, flattened to create a parking lot for its successor. At the huge grey Universal Center, located a couple of hundred yards from condemned tenements which have become warrens of crack houses, the minimum ticket price is around $60. But not all Chicago residents take an unalloyed pride in their team's achievements. For Marty Preibe, a 35-year-old hotel bell captain, the Reinsdorf–Krause–Jordan Bulls symbolized the commercial corruption of what was once a game played for the pleasure of working people and their children.

'I used to live and breathe basketball,' he told me. 'When I was a kid and we lived halfway between here and Detroit, my dad used to take me to see the Pistons. He'd put a twenty dollar bill in his pocket and out of that he'd pay for parking, tickets and food for both of us. We had such fun. The crowd at Cobo Hall really knew basketball. They could appreciate a good defence, when someone was working hard for rebounds. It wasn't just about who scored the most points.

'Then when I went to college in Seattle I'd go see the Sonics. I'd buy a $5 ticket for a nosebleed seat and if there were free places at courtside nobody minded if you walked right down and sat there.

But then the salaries started going crazy, and the players started having their pictures taken in front of corporate logos, and the best seats got taken by the corporations, and I haven't been to a game in five years. It's not a game for working people any more.

'What happened was that the players became businessmen. They may have a union, but they're such hypocrites. They were talking about solidarity during the lockout. But, you know, Nike laid off 63,000 workers in Maine, all union people, and took their jobs to Korea, and then to Indonesia, where they don't have unions, and the players didn't say a thing.'

In fact, the 'workers' were generally felt to have come off much worse than the bosses in a dispute that was principally concerned with the division of the NBA's $2 billion annual revenues. The owners managed to win agreement on a mechanism that will rein back the runaway salary increases of recent years, although it would be hard to describe as a defeat any settlement that gives a rookie player, fresh out of college, a statutory minimum annual income of $275,000.

So as the NBA winds up the hype for an abbreviated fifty-game season scheduled to begin on 5 February, the 35-year-old Jordan, still pulling down around $80 million a year from corporate endorsements, is off to a life of golf (he was clowning with Charles Barkley at the Bob Hope Classic this week), gambling and a seven-a-day cigar habit.

Rodman, aged 37, said on Tuesday that he wants to pursue his Hollywood career and give more time to his marriage to Baywatch star Carmen Electra, but on Thursday he was making tentative noises about playing again, although probably not in Chicago. Pippen, 33, will pick up an estimated $80 million over five years for joining Barkley and Hakeem Olajuwon in Houston, turning the Rockets into serious contenders for the championship; Longley's five-year deal with Phoenix is worth $30 million; and Kerr, the three-point specialist, will make $11 million for a similar spell at San Antonio.

Farewell, then, to an Air-a, as the display window of a State Street department store put it this week, in bold lettering above a display of Jordan memorabilia. Chicago knows it will not see his like again. But this is a tough and businesslike town, not given to despair. 'What happens next?' John Castelli mused, leaning against his limo's door. 'That's the thing about sports. You never know.'

WASHINGTON, DC, 21 OCTOBER 2001

THE DUNK CAME with seven minutes and twenty-four seconds of the third quarter remaining in Saturday night's game, and it provoked a roar so loud that the stadium threatened to rise off its foundations. Michael Jordan was not just back. Once again he was walking on air.

He had been scoring with jump shots and free throws all night, guiding and goading his team of rookies and unknowns. Only half a minute earlier he had left a master's signature on the night when he leaned back into his opposing defender, a jostling 21-year-old rookie named Richard Jefferson, before pushing himself forward to find a yard of space, then turning and finding the basket with a 19-foot jumper that left his hand as he was falling backwards into the sidelines, everything sacrificed to the heart-stopping accuracy of the shot.

But it was the dunk, coming at the end of a long, arcing drive, with defenders falling away from him like ghosts meeting daylight, that removed any doubt. For the next two years, 23 JORDAN is going to be more than just a number and a name above a peg in the Washington Wizards' locker room.

'Obviously, Michael was magnificent,' his coach, Doug Collins, said, reflecting on a performance in which Jordan, after three years out of the game, had scored 41 points in a total of thirty three minutes on the court. 'But he never ceases to amaze me.'

When Jordan announced his return three weeks ago, after months of rumour and deliberation, there was no shortage of observers ready to cast doubt on his wisdom. Coming back successfully at the age of 32, as he did in 1995 after an unsuccessful stab at playing pro baseball, was one thing. At 38, they said, he might still have the mind for basketball, but not the body. And however much he said he loved the game, however much he was prepared to sacrifice to get himself back into shape, he would no longer have the dunk. His Airness would now be as earthbound as those on whom he had once looked down.

On Saturday night, in front of a crowd of 20,674 in Washington's

MCI Centre, Jordan played his first pre-season game in his new home. In the end the Wizards lost to the New Jersey Nets by 102–95. But the more significant statistics were these. Jordan was in action for thirty-three of the forty-eight minutes. While he was in the game, the Wizards outscored the Nets by 82–57. While he was resting, his team-mates were overshadowed by 13–45. The most dramatic illustration of the difference he makes came in a five-minute spell in that dizzying third quarter, when the dunk was among the 16 points he scored to drag the team back into contention, with the crowd going wild. Then Collins pulled him off to give him a breather, and the team fell apart again.

'I'm feeling good,' Jordan said. 'That's a good sign. The bad sign is that the team's going to have to elevate to stay in tune with what's happening with me. I think this was the first time they've had the feeling of what it's like to be on the same court when I get into those rhythms. That's something they're going to have to learn. They're young kids and they're going to have to grow up quick.'

As the coach had noticed in earlier pre-season games, his colleagues – several of whom were members of the squad that finished bottom of the NBA's Atlantic division last season – are so overwhelmed by Jordan's presence that they stand back and wait for him to deliver the goods. They see not a team-mate but the legend who won six championships with the Chicago Bulls between 1991 and 1998, and whose worldwide fame lifted the NBA to a new level of popularity. And they freeze.

'They're playing in awe of him,' Collins said. 'Tonight I didn't want to keep him out there, but he was the only thing giving us any stability. Is that scary? Yes, it is. If he doesn't score or make something happen, we struggle. When he wasn't out there, we were bad.'

The other players may be further inhibited by the knowledge that Jordan also functions as the Wizards' president of basketball operations. He bought a 10 per cent stake in the franchise during his retirement and took control of the team's affairs. Under the league's rules, in order to play again he had to sell his stake – for a reported $20 million – but he remains the man who hired Collins, one of his early coaches in Chicago, to take charge this season, and who engineered the arrival of such players as Kwame Brown, a raw

19-year-old forward fresh out of high school in Georgia, and Christian Laettner, a 32-year-old forward whose talent is unquestioned but whose temperament has led his four previous NBA clubs to let him go. Now Jordan's responsibilities are divided in a way that will require an extremely skilful deployment of all his energy and expertise.

'It took a lot of work to get back to this point,' he said on Saturday night, already changed back into a cream suit, cream shirt and cream tie. 'I had to shed about 25 pounds. I have no foot problems, no knee problems, I'm getting my rhythm and my timing back, and I feel like I'm starting to get my wind. Today I took a big step in the right direction. That's for me personally. But it was a backward step in terms of what the team has to do to get into a competitive mode.'

He has the corner peg in the locker room, tucked away behind a cupboard, out of the sight of anyone who sticks a head through the doorway in the hope of getting a peek at the world's most famous sportsman. It sums up the dilemma facing Jordan as he begins his second coming, his appetite for domination reawakened but tempered by the knowledge that he is no longer surrounded by the Pippens and the Rodmans who helped him turn the Bulls into a basketball equivalent of the invincible Real Madrid of the 1950s.

Lingering behind after he had said his goodbyes, his younger team-mates were clearly chastened by the experience of failing to meet his standards by such a margin. 'Michael is such a great player,' said Etan Thomas, a 23-year-old rookie centre, 'and he's able to do so many things that when he's out there, that you do have the tendency to just watch him.'

'It's a fine line,' Courtney Alexander, a 24-year-old guard, said. 'You want him to have the ball, but at the same time we do have other guys on the team with the ability to score. We have to help him.'

Jordan's motivation has been endlessly debated. 'There's an itch that still needs to be scratched,' he said when he announced his return, 'and I want to make sure it doesn't bother me the rest of my life.' He has talked about doing it for 'the love of the game', and his first year's salary, a million dollars, will be donated to the bereaved families of the September 11 attack on the Pentagon.

But sceptics might point to the corner of 12th and J streets, three blocks from the arena, where a huge mural advertises Jordan's new line of sportswear, a Nike brand that generates an annual $300 million in sales. He is also said to be planning to open a restaurant in the city, along the lines of his successful enterprise in Chicago. Sales of Wizards season tickets have rocketed and the club will earn a great deal more from TV exposure this season. Replica vests with the number 23 and Jordan's name on the back are already walking off the shelves at $145 each. And there's hardly enough material in them to blow your nose on.

Cynicism is the natural response to that sort of thing. But in Jordan's case, after witnessing the beauty and the euphoria of those five minutes in Saturday night's third quarter, it was tempting to conclude that sometimes a man can indeed focus on the bottom line and still reach for the sky.

RUGBY STRIKE
Market Forces

PENNYHILL PARK, 21 NOVEMBER 2000

THE FINAL ACT in the protracted and painful transformation of English rugby union from the preserve of Barboured amateurs into a fully professional business controlled by agents and lawyers took place in a Surrey country club yesterday, when the entire England squad went on strike over a contract dispute and were ordered to pack their bags and go home.

After their manager, Clive Woodward, heard that the squad had voted unanimously in a secret ballot to reject the latest pay offer from the Rugby Football Union, and would be withdrawing from Saturday's match against Argentina, he told all twenty-two players to leave the team's headquarters and to spend the night examining their consciences. Only if they return for a training session at 11 a.m. today will they be considered for selection for the match at Twickenham, for which around 60,000 tickets have been sold. If they fail to show up, he promises to put together a side from whatever resources are available to him.

At yesterday's press conference, Woodward said he felt

'betrayed' by players with whom he has worked for the past three years and who, after capturing last season's Six Nations championship, beat Australia, the world champions, last Saturday. 'The players had my full support,' he said. 'I don't think they were being greedy. But after seeing the offer, I can't believe they haven't accepted it.'

He was particularly critical of 'three or four strong characters' among the senior players. 'They've made a huge mistake,' he said. 'A lot of the younger guys will be driving home now, panicking and wondering what the hell they've just done.'

Most of the squad had already left the Pennyhill Park hotel, just outside Bagshot, when an ad hoc committee consisting of three senior players – the present captain, Martin Johnson, and two of his predecessors, Lawrence Dallaglio and Matt Dawson – emerged into the courtyard. Accompanied by Alan Edwards, a public relations man better known for advising the Rolling Stones and the Spice Girls, they put their side of the argument to reporters who had gathered expecting to hear nothing more exciting than Woodward's team selection for Saturday's match. Instead the journalists were witnessing the apparent meltdown of the one area in which rugby union, riven in recent years by the stresses imposed by the sudden influx of money from satellite television, had retained its unity.

At the heart of the dispute is a disagreement over the complicated formula determining the balance between fixed match fees and win bonuses stipulated by the four-year deal. Although neither side would be precise about figures, the RFU is offering a split under which the players would each earn about £65,000 for winning all this season's eight matches, plus a top-up bonus, and about £25,000 for losing them all. The players, perhaps mindful of the painful experience of watching a Grand Slam win bonus go down the drain against Scotland in the final match of last season, want to raise the proportion represented by the guaranteed match fee.

This income comes on top of regular salaries from their clubs, which range from about £60,000 a year for the least experienced players to perhaps £120,000 for the most senior. Added to all this, for the international players, is a system of payments for intellectual property rights – in other words, for the use of their images as part of sponsorship and advertising deals. This, the RFU say, is expected to swell the players' pot by up to £2 million over the four years of the deal.

Johnson read a prepared statement in which the players were highly critical of the way in which the negotiations, described as 'frustrating and inconclusive', had been conducted by the 'old-fashioned, patronising and arrogant' RFU and in particular its chief executive, Francis Baron.

'The issue from the players' side is one of principle,' Johnson said, 'and their main drive is to bring the sport into the twenty-first century, and ensure that as performers they get something approaching a fair deal to bring them in line with other sports. Most rugby players earn a salary commensurate with many Premiership soccer players' weekly drawings, so there is no question of greed being a factor here. Our careers are very short and all we are asking is a fair share of the substantial income that these games generate. The players have made attempt after attempt to resolve the situation and we have been met by nothing other than prevarication, excuses and general delaying tactics. We will not be turning back.'

The negotiations began in August, six months after the squad had put their collective financial affairs into the hands of CSS Stellar, a sports management company that also supervises the commercial affairs of the England soccer team and which is largely controlled by former employees of Mark McCormack's International Management Group. On 26 October, Baron left a meeting under the impression that he and his board had agreed a deal with CSS's Julian Hill and John Simpson.

Yesterday Hill and Simpson were at Pennyhill Park and said that although they had indeed recommended the RFU's offer to the squad, it was the players themselves who decided to turn it down and go back in search of improved terms. The agents also pointed out that although the required shift in the balance between fee and bonus payments would not affect the RFU's budget, the players were unhappy to be receiving a total sum equivalent to only five per cent of the RFU's receipts from internationals, estimated at £2 million a match.

The first serious rumblings of the dispute were evident to the team management early last week, a few days before the match against Australia. Johnson called Woodward to tell him that, at the next day's press conference and open training session, the squad would be staging a protest against the RFU's apparent unwillingness to resume negotiations by wearing their shirts and tops inside out, so that the sponsors' names could not be seen.

Woodward met the players the following morning and told them that if they refrained from 'pratting about' in the build-up to the match, he would arrange a meeting between their representatives and the RFU management board. 'I gave them my word on that and they agreed to it,' Woodward said. 'I asked them to put it out of their minds and concentrate on the match, which they did, with the results we all saw. My words to the players then were to get it sorted out one way or the other because I didn't want to go into another match under that sort of threat.'

On Monday night the management board, led by the RFU's president, the former international forward Budge Rogers, met the three senior players and the men from CSS. 'We spent four hours talking,' Baron said yesterday, 'during which we offered a number of improvements to the package. It would be an understatement to say that we were shocked when it was not only turned down, but turned down with the immediate threat that they would not play for England on Saturday.'

A seemingly petty incident might have concentrated the players' minds or at least convinced them that the RFU did not have their best interests at heart. As part of the new contract package, the RFU announced its intention to reduce their allocation of free match tickets from three to two. Although the reduction was subsequently rescinded, this was probably the factor that led Johnson to refer to the board's attitude as 'feudal' yesterday.

'I have a terrible feeling that there's something going on here that I don't know about,' Woodward said, hinting at dark forces behind the players' unprecedented resort to industrial action. He denied a suggestion that he was referring to the influence of the players' clubs, among whom there is a belief that they should receive greater recompense for providing the personnel for the England side.

'I just hope that whoever plays on Saturday gets a standing

ovation from the English public,' the manager added, musing on his imminent selection problem.

Martin Johnson, asked if he would be returning for today's training session, answered in a single word: 'No.' But as he threw his bags into the boot of his top of the range Audi, the last of the players to leave the team hotel, someone said they hoped he'd be back soon. 'So do I, mate,' he replied. 'So do I.'

FOUR DAYS LATER

A S THE DUST settles on the Battle of Pennyhill Park and the scene is set for hostilities of a different kind at Twickenham this afternoon, once again stories are being written about the 'irreparable damage' done by a commercial dispute to the emotional fabric of a sport, as expressed in the relationship between its players, coaches, administrators and spectators.

It makes a good story but it is evident nonsense. Did the Kramer Circus kill off big-time tennis in the 1950s? Did the strife over the ending of football's minimum wage forty years ago diminish the public's interest? Did the all-night sit-in of grand prix drivers at Kyalami in 1982 destroy the audience for Formula One? All that happened to rugby union this week was that the game took a belated step along the road to matching its professional status with professional behaviour, which includes a right to full participation in the free market economy and all that it entails, for good and ill.

There was a similar wave of reflexive tut-tutting two weeks ago when Tiger Woods criticized the US PGA Tour for not paying him enough money and for trespassing on his 'intellectual property rights', meaning his right to control the use of his own image. In other words, Woods has a personal endorsement deal with Buick and he objected to playing in a tournament sponsored by Mercedes-Benz. 'This is the type of thing that drives us crazy,' said Mark Steinberg, his agent at Mark McCormack's International Management Group. 'It's an infringement of Tiger's rights.'

Woods won $9,188,321 in prize money this year and in September he signed a five-year deal with Nike worth $100 million. His income from endorsements alone in 2001 is predicted by *Golf World* to be $54 million, from a dozen companies. 'There's a lot the public doesn't understand and doesn't know about,' the world's number one golfer said when he realized ordinary people were coming to the conclusion that, like England's £100,000-a-year rugby players, he was being greedy. And, again like the rugby men, Woods was not necessarily his own best advocate.

But as his father Earl Woods said: 'Tiger holds all the cards.' The fact is that when Woods is not playing in a PGA tournament, its audience drops by 60 per cent. In the world of professional sport the size of the TV audience determines everything.

Richard Williams, the father of Venus and Serena, whose financial affairs are also handled by IMG, was quick to jump on the theme. 'You don't want players thinking they've got a bad deal,' he said. 'The rankings don't mean anything. For example, Anna Kournikova has never won a tournament but, like Venus and Serena, she puts a lot of people in the stands. She also should share in the revenue. When I was a department manager, every time my people put out more work, the company gave us a bonus. No one can argue that Venus and Serena haven't raised attendance and television packages. Why not allow them to share in the revenue packages? It's only fair.'

Fairness, of course, has nothing to do with it. Capitalism rewards winners, and against that background it is hard to make a coherent counter-argument. After Woods stunned the entire world of sport by winning the US Masters, his first major as a professional, in 1997, the US PGA Tour was able to sign a new TV deal worth $500 million. On what grounds should he be denied the chance to participate in the prosperity he did so much to create?

'What you have to remember is that without the players there wouldn't be any sport,' the agent Jon Holmes, who has represented Gary Lineker, Mike Atherton, Will Carling, Rob Andrew and Emile Heskey, argued this week. 'I'd rather they got the money than a lot of other people. And it's not just sport. High flyers in all sorts of businesses are earning much more money today.'

Today, in this sense, began in 1959, when Arnold Palmer, the world's number one golfer, met McCormack, a Cleveland lawyer who had spotted an area of activity with an untapped potential for economic growth. Adi Dassler, who built a commercial empire by getting the top athletes to wear his Adidas shoes in the 1930s, had been the first to recognize the riches that could be wrung from sport. McCormack was the first to see that the sportsmen and women themselves could become the principal beneficiaries, and had soon turned Palmer from a $20,000-a-year man into golf's first millionaire.

'Arnold is the one who got it all started,' said Tiger Woods, and all else has flowed from that pioneering coup, including the £18 million that Leeds United are paying this weekend to secure Rio Ferdinand's services, made possible by the Premier League's revenues from the sale of television rights. This, too, was foreseen by McCormack, who made it his business to get into both the negotiation of such rights and the production of the programmes to which they gave birth.

So it was no coincidence that, when England's rugby union international players went on strike this week, in the wings were a group of men who learned their trade as IMG employees. Julian Jakobi, the managing director of CSS-Stellar who handle the commercial interests of England's rugby and soccer teams, left McCormack in order to steer Ayrton Senna into a position where he rivalled Michael Jordan for the title of the world's highest-paid sportsman.

'It all comes down to market forces,' Jakobi said yesterday, echoing the words of every other sports agent I spoke to this week. 'People pay to see players, not administrators. If you have a special talent, people are prepared to pay to see you exhibit it. It's important that the people who run the sports understand that. Twickenham is used only a dozen times a year, which puts the RFU under pressure to service the loan they took out to build the stadium. But why should the players be underpaid in order to help them out?'

Different sports have confronted the challenge of professionalism with different levels of alacrity. Rugby union, most outsiders agree, is near the back of the grid, along with athletics. At the front, both Jakobi and Holmes pointed to the Premier League, which recognized that the elite requires its own administration, and to Formula One, which has been run for twenty years by Bernie Ecclestone as a virtual personal fiefdom, its participants' loyalty ensured, once again, by their share of vast broadcasting revenues and by the income from sponsors attracted by the worldwide TV audience.

'Ecclestone is a good businessman,' Holmes said. 'Like the NFL, he satisfied the public's appetite by not overdoing it. He knows which bits sell and which bits don't, unlike rugby – or cricket, which persists in trying to promote the county game even though it's obvious that people don't want to watch it. In my opinion the roots of the betting scandal are to be found in cricket's failure to sort itself out and pay the top players properly. A lot of sports are being run by people who don't understand the rules of commercialism and have failed to make the right decisions.'

'There's a lot more to come from sport,' Edward Freedman, Manchester United's former merchandising director, said yesterday. Freedman now runs icons.com, the footballers' website. 'Players are going to get even more powerful. Image rights is the next big thing. If the clubs are going to share a TV deal worth a billion pounds, why shouldn't the players get five or ten per cent?' But how would it be divided up? 'Someone is going to have to sit down and work that out.' And no doubt, with future millions at stake, someone will.

In a way the most telling element of the rugby strike was the decision of the RFU management board not to discipline the players. Five years ago their predecessors stripped Will Carling of the captaincy merely for referring to them as 'old farts'. This week Budge Rogers, the RFU president, said: 'We didn't consider disciplinary action because this was a whole-squad decision.' What he meant was that, whatever his negotiators might claim, the players had finally got the upper hand.

Julian Jakobi was not directly involved in the Twickenham negotiations. His time this week was occupied with preparations for the flotation of CSS-Stellar on the alternative investment market, projected for 12 December. To those with an eye on sport's bottom line rather than its scorelines, there was the week's real winner.

MIKE TYSON
His Own Worst Enemy

THIS IS, ACCORDING to Mike Tyson yesterday, 'just another fight'. A few seconds later, in the kind of apparent contradiction that gives a surface expression to the fault lines running through his character, he was saying how important it was to him. 'I'm gonna blaze,' he claimed, although in most people's view a couple of small sparks ought to be enough to do the job.

Just about the least interesting aspect of Tyson's visit to Britain is the matter of the event scheduled to take place at around ten o'clock tomorrow night in a Manchester arena, when the former undisputed heavyweight champion of the world meets Julius Francis, a man whose name, until a few weeks ago, was hardly known outside the ever diminishing number of boxing cognoscenti. In terms of sporting contests, this is a mismatch of such towering absurdity that it would be unimaginable in any sport other than the eternally surreal and value-free world of heavyweight boxing.

In other ways, however, this shameless farce is providing a great deal of food for serious thought. Tyson's arrival, and the remarkable scenes played out in London and Manchester over the last week, have opened up a few frayed seams in our society, exposing layers of shoddiness that lie beneath the surface of New Labour's Britain.

At yesterday's pre-fight press conference Tyson was asked to describe his reaction to the way he has been received. 'I'm pretty flattered,' he said. 'But I'm truly here to do some work. After I've done my job, we're going to have some fun with the British people.' Many observers would say that he and his promoter, Frank Warren, have been having fun with the British people from the moment the fighter stepped off Concorde – and even before that, given the way some of our minor politicians were so anxious to promote the fight, and themselves, by arguing about the legitimacy of allowing him into the country.

Every drop of the deluge of publicity has served Warren's purposes. After the 21,000 arena tickets sold out within two hours, the promoter's priority was to help Sky Sports sell subscriptions to the pay-per-view live broadcast. The rest of the British media fell over themselves to help, and their audience needed no second invitation to join in. The American correspondents following Tyson across the Atlantic have looked on in amazement at the immoderate behaviour of their supposedly cool and reserved cousins.

A sense of foreboding about tomorrow night's event was hardly eased by the sequel to Tyson's tongue-in-cheek suggestion, made in a Sky TV interview, that those without tickets should break into the arena, just as he had when, as a boy, he wanted to see one of his own idols, Roberto Duran. 'I would break in,' he said. 'I would rally a bunch of guys in the street – "Come on, come on, they can't stop us" – and crash right through the gate.'

It was a stupid thing to say, even in fun, but it was made worse when a London news radio station broadcast a reference that suggested Tyson had been perfectly serious. When I talked to the radio reporter responsible for the item, he described Tyson's tone in the interview as 'light-hearted'. When I asked him about the calculated alteration of tone, he said, 'That's Tyson for you, isn't it?' – as though the boxer's foolishness absolved anyone else of the need to show a normal sense of responsibility.

There have been times in the past fortnight when Britain seems to have lost its head, in a variation of the pattern seen when Tony Blair came to power, when the Princess of Wales died and when David Beckham was sent off in Saint-Etienne. This is what has astonished the normally worldly reporters from the American newspapers. Modern Britain, they correctly surmise, is a country that cannot bear to exist without novelty, without a current sensation. Tyson's arrival is like a guest appearance in the never-ending national soap opera.

The exploitation is mutual and it has made quite a spectacle. Tyson was mobbed in Bond Street and in Brixton, giving the illusion that his appeal crosses barriers of race and class. He has flaunted a diamond-encrusted watch costing more than the £350,000 that Francis will earn from Saturday's appearance, before speaking plaintively about his 'pain' – which, of course, no one understands. When he arrived in Manchester on Wednesday evening, he appeared on the balcony of his hotel suite to salute the thousand-strong crowd assembled outside in Peter Street, showing himself like Eva Perón to her shirtless ones.

Tyson in Britain has been a genuine phenomenon: a person in whom celebrity, notoriety and criminality create an unbroken spectrum of popular appeal. When he was merely the world's most dangerous boxer, he was nothing more than famous. His crimes turned him into something else, and in the past few days he has appeared in the guise of everything from a fallen angel to a revolutionary icon.

And, because he is intelligent, he knows it better than anyone. 'I'm the guy who makes the whole freak show happen,' he said earlier this week, talking to a Sky reporter and displaying a hint of the self-disgust that sometimes tempts even the unfriendly observer to experience a twinge of sympathy. In his own analysis, the phenomenon has two sides. 'Michael and Tyson are two different people,' he said. 'To my children and my wife I'm Mike and Daddy, but I'm Tyson here. Tyson is nothing. Tyson is just a freak. Tyson is somebody that generates a ton of money.'

This kind of self-exculpatory nonsense can hardly be in tune with his allegiance to Islam, and he had the grace to acknowledge it yesterday. He had been affiliated to many religions, he said, including Christianity. 'Islam is what I am naturally, without having to try. But that doesn't mean I'm a good person just because I'm a Muslim. If a Christian can live in a righteous way, that's a good person. We're all judged by our deeds and our conduct.'

To judge by his reception on the streets of Britain, Tyson's unworthier deeds – including the convictions for rape and a road-rage attack, the admitted beating of his first wife, and the munching of Evander Holyfield's ears, all examples of sudden and uncontrollable violence – have done nothing but inflame his popularity. For days it has been almost impossible to turn on the TV news without seeing youths in Brixton or Moss Side testifying to their reverence for a man they see as a 'role model'. On the face of it, there could hardly be a more powerful testimony to the impoverishment of the culture in which they have been raised. But from time to time, between the bursts of arrogance and self-pity, Tyson's intelligence can't help breaking through.

'We need our community leaders to have faith,' he said, improvising an answer to a question about the violence on the streets of Manchester. 'We have a lot of community leaders who don't have faith in the people, who promise them everything and give them nothing. We have to have leaders that the community can believe and trust and respect. Respect is a powerful word, more powerful than love. When you have somebody you can respect, you're able to change things around. What people want is food and jobs. We know we're not supposed to be killing people. We have to stop this.' With his claim that he is going to 'kill' Francis in the ring tomorrow, however, he was not exactly helping to reduce the emphasis on violence.

He also added a piece of special pleading that would raise no dissent within any belief system based on the forgiveness of sin: 'We have to do something about the laws saying that just because you've made a mistake and you've been in prison and you've got a record, that doesn't mean it's over for you and that you're a piece of trash and that you should be tossed away like a used towel.'

A lot of used towels can be laundered with £10 million, which is his reward for tomorrow night's labours and which ought to be all the evidence he needs that the world accepts him. But the sense of rejection, however illusory, is at the root of his appeal to young men who call him a role model. It is what unites them, and his own convoluted logic suggests that he could not manage without it. 'If everybody loved me, if everybody was my friend, I'd be an enemy to myself,' he said yesterday. 'When people love me, I know who loves me. When people hate me, I know who hates me. So if everyone loved me, people would hate me without me knowing.' No danger of that in Britain, where opinions have been so sharply divided and no one has been reluctant to tell him where he stands.

MILLE MIGLIA
Round Trip

BRESCIA, 14 FEBRUARY 1998

To THE GREAT Fangio, who had learned his craft on week-long marathon contests across the Andes, where the drivers chewed coca leaves to ward off altitude sickness, it was simply 'the hardest race'. He won five world championships and became synonymous with his sport, but he never conquered the Mille Miglia. There's a photograph of him during his final attempt to win this most amazing of motor races: a thousand-mile circuit of Italy's public roads. Taken in 1956, it is a classic study of sporting despair. Fangio's big Ferrari has come to a halt at the Rome control point, halfway round the course. He's been racing for six hours, slamming through the piazzas of medieval towns, hammering along the straight Adriatic coast road at 160 miles an hour, sliding up and down the Abruzzi mountains, bumping over tramlines and level crossings, taking his car within millimetres of rock walls and precipices.

It's been raining since the moment he started, a cold April rain, and the water has been spraying up into the cockpit through a hole cut by his mechanics the night before, while they were repairing a leaky fuel tank. He's sitting in a pool of freezing water. In Ravenna, he stopped and had another hole cut in the floor, hoping that the water would drain away. Instead, more water blew in through the new hole. In the picture he's surrounded by race officials and policemen, all leaning over him, wrapped in hats and waterproofs, grinning and gesticulating their encouragement. Fangio is looking straight ahead. His mouth is shaped in an expression of bitter defeat. Behind his leather-rimmed goggles, his eyes show nothing but exhaustion. He wants to stop but he carries on to finish fourth, one of 182 cars to complete the course out of 365 starters. 'I was half-frozen and half-dead,' he said many years later. 'Never in my life have I suffered so much as on that day.'

Nothing today marks the spot at which he started and finished that terrible journey, the point from which some ventured to find glory and others set off to meet their death. There is a small, anonymous park in the shape of a flat isosceles triangle, where the via Venezia meets the via Rebuffone on the eastern outskirts of Brescia. But no sign suggests that here was the grandstand from which, between 1927 and 1957, privileged citizens could sit once a year and watch through the night as a procession of cars were flagged away at one-minute intervals, launched into a contest whose nature and format seem almost unimaginable today.

And that's where I was sitting on an unseasonably sunny day in February, installed in the driver's seat of a new red Alfa Romeo coupé and thinking about how I had been just old enough, when the race was held for the last, fateful time in 1957, to cut out the photographs from motoring magazines and paste them into a scrapbook. More than forty years later I was about to retrace the route made famous by Fangio, Tazio Nuvolari, Stirling Moss and many others. But no one would be closing the roads, switching off the traffic lights or holding the level crossings open for me. And I had a rule: no motorways.

The post-war editions of the race attracted anything up to 500 competitors, and they came in all shapes and sizes. On the ramp in the via Rebuffone, they started with the slowest. Local amateurs in souped-up Fiat Topolinos with racing numbers hand-painted on the bodywork were followed by Spanish noblemen, Italian film directors and Argentinian world champions in cars built and prepared specially for racing. One after another the drivers paused on the ramp, smiled for the cameras and the crowd, revved the engine, let in the clutch and roared off into the night on a great loop that would take them across to the Adriatic, down the coastal road, over the Abruzzi mountains to Rome and back through Tuscany and the Apennines to the same stretch of boulevard in Brescia.

Races from city to city were how motor racing had begun, but they had almost died out by 1927 when four men – two aristocrats and two journalists – devised an event that would bring publicity to Brescia, their home town, as well as satisfy their love of motor racing. In the end they created a legend. Count Aymo Maggi and Count Franco Mazzotti, friends since boyhood and keen amateur racing drivers, joined up with Renzo Castagneto and Giovanni Canestrina to plan a race that would circumnavigate half of Italy. When Castagneto estimated that the cars would cover a distance of about 1,600 kilometres, Mazzotti responded: 'That's a thousand miles. Why don't we call it the Coppa della Mille Miglia?'

The first winner, Nando Minoia, covered the course in just over twenty-one hours, averaging 47.9mph in a car built by OM, a Brescia firm. Over the next thirty years the average speed would double, until in 1955 Stirling Moss and his Mercedes set the all-time record at just over 98mph, completing the course in ten hours and seven minutes. Alfa Romeo and Ferrari each won the race eight times. But it was a Ferrari that finished off the race, on 30 April 1957, when the car of the Spanish playboy and sportsman Fon de Portago – the charismatic Don Alfonso Cabeza de Vacay y Leighton, 17th Marquès de Portago – and his American co-driver crashed only 25 miles from the finish, killing nine spectators and throwing its crew to their deaths. And that, thanks to an outcry in the newspapers and stern words from the Vatican, was the end not only of the Mille Miglia, but also of racing on the open roads of mainland Europe.

In the forty years since that day, the legend has grown in strength. Count Maggi, the founders' leader, refused to countenance the modification of the event into some sort of reliability run, but years after his death a bunch of exotic old cars again began to assemble at the original scrutineering point in Brescia's Piazza di Vittoria and to make its way around Italy in a historic parade, an event restricted to those with the money to keep a 1930s Alfa or a 1950s Ferrari in the garage. The rest of us could only dream.

Since Piero Taruffi achieved his lifetime's ambition by winning the final edition, the image of the race has lost none of its power. The famous dramas – the stories of Nuvolari, for instance, switching off his headlights in order to catch his bitter rival Achille Varzi unawares just before the finish, or, another year, continuing despite losing half his car's bodywork and most of its suspension – overshadow anything to be found in modern motor racing. But if I had always imagined that driving a thousand miles round Italy in half a day was a remarkable feat, only by trying the course myself did I get something close to a real idea of what the Nuvolaris and Taruffis achieved. Afterwards, what had always looked extraordinary now appeared simply incredible.

It was a Wednesday lunchtime when I set off, with seventy-two hours to complete the journey. The Alfa, straight from the factory, was a new GTV coupé, with a 24-valve three-litre V6 engine and properly painted Italian racing red, albeit a brighter shade than the rich cherry of the cars sent into battle sixty years earlier. Driving with only maps and reference books for company, I set the car along the first leg of the course, eastward through Verona to Padua. This is a region of Italy in which beautiful Renaissance cities are separated by endless industrial zones. By day the roads are no fun to drive; nor was it a pleasure to think about the things I was missing: the Roman arena at Verona, built for a crowd of 25,000; the work of the architect Palladio at Vicenza, his home town; the Church of the Hermits at Padua, with Mantegna's frescoes. All these wonders registered only in the Alfa's rear-view mirror.

For me, during these few days, history had to mean something different. In the opening mile, for instance, I thought of the cars pushing up through the gears as they passed between the two walls of human flesh that obscured the line of the corners on race day. After eight miles, nearing the shore of Lake Garda, I remembered that this was where Moss, the last starter in the last of all the Mille Miglias, had ended his race when the brake pedal sheared on his Maserati.

At Padua a big right turn took me down towards Rovigo and then on to Ferrara. There, 150 miles from my starting point, I found a room in the Hotel Touring, less than a hundred metres from the Castello Estense, headquarters of the d'Este family who ruled the city from the thirteenth to the sixteenth century. In the morning, roused by the bells of the Duomo, I set off in bright sunlight, leaving through the arch at the western gate and immediately discovering a change of mood.

From Ferrara to Ravenna and on to Forli, the scenery cleared to reveal the grace of rural Italy. No more ceramics factories and supermarkets. In their place, neat copses and farm buildings punctuated the landscape. The traffic thinned out and the curves and bends began to reveal themselves, encouraging the Alfa to show its qualities.

By contrast, the drive from Rimini to Pescara involved about 170 miles of virtually straight coast road. In the summer the route would be jammed with holidaymakers: in February it was practically empty, making it possible to see how the big sports cars of the 1950s could sustain the speeds that would keep their average for the whole race close to a hundred miles an hour despite the difficult mountain roads still to come.

It was twilight when I turned right at the train station in the middle of Pescara and began the climb into the Abruzzi. After Popoli the bends started to twist into hairpins, and while I was crossing a vast and spookily empty plateau the full moon came up from behind the snow-capped mountains, irradiating the landscape with an unearthly orange glow. Not much further on, in L'Aquila, a large hilltop town set within a ring of mountains, I checked into the Hotel Castello. I had 350 miles to my credit in the day, meaning that I'd reached half-distance.

The next day promised the greatest pleasures of the whole trip, since it involved the three great mountain passes on which the best drivers could make their skills pay dividends. But first came the run down from the Abruzzi to Rieti, after which the scenery changed again. A certain lushness – olive groves, clusters of pines – took over on the via Salaria as the valley gave way to the outskirts of Rome. Here, in 1953, in a grandstand set up on the northern side of the Villa Borghese, Ingrid Bergman sat surrounded by photographers, waiting for the arrival of an exhausted Roberto Rossellini, who retired his Ferrari at the control point and went home with his consort. The saying that 'He who leads at Rome will never win the Mille Miglia' held true until 1955, when Moss and his navigator, Denis Jenkinson, swept into the city to discover that they held a lead of nearly two minutes over their nearest competitor. At Brescia they would still be in front, by more than half an hour.

The race left Rome by the via Cassia. Again the sort of sights that would have detained any conventional tourist – the sandstone caves of Sutri, for example – became no more than a blur in the mirror. And then, between Vetralla and Viterbo, the trace of the old road disappeared altogether, replaced by a high-speed dual carriageway. But after Montefiascone it narrowed again before revealing an elevated view of the serene Lake Bolsena, quickly descending to the water's edge and continuing around the eastern perimeter before heading north to the first of the mountain climbs. There, on the hill called the Radicofani, an ancient shepherd turned towards the howling Alfa with a gaze that might once have encompassed the passage of Nuvolari.

In the southern reaches of Tuscany the road began to wind and undulate as it passed monasteries and vineyards. Siena is one of those towns in which a modern one-way system makes it impossible to travel the exact route of the old race; half an hour later, Florence proved very different. Here the checkpoint was on the Piazzale Michelangelo, high above the Arno, where the tourist can stop and look down over the city's splendours. For the racers, however, there followed a fast slalom down to the river and a sweep along the eastern side of the inner ring road to the via Bolognese, which heads north and is known, as it leaves the city, as the via Biondetti, in memory of Clemente Biondetti, a wealthy Tuscan amateur who was the only man to win the race four times.

A narrow, tight climb out of the city, hemmed in by harsh stone walls, led to a different world. The lushness of Tuscany yielded to scruffy fields and abandoned mansions. But with dusk came the Futa and the Raticosa, the two historic Apennine passes, where the Alfa came into its own, squirreling around the hairpins and leaping up the short straights with such alacrity that it was almost possible to overlook a personal aversion to front-wheel drive (if God had wanted cars to be driven by their front wheels, wouldn't he have told Enzo Ferrari?). At the summit of the Futa, just past an *albergo* virtually unchanged since the first race went by, there stands a vast, meticulously maintained and well-visited German war cemetery, a reminder of how effectively Hitler's troops delayed the progress of the US Army in 1944, and at what cost.

From the 4,000-foot peak of the Raticosa came a long, arduous descent back to sea level. The tangled outskirts of Bologna made it difficult to get a fix on the old itinerary, but the exit was clear: another rendezvous with the arrow-straight via Emilia, this time towards the most significant city in Italian motor racing.

Modena was the home of Enzo Ferrari, whose involvement with the Mille Miglia began as a spectator in 1927, took in a ninth-place finish as a driver in 1930 and continued as the entrant of winning Alfa Romeos before he began to build cars bearing his own name. As the post-war races entered the city, the cars swept past the original headquarters of the Scuderia Ferrari and through the Largo Garibaldi, a square where Ferrari kept his home in a tall, dark house. The night I arrived, workmen had just manoeuvred a 20-foot high statue into place, to be unveiled a few days later, on the centenary of his birth.

From his new vantage point, Ferrari can keep an eye not only on his old home and on the site of the Scuderia's premises, but also on the building (now a bank) that was once the Hotel Real, where he would repair at night to plot with his cronies and, according to his less dewy-eyed biographers, avail himself of the services of the local whores. I, by contrast, spent a chaste night at the Hotel Canalgrande, owned by Alessandro de Tomaso, an Argentinian wheeler-dealer who arrived in Modena in the 1950s, raced briefly in Formula One and later took over the Maserati company with the assistance of his wife, the American heiress Isabel Haskell.

The route out of the city sweeps past the noble buildings and statues of a tree-lined avenue before regaining the via Emilia in the direction of Parma and Piacenza. As with the opening section of the course, industrial activity has obliterated most of the road's charm, and not until I turned sharp right at Piacenza, cutting back along the straight and empty road to Cremona and Mantua, did the sights improve. Here, too, the speeds rose sharply again, despite a hint of Lombardy mist diffusing the morning sunlight. High averages were possible all the way back to Brescia, where the finishers were greeted on the via Rebuffone by huge crowds and the trilby-hatted Renzo Castagneto waving a chequered flag. But first – for me – there were homages to be paid. In Mantua the municipal cemetery holds the mortal remains of Tazio Nuvolari, who died in 1953, aged 61, only three years after retiring from the cockpit. I bought him some roses – yellow, his lucky colour – from the stall across the road and went to read the inscription above the tomb: 'Correrai ancor più veloce per le vie del cielo' – 'You will race even faster along the roads of heaven'.

Nuvolari, a notorious daredevil, passed away in his own bed. But between Mantua and Brescia, 25 miles from the finish line of the Mille Miglia, on a perfectly straight stretch of deserted roads, stands an elegant white marble memorial bearing the names of Portago, his co-driver, Ed Nelson, and the members of the public whose deaths put an end to the race in 1957. The spectators had walked up the road from Guidizzolo, the next village, a distance of just over a mile, hoping to watch the cars as they went by at full speed before braking for the corner around their parish church. When the left front tyre of the Ferrari burst at about 160 miles an hour, the car cartwheeled straight into them. 'Life has to be lived to the full,' Portago had told the wife of his team-mate Peter Collins at dinner the night before the race. 'It's better to be wholly alive for thirty years than half-dead for sixty.' He was 28.

I finished the route, returned the borrowed Alfa, and made it to the airport with half an hour to spare. I can't imagine many other people being interested in such a drive – at least, not under the same conditions, which meant driving as hard as possible for three days, with complete concentration, ignoring a thousand miles and two thousand years of art and architecture. But if you want to know the truth, I felt that the journey had changed me, as good journeys should. Through an act of tribute I'd repaid a debt to the people whose feats had given me such pleasure; and by the repayment, that pleasure had been further enriched.

THE VIEW FROM THE HIGH BOARD

V

MARADONA

The Virgin and the Gypsy

ROSARIO, ARGENTINA, 9 OCTOBER 1993

THEY CARRIED THE Virgin of Rosario home on Thursday, up the hill to the cathedral that bears her name, past the giant memorial to *la bandera* – the Argentine flag – which faces the broad River Parana. Two thousand people had celebrated an open-air mass in the sunshine of a spring afternoon in Argentina's second city, praying and singing together and listening to choirs and a military band, closing the solemnities with the national anthem. As the Virgin's statue was borne aloft in its glass cabinet, the congregation waved handkerchiefs in affectionate salute to their patron saint.

On the fringe of the crowd, a few yards away from where a middle-aged woman in a cream woollen twin-set and good shoes knelt to confess her sins to a priest half-dozing in a canvas picnic chair, a small market was doing brisk business in votive offerings: candles, artificial flowers, pink plastic rosaries, tiny images of the Virgin framed in black velvet. And, in the midst of these sacred objects, there lay a pile of posters of a small figure in a red and black shirt, balancing a football on his left instep, his dark boy-man's face familiar from a thousand moments of triumph and shame.

'*Gracias, Diego,*' the message on the poster read. '*Bienvenido a Rosario. Esta es tu casa.*' Thank you, Diego. Welcome to our town. Now it's your home, too.

The Virgin and the gypsy. Home at last.

An hour after they settled the Madonna back in her resting place next to one of the cathedral's great brown marble pillars, Rosario's other saviour – the phrase is the local paper's, not mine – was preparing to receive the Virgin's benediction. Diego Armando Maradona left his suite on the top floor of the four star Riviera Hotel with his wife, Claudia, and their two small daughters, to be driven the mile and a half to a decaying concrete bowl in a civic park. This was where the greatest footballer of his generation was scheduled to attempt the resurrection of his career. And, for good measure, the hopes of his nation.

Here, too, the votive offerings business was enjoying a bonanza. Trade was booming in red and black shirts bearing the magic number 10, key rings and duffel bags and headbands and sun visors and plastic bugles all emblazoned with the sacred name.

When he had changed into his new kit, when the fireworks and ceremonies in the stadium had finished, he came out of the tunnel, his daughters – Dalma, aged six, and four-year-old Giannina, both now wearing miniature replicas of the red and black uniform – clutching his hands. As the crowd erupted and the flash-bulbs popped, a large commemorative plaque was thrust into his hands. 'May Our Lady of Rosario protect you as a man and as an idol,' it read, 'and may today's miracle provide an example of faith, hope and charity. Welcome back to life! From the city of Rosario and its people.'

So why did Diego Maradona, 32 years old, choose to return to the game in a place like this, in the shirt of a provincial team nicknamed *Los Leprosos* – the Lepers? For not only is Newell's Old Boys far from being the most important club in Argentina, it isn't even the most important club in Rosario. 'Don't do it, Diego,' the historian Osvaldo Bayer implored in a newspaper column. 'Think about those of us whose faith is vested, man and boy, in Rosario

Central. Don't do it. Don't make us turn our backs on you. Don't play against the glorious blue-and-yellows. Che Guevara is looking down at you from heaven ...'.

Guevara, born in this town of a million people on the banks of the Parana, was a lifelong fan of the 'blue-and-yellows' – Rosario Central, the club formed at the turn of the century by a group of British railway engineers and named after the station they built. The British were the founding fathers of Argentine football, and in 1903 a second club was established in Rosario by former pupils of Isaac Newell's Anglo-Argentine Commercial School. Newell's Old Boys was the club's name, and still is, even though the British long ago took their profit from Argentina and went home, bequeathing to the Spanish and Italian settlers the railways, a replica of Big Ben in Buenos Aires, the rules of a few games – football, racing, polo, rugby – and a handful of surnames.

A few months ago, when Maradona began to think about a return to football in Argentina after a decade in Spanish and Italian exile, Newell's Old Boys were not the obvious choice to sign the man who led his country to victory in the 1986 World Cup. Argentinos Juniors and Boca Juniors, the metropolitan clubs with whom he had played during the first part of his career, seemed more obvious favourites; both showed an interest. But Walther Cattaneo, the president of Newell's, worked hard on his negotiations with Maradona and his manager, Juan Marcos Franchi, persuading them that their future lay 200 miles up the river.

There was consternation in the capital when Maradona announced his decision. He is a Buenos Aires boy, after all. Rosario has a nice little municipal art gallery, a dilapidated racetrack, a few cinemas and the mortal remains of General Belgrano, but, marooned between the endless flatlands of the pampas and the swampy wastes of the Parana delta, it can't compare with the big city.

'The key to the decision was the passion shown by the club's management,' Franchi said, while Maradona himself mentioned the outstanding qualities of 'El Indio' – Jorge Solari, the coach of Newell's. 'I knew him before, of course,' Maradona said, 'but this time we really got talking. He filled my head with football. We talked for two hours. About players and tactics. That convinced me.'

But Maradona also had another, more arcane explanation for his decision, one that touched on his peculiar fortunes over the past couple of years.

Life was particularly good for Diego Maradona between 1986, when he held the World Cup aloft in Mexico City's Aztec Stadium, and the spring of 1990, when he led Naples to their second Italian championship. That summer, though, his world started to come apart. The erosion of the legend began in Rome, where Argentina lost a dreadful World Cup final to West Germany in July; less than a year later the Italian league authorities suspended him for fifteen months after traces of cocaine had been detected in a regular anti-doping test. And there was more: a phone tap appeared to reveal his involvement in a network of drug dealers and call girls, while rumours of his supposed connection with the Camorra – the Neapolitan mafia – began to circulate. Suddenly the bloated, distraught features of an overweight and shame-faced Diego Maradona, caught by the flash-bulbs while being bundled into police cars and courtrooms in Italy and Argentina, became a regular feature of the news pages.

Maradona never went back to Naples. Instead, last year he returned to Spain, to play for Seville, whose manager, Carlos Bilardo, had guided Argentina through the 1986 and 1990 World Cups. Maradona cost Seville just under £5 million, the same amount as Naples had paid Barcelona for him seven years earlier, but the Spaniards didn't get the same dividend. He played only twenty-six games for them, scoring five goals, before falling out with Bilardo, who substituted him in a match against Burgos in June. 'I'm going to have this out with Bilardo, man to man,' he said. 'If, that is, Bilardo is a man …'. It was Maradona's last appearance in a Seville shirt.

Bilardo was not the first of his country's senior coaches to cross Maradona. César Luis Menotti, the author of Argentina's first World Cup triumph, in 1978, had angered Maradona, then a mere 17 years old, by leaving him out of that tournament because he considered him too young. Their relationship never really recovered, and a subsequent reunion at Barcelona in 1983 was unproductive.

Menotti and Bilardo represent the twin antithetical impulses of Argentine football. An apostle of all-out attacking play when he managed Huracán in the league, at a time when Argentine football was beset by violence and negativity, Menotti held on to his philosophy as manager of the national side. 'He just told us, "Get on the field and invent"', said René Houseman, one of his players.

Bilardo, a member of the notorious Estudiantes team of the 1960s, came from the opposite camp. His teams' brutal pragmatism recalled the observation in a Borges story that football was what post-colonial Argentina had been given as a replacement for the old pastime of knife-fighting. 'We knew nobody liked Estudiantes,' Bilardo said, 'but we got results. And that's what counts. Very few fans really like lyrical football. When their team is winning 1–0, they can't wait for the final whistle.'

The poet and the pragmatist – and Diego Maradona managed to disagree with both of them. With their successor, too – Alfio Basile, a Racing Club defender of the 1960s whose philosophy of football is said to fall somewhere between Menotti's rapturous attacking and Bilardo's unapologetic negativity.

Maradona played in Basile's selections until only two months ago, when he found himself omitted from the squad for the vital World Cup qualification series. Looking at Maradona's form, Basile hardly needed to justify his decision; no doubt, too, he was basking in the deceptive security of a thirty-match unbeaten run. Maradona, though, was livid. 'I wouldn't play for Basile again if he came begging on his knees,' he spat.

The manager's plans were working out perfectly until Colombia arrived to play the final group match in Buenos Aires last month. Freddy Rincón and Faustino Asprilla ran amok, leading a 5–0 trouncing that left a humiliated Argentina needing to win a two-leg play-off against Australia if they – twice winners and once runners-up in the last four World Cups – are to qualify for the 1994 tournament in the United States.

As the Colombians' score mounted, a chant arose in the stadium. 'Ma-ra-do-na, Ma-ra-do-na …'. The fans' thoughts were turning to a saviour.

'I felt bad watching that match,' Maradona said last week. 'I don't believe the difference between the teams was five goals. Two–nil would have been about right. And I wouldn't have wanted the possibility of returning to the national team to arise simply because we hadn't qualified directly for the World Cup. Anyway, it's wrong to think that Argentine football died that night. It just took a wrong turning. And it certainly didn't deserve what *El Grafico* did.' The Buenos Aires sports magazine had appeared in the week following the match with an all-black cover.

After his estrangement from Seville and his rejection by Basile, Maradona took the summer off. He gathered up his family, his father and mother too, and went off to Esquina, the small town in Corrientes province where his parents had started life. There, 400 miles from Buenos Aires, Maradona went fishing every day. He breathed clean air. And he started to recover something of his old self.

It was in Esquina, Maradona suggested, that he formulated the philosophy which he now claims was responsible for his decision to join Newell's Old Boys. 'It was something to do with the officers and coaches at the club, but also with its history. I have a lot of respect for the people who contributed to the growth of football in Argentina, and Newell's has given it a great deal. I chose it because of the history of the club, and also because it's in the interior of the country. It might seem like a cliché, but this year I've been lucky enough to travel all over Argentina, to look at my country and get to know it, and I began to realize that whole areas of it have been neglected. I want to decentralize football. It can't be good to have twenty top teams inside twenty square kilometres.'

With these thoughts in his head, or so he says, he returned to Buenos Aires after his holiday. While Franchi conducted negotiations with prospective new clubs, Maradona went training with the players of Chacarito Juniors, a third division club. He began a regime of three sessions a day and the fat started to fall from his frame. In a matter of weeks he lost 30 pounds, coming down to what his personal trainer, Daniel Cerrini, calls his ideal weight – a pound or two above 11 stone. Currently, in fact, he is 7 pounds lighter than when he lifted the golden trophy in Mexico seven years ago.

'You will find,' Osvaldo Ardiles said just before I left London for Buenos Aires, 'that Argentina is going through its Thatcher years.

Inflation has just about disappeared. There's a boom, of sorts. Footballers don't need to go abroad to earn good money.'

The Argentina to which Diego Maradona returned this summer is certainly very different from the one he left in 1982, when Barcelona paid Boca Juniors $10 million for his transfer. At that time, under the military dictatorship, his native country was on a ramp that led, under the subsequent Alfonsín administration, to the problems associated with an annual inflation rate of 20,000 per cent. 'In those days,' I was told, 'you could stand in line in a bank in Buenos Aires waiting to change your dollars for pesos, and double your money by the time you reached the front of the queue.' That was the sort of instability that led generations of Argentinian footballers to Europe: Alfredo Di Stefano with Real Madrid in the 1950s, Omar Sivori with Juventus in the 1960s, Mario Kempes with Valencia in the 1970s, Osvaldo Ardiles with Tottenham. According to Ardiles, those days are over, thanks to Carlos Menem, an aggressive free marketeer who is the current president of the republic.

Menem was giving five-minute audiences to Michael Jackson and Ayrton Senna in Buenos Aires on the day Diego Maradona made his comeback in Rosario last week, but there is no doubt where the president's true interest lies. A good showing in the World Cup – or at least a showing at all – will do him no harm. And the return of a fit Maradona to the national side represents the best guarantee of that.

Somehow, Walther Cattaneo raked together $4 million to buy Maradona's contract from Seville. The player's salary at Newell's is said to be about $25,000 a month. Cattaneo claims that 'friends of the club', which has 10,000 members in Rosario, have come up with the sum, but the involvement of big business – perhaps Pepsi-Cola and Yamaha, who sponsor the team – is suspected.

For Maradona's first training session, 30,000 people turned up to watch. 'Now I know I haven't made a mistake,' he said. 'I wanted to hug them all, one by one. It's like starting to live again.'

He and Basile publicly kissed and made up. 'Maybe we were just hotheads,' the coach said, hinting that he only had to have proof of Maradona's fitness to add his name to the squad already announced for the games against Australia. 'Maradona doesn't have to be on any list,' asserted the president of the Argentine FA, Juan Grondona. 'We're waiting to see what happens when he plays a few games.'

Last week the club took advertisements in the local daily paper, *La Capital*, pleading with the fans to turn up for Maradona's first match, a friendly hurriedly arranged against Emelec of Guyaquil, who are managed by a former Newell's player and include several members of Ecuador's national squad. The admission prices were set at $20 for the terraces and $50 for the grandstands. 'This is the only sacrifice the committee will ask of the club's fans,' the advertisement read, 'in order to keep the world's best player in our team.'

The committee didn't need to beg. An hour before Maradona's scheduled arrival on the pitch, the fans were hanging off the floodlight gantries, dancing on the grandstand rooftops and dangling their legs over the walls of the moat that surrounds the playing area in an effort to bear close witness to something that *La Capital* itself described as 'an event comparable with few that have taken place in this city'. Hardly an inch of space remained in the stadium, whose capacity is more than 30,000, so there was general hilarity in the press box when a piece of paper came round announcing the official attendance as 21,652, with takings of $586,310. A bad night for the taxman, someone sniggered. To his credit, Cattaneo later admitted the apparent discrepancy and announced an inquiry. Since Newell's Old Boys' average league gate is somewhere below 10,000, the effect of Diego Maradona on the club's receipts is likely to be a continuing focus of interest; and for the rights to a live transmission of this single non-competitive match, the Argentine television network Telefe paid Newell's $800,000. Quite a decent first return on their investment.

However many of them there may or may not have been, the fans got their money's worth. In a spectacular pre-game carnival the scene was set by 300 schoolboys affiliated with the club's coaching scheme, who ran through their repertoire of dribbling skills: the *fintas*, the *amagues* and the *gambetas* that are more like dancefloor moves than the sort of thing you'd find being taught to English apprentices and for which, indeed, there are no equivalent English terms.

After the boys had covered the playing surface with giant red and black banners, after the fireworks and the laser show, it was another boy's turn to do his stuff. For no matter how many gruesome headlines he may generate, the heart of a boy continues to beat within the adult breast of Diego Armando Maradona.

This was a friendly match, of course, and the Ecuadorian team, whose style of football is pitched somewhere between the silky speed of the Brazilians and the obsessive neatness of the Colombians, clearly did not consider it part of their duty to spoil the party. Nevertheless, even in this context Maradona's contribution was not without genuine significance.

Looking sleek and alert, he strutted and jogged with that familiar chest-out, elbows-back, head-up arrogance, immediately justifying his assumption of the team captaincy. With his first touch, in the opening minute, he stunned the ball on his chest and, bringing God's own left foot into play, hooked a 30-yard pass over his shoulder into the path of Carlos Torres, his right winger. Three minutes later he was hurtling into the area to fling himself at a cross from Gerardo Martino, sending his header just wide. Before long he was coming short for a corner and scissor-kicking a dangerous cross, then flicking the ball over a defender's head, next forcing a save from the Emelec keeper with a rapturously acclaimed *bicicleta*. He even showed us a glimpse of the *amasada*, the magical drag-back with which he took the ball away from Peter Reid that day in the Azteca in 1986 and began the long slalom that carried him past four England defenders and ended with the goal of all goals.

In ninety minutes on Thursday night, according to the Buenos Aires daily *La Razón*, he had possession of the ball no fewer than 102 times, making sixty-two successful passes, having five attempts on goal, taking four corners and one free-kick, and being penalized three times (one of them for a foul). And, in the seventieth minute, the Virgin of Rosario turned her face towards him and gave a big, beautiful smile.

Accepting a pass from Alfredo Lopez, Maradona ran across the face of the penalty area from left to right and, without warning, aimed a shot at the top left-hand corner. With, unusually, his right foot. The ball flew in a tantalizing, unstoppable arc over the right shoulder of Emilio Valencia, the Emelec goalkeeper, and just inside the angle of bar and post.

There was a split-second of silence. No one could quite believe that it had happened. And then you'd have thought they'd won the World Cup again.

Understandably enough, in his first game for four months, Maradona slowed almost to a standstill in the last ten minutes. 'In three or four games' time,' Alfio Basile said afterwards, 'he should be in perfect condition. The key is just for him to keep on playing. Tonight he felt the pressure of the fans' expectations, and he wanted to show them everything he knows. But how could we ever forget his talent? He did three or four wonderful things in this match. That header, that bicycle-kick …'.

Even Bilardo joined in. 'It was a pleasure to see Diego in action again,' he said. 'There's no doubt he'll show us again that he's the best in the world. And that's very important for the convalescence of Argentinian football.'

Maradona himself arrived at his press conference in a loud green jacket, diamonds winking from the gold ring in his left ear. 'I felt very good,' he said, although he seemed breathless and his tanned face looked drawn, like that of a jockey on a wasting regime. 'Of course I'm still short of match fitness, but I'll get there. Little by little, day by day.'

Outside in the distance, the bugles and the car horns blared their joyful fanfares down the avenues and boulevards. Homeward bound, the fans were chanting in praise of their new saviour, and taunting their enemies. 'Let's have a minute's silence for Rosario Central,' they sang, 'because they're already as good as dead.' A local celebration, perhaps, but its echoes may soon be heard around the world.

JACK NICKLAUS
Golden Sunset

'O N THE TEE, Jack Nicklaus.' For the last time in the Open championship, the crowd around the Royal & Ancient clubhouse sent up a cheer to greet the announcement of the arrival of the greatest golfer of them all. Well, maybe for the last time. 'You should never say never,' he pointed out afterwards, hinting at a slim possibility that he might accept an invitation to come back in 2005, when the Open returns to St Andrews, where in 1970 and 1978 he won two of his record eighteen major championships.

But it was always probable that yesterday's round would be the farewell performance, since he started the day at five strokes over par and odds-on to miss the cut for only the fifth time in his thirty-seven appearances in the tournament. As he strode the sundrenched course in his buttermilk shirt and beige slacks, the galleries gave him a reception that resembled a giant Mexican wave, 7,115 yards and five hours long.

He started in the most wonderfully promising of ways, with a

40-foot putt that gave him a birdie at the first hole, where he had made double bogey on Thursday after paying a visit to Swilken burn. 'That was worth it for the whole day,' an American woman in the gallery remarked as the tumult died down and Nicklaus moved on with the small wave of acknowledgement that he was to repeat hundreds of times during the round.

Off the second tee he hit trouble, calling for a consultation with the rules official and taking a free drop. The negotiations had spectators in stitches. 'It doesn't make any difference to me,' Nicklaus said with mock asperity as they disagreed over the procedure. 'I'm going to drop it here anyway.' And as he settled to the shot, he remarked, to no one in particular, 'I'll chop it up there and go chase it again. That's what you do with this game, isn't it?'

No one has ever been in a position to analyze 'this game' with more authority. When Nicklaus played his first Open, at Troon in 1962, the Beatles were still a few months from releasing 'Love Me Do' and John F. Kennedy was in the White House. Nicklaus tied for thirty-fourth place on his debut, but in his first twenty years at the championship he not only won three times, but also finished in the top five on all but two occasions. It was this kind of consistency that made him the first golfer to reach career winnings of $2 million (in 1973), the first to $3 million (1977) and the first to $4 million (1988).

Yesterday he put his opening round behind him and took the front nine by storm. He putted from 50 feet to within eight inches for par on the 2nd and just missed a twelve-footer for birdie at the 3rd. Finding himself among the buttercups off the tee at the 4th, he dribbled a three-wood from one mound of rough to another, but then – perhaps having overheard a fellow in the gallery say, 'That might have been a wood shot for someone like Tiger' – responded by hitting such an exquisite wedge that he was able to rescue his par.

He drove 320 yards on the par-five 5th, way beyond his playing partners Angel Cabrera and Mark James, and rolled a 25-foot eagle putt past the rim before knocking in a three-footer for his second birdie. After he had surveyed the 6th green with such intensity that he appeared to be interested in buying the freehold, a 12-foot putt secured his third. Maybe, he was thinking, he might be spending the weekend in St Andrews after all.

'Aye, it scares a lot o' them, but it'll no' scare Jack,' a spectator told his neighbour as the group headed into the Loop, the complex of holes from the 7th to the 11th. But Nicklaus's first reverse came at the par-three 8th, where he missed a short putt to drop back to two under for the day.

Behind him as he bent over his second shot on the 9th fairway, a hawk hovered in the heat haze and suddenly stooped on its prey. Once that predator would have been Nicklaus. But as he went through the rest of the Loop, making his pars safely enough, he started to look tired. Behind the 12th tee he put his hands on the top of his golf bag, stretched his legs out behind him, rested his forehead on the rim of the bag and bent into an exercise that appeared to be designed to ease his back. Five minutes later he had three-putted from 30 feet and dropped another shot.

By now play was stuttering to a halt with infuriating frequency, the players kicking their heels for five and even ten minutes at a time as they waited for greens and tees to be cleared and for the occasional crossover to be negotiated. It gave the spectators a prolonged opportunity to gaze upon the old champion for the last time, although a 60-year-old cannot have found it easy to maintain his rhythm in such circumstances. At the 14th he two-putted to relinquish the last of the day's gains and misjudged the wind at the Road hole before underhitting a pitch and again taking two putts to go one over for the day.

As he walked onto the 18th tee, the packed galleries prepared their welcome. After sending a sensible drive down the middle, laying up just the far side of Grannie Clark's Wynd, he performed a ritual final crossing of the Swilken burn bridge and sent a beautiful second shot to within five feet of the pin. Cabrera and James holed out to make their pars. All it needed now was one last putt for a birdie, and a par round with which to close Jack Nicklaus's glorious career at the Open.

Fate had other ideas. Sport is not designed to satisfy sentimentalists, among whom Nicklaus has never claimed membership. He missed his final putt, signed a card reading 73 for the day and 150 for the two-round aggregate, and that was that. All over. From now on, if you want to see Jack Nicklaus in action in a major championship, you will have to go to Augusta National, where he is guaranteed a starting place in the US Masters until he drops, and has indicated that he will accept it.

Ten minutes later, Tiger Woods walked on to the first tee to set off on a round that would take him a stage further on the route to his first Open championship. The sense of a baton changing hands was among the more poignant elements of an already emotional day, and Nicklaus was happy to endorse its symbolism.

'Every time I switch on the television he holes a putt,' the former champion said. 'He's an awfully good player. He has a very good head on his shoulders. But it's easy to have a good head on your shoulders when you don't worry about making anything from 15 feet in. You know you're going to make it, why worry about the problems? There were periods of time when I was doing exactly what he is doing. When you get that, boy, the game becomes easy.'

The difference, he felt, was that whereas he had faced competition from the likes of Palmer, Player, Trevino and Watson, all multiple winners of major championships, Tiger is playing in a void. 'Right now he's the dominant player. Everybody has thrown up a white flag and surrendered. He's good for the game, but he has to have challengers for the whole thing to be right.'

So now Jack Nicklaus is a memory, just as the Open is now a memory to him. 'I had great times,' he said. 'It has always been my favourite event. There has always been a sense of history that I've enjoyed so much. So many of the great golfers of the past have played on these courses.'

From yesteryear's Old Tom Morris to tomorrow's Tiger Woods, the history of the Open is a parade of great champions. One day Jack Nicklaus's records may be surpassed, but there is unlikely ever to be a farewell to match the golden glow that bathed the Golden Bear as he slipped away from the 18th green yesterday and walked into legend.

ROD LAVER
The Rocket

THE FIRST VOLLEY, an angled forehand, slants across the court, grazing the red clay just inside the line. The second, a blocked backhand, slides down the tramlines and into the backboard. The third, backhand again, bisects the court in a blur, leaving the opposing pair of players motionless, stranded, as though the clay were tar, tugging at their shoes.

Forty–love.

Neither the baseball cap, the abstract doodle dribbling in green, blue and yellow down his shirt, nor the oversized graphite-bodied racket can disguise the outline. The rolling, bowlegged walk is still as it was when he ruled the world; so is the angle of the head and the long nose, tilted up like an alert bird.

On the stone terrace of one of the outside courts at the Foro Italico, a middle-aged man in a business suit smiles, shakes his head and turns to his neighbour.

'*Sempre giovane, eh?*'

You bet. Forever young.

His left forearm is thinner now, no longer twice the circumference of his right. Twelve inches in circumference at its widest point and seven inches at the wrist. That's what everyone remembers. That and the general agreement that the Rockhampton Rocket was the greatest tennis player the world had ever seen.

Nowadays he doesn't like to make too much of the forearm. When pushed, he mentions in a doubtful sort of way that Howard Cosell, the American TV sportscaster, once claimed it was the same size as Floyd Patterson's. 'Patterson was a great champion,' Rod Laver says, 'but I don't know what the analogy means.'

Laver, 54 years old, looks down at the forearm in question: pink, with sandy hair, the sinews still visibly defined. It's resting on a coffee-shop table in a hotel in Rome, where he has arrived to play a tournament on the ATP seniors circuit, a sideshow to the Italian Open. On court, at rest or in motion, his silhouette is unmistakeable.

'Other players guided their strokes,' wrote Gordon Forbes, the South African who was Laver's contemporary and friend. 'Rodney fired his at predetermined points.' Laver was only five feet eight inches tall, but that forearm gave him a special power and, more important, control beyond that of much bigger men. He developed it as a boy in Queensland, playing constantly. 'I always played with a fair degree of wrist,' he says, 'so there was a little extra pressure on the forearm. Plus squeezing a tennis ball or one of those spring machines. When the arm got strong, you could pull off shots that weren't normally possible. And having a strong arm allowed me to put a lot more spin on the ball.'

How many times would Rod Laver have won the Wimbledon singles title had he not signed on with the professional circus in 1963? After all, every time he walked into the All England Club between 1959 and 1969, they might as well have given him a bye straight to finals day.

In 1959, as a 20-year-old, he lost to Alex Olmedo of Peru in a final described by David Gray of the *Guardian* as 'a pallid, shapeless affair, full of nervousness and errors'. That year he also won the mixed doubles final (with Darlene Hard) and lost the men's doubles final (with Bob Mark), playing a total of 533 games in the fortnight – 299 of them on the Centre Court, a total of eleven hours and thirty-three minutes in the big green temple. He lost the men's singles final again the next year, a much better match – two hours, four sets – won by a fellow left-handed Australian, Neale Fraser. And with that his SW19 apprenticeship was complete, his dues paid. In 1961 he flattened Chuck McKinley of the US in straight sets, 6–3, 6–1, 6–4. And in 1962 he annihilated another compatriot, Martin Mulligan, 6–2, 6–2, 6–1. (That was the year when all four men's semi-finalists were Australians, the others being Neale Fraser and his brother John.)

Wimbledon 1962 was the third stage of Laver's first calendar-year grand slam. This was, as it remains, the supreme achievement, and only Donald Budge, in 1938, had done it before (Laver apart, no one else has done it since). Yet there was something missing. You can only play the guys who turn up, as they say; but among the guys who weren't turning up in those years were fellows by the names of Hoad, Rosewall and Gonzales. They were the pros, which meant they were the best players in the world. If he really wanted to prove himself, Laver had to join them. He waited only to compete in the winning Davis Cup team for the fourth year in a row before signing pro forms in January 1963. That kept him out of Wimbledon for five years.

When he returned, of course, he won the next two titles. Take this in conjunction with the knowledge that, in four of the intervening five years, he won the pros' main event, the World Indoor Championship, in front of packed late-night crowds at the Empire Pool, Wembley. So how many Wimbledon men's singles titles would he have finished up with in other circumstances? Six? Seven? Eight?

Laver says he doesn't regret his decision. 'I wanted to play against the best at the time, and most of the best were pros. There was a good band of past champions and they weren't all that old.' In 1962 Pancho Gonzales, at 34, was the senior pro; Hoad and Rosewall were 28 and lying in wait for their fellow countryman, anxious to prove that their skills hadn't been eroded by the years on the road, playing on the boards, under the floodlights, in a different town – often in a different country – every night.

'It was a shock to see their game unfold in front of me,' Laver remembers. 'I was playing Hoad and Rosewall on alternate nights, and I didn't really know much about their game. I'd played them as a kid, before they turned pro in '57. Hoad was probably the person I most looked up to and tried hardest to emulate. It seemed to me that they never missed a ball, they hit it a little harder and they were more accurate. So you had to play your best tennis all the time.'

To start with, he didn't win much. It took him two or three months and more than a dozen matches to beat the glamorous Hoad, who had turned pro after beating Rosewall in the 1956 Wimbledon final. 'When he was in shape, Hoad was the most difficult. By the time I turned pro, he'd lost the desire to be a day-in, day-out competitor. He'd had a lot of injuries. But he said to himself that I'd won the grand slam, whereas in 1956 he'd won three grand slam tournaments – he'd lost the final of the fourth to Rosewall. To an extent, he was representing the pros. It wasn't exactly a vendetta, but it was a very concentrated effort on his part. And on Rosewall's, too.'

Indeed, Hoad and Rosewall put their names to Laver's contract, guaranteeing him $110,000 against prize money over three years. 'If I didn't make that back in the period, they were supposed to put up the difference. In fact, I made it back in just over two years.' Good times, but a tough life. 'The second time I came to Europe with the pros, we played twenty-eight matches in twenty-eight days, in four or five countries, a different city every night. In Spain we wouldn't start until ten or eleven at night, finishing at half past two or three o'clock in the morning. And by the time you got your system back to normal after competing, it would be four o'clock. You could only snatch a couple of hours' sleep because you'd have to be ready for a plane or a train at eight.'

And what about the old accusations that it really was a circus? That the matches were fixed?

'Well, there were certainly nights when a player didn't perform because physically or mentally he wasn't with it. You can't hold up every night. But the money was divided according to who won and who lost. It wasn't just a question of a fee for turning up.'

Nevertheless, no one was more pleased than Laver when tennis went open, prefaced in 1967 by an eight-man all-pro tournament on the Centre Court at Wimbledon, organized by the All England

Club and televised by the BBC. 'Some of the amateur officials wanted it to fail,' he remembers. 'But on the last day we just about filled the Centre Court – the only time it's ever been used outside of the championships, I believe.' He beat Rosewall in a five-set final and the next year they were back in the fold for good.

'It was a thrill. In a way I was given a reprieve. I'd said to myself, I'm a pro, I'm out of the amateur world, and I'd accepted that. To be given a chance to go back again, it was fairly special. All the pros felt that way. We went to Bournemouth first, where Ken beat me in the final. [Field Marshal] Montgomery presented the prizes – it had all gone round 360 degrees, back to the amateur world, the world of meeting the Queen. And when we went back to Wimbledon for the championships, to the same locker room, the same attendants, the same crowds, it was like picking up where you'd left off five years earlier.'

Which is what he did, despite the amateurs' best efforts. 'They wanted to beat us, all right. They felt they had something to prove, and so did we – that we weren't just a bunch of guys who went round playing fixed matches. In the locker room there wasn't a real big welcome back.' Was there, in fact, resentment? 'No. But they wanted to win. I enjoyed the pressure. It was a click that got me concentrating. Whenever I walked out on to a court at Wimbledon – the Centre Court, Court One, wherever – the atmosphere was there, and it brought another dimension to my game.'

In the first open final he played Tony Roche, yet another Australian, who had spent the previous year with a pro group known as the 'Handsome Eight'. 'Tony was a lefty, which made me a bit apprehensive because I'd hardly played against a lefty in five years – I was the only one on our tour. Nor had we played much on grass in that time. But I guess I felt pretty good about my chances. He was an extremely good doubles player and he'd won a lot of singles titles, but on that day … well, maybe he didn't play as he'd planned.' It went in straight sets: 6–3, 6–4, 6–2. The king was back, pocketing a $13,000 cheque rather than the £10 voucher he'd been given along with a handshake in 1961.

His fourth and last Wimbledon singles title, against John Newcombe, came during his 1969 repetition of the calendar-year grand slam, an achievement that bettered his 1962 feat since it was against all comers. Newcombe actually gave him a moment of anxiety: 'Set-all and 4–1 down. He was a tough opponent, a thinking person on the court. He tried to wear me down and get me out of my rhythm. That's what I did to people, too, so I knew what was happening to me.'

Laver didn't believe in worrying. 'You do the best you can. If you don't play your own game, you're going to lose anyway. If you start to worry about the importance of the win before it happens, you're going to have yourself in a complete panic. You play the shots as you see them. That, and don't start wishing the shots to go in. When you start wishing, you're in trouble.'

He fell on his racket handle and sprained his wrist in Boston during that second grand slam year. Then there were problems with tennis elbow. He was back at Wimbledon in 1970, going down to a headline defeat by Britain's Roger Taylor in the fourth round; the following year he lost to Tom Gorman. He retired to California, to the wife he'd married in 1966 and the son they'd had a couple of weeks after the last of the four grand slam victories in 1969, concentrating on running a tennis holiday-camp business with Roy Emerson and various other involvements with tournament sponsors and equipment manufacturers.

And does he still play tennis every day?

'No. If I don't have something specific coming up, I may not play for months. It depends. I have to exercise a little more now, to avoid the aches and pains.'

Aches? Pains? Just watch that silhouette, scampering into the back-court to make a retrieval, winding up the left arm and whipping the ball back with interest. The Rockhampton Rocket. The greatest, yes. An immortal. And forever young.

SEVERIANO BALLESTEROS
O'Grady Says

MADRID, NOVEMBER 1994

IT'S NINE O'CLOCK in the morning, and black rain is smudging the hills above Madrid. Away in the distance, the city's cathedrals and palaces look like a painting that's been dropped in a puddle. There's standing water all over the golf course, and the second round of the Spanish Open is going to be delayed for an hour, maybe more. The players' restaurant is full of men in loud knitwear, talking and drinking coffee and playing cards. Outside, only one figure moves.

Just off the practice green, sheltered by a fir tree, the greatest golfer of his generation is trying to tune up his basic bunker shot. He settles into his stance, feeling the sand through the soles of his shoes, hips and shoulders bouncing up and down. Half a dozen hardy spectators cluster round in the murk, watching intently. Suddenly one of them pipes up.

'You look like a cowboy,' Mac O'Grady tells Severiano Ballesteros, parodying the bow-legged posture.

The three-time Open champion laughs. Then he settles again, swings and floats a near-perfect chip 25 feet to the pin.

'Good,' O'Grady says.

'Really?' says Ballesteros. 'But am I too far inside?' He repeats his swing, exaggerating it.

'No, no,' O'Grady replies.

'Are you sure?'

'Yup.'

It's a strange thing. Severiano Ballesteros, 37 years old, celebrating twenty years as a pro golfer this spring, winner of sixty tournaments, with prize money of more than $1.5 million, is looking almost beseechingly at his companion, a man of whom few people – even armchair golf fans – have ever heard. Yet people are saying that Mac O'Grady is the man who brought Seve Ballesteros back from the dead.

The day before, when the sun shone hard and true and gentle zephyrs cooled the wooded Castillian slopes, O'Grady had been following Ballesteros around the switchback championship course at Club de Campo, a camcorder clamped to his shoulder and a large yellow notebook sticking out of his shoulder-bag.

The word was that neither Seve nor O'Grady want to talk about whatever it was they had done to ensure that, the previous Sunday, Ballesteros walked up to receive the winner's trophy for his first tournament victory in two years – the Benson and Hedges International at St Mellion, where he led with perfect serenity through all four days and went from 164th to first in the European Order of Merit.

Ballesteros's slump had gone so deep that in fifty tournaments between Majorca 1992 and St Mellion 1994 he made only four top-ten finishes, while missing the cut no fewer than seventeen times. In 1993, for the first time in seventeen years, he failed to win a tournament on the European tour, finishing a weedy forty-second in the money list. But last week there was only one headline: 'Seve's back.' And the stories multiplied – about his reaction to the absence of an invitation to this year's US Open, about his resignation from the European Ryder Cup committee over a possible conflict of interests concerning the choice of venue for the 1997 competition, about how his third son will be born during the British Open in July. Severiano Ballesteros was news once more.

'We're trying not to talk about it right now,' O'Grady said as he put down the camcorder on the fringe of the 15th green to shake hands and establish eye contact in the way Americans do. In his Titleist baseball cap, his Ray-Ban Clubmasters, his patterned purple sweater and his white golf shoes, he cut a figure indistinguishable from the 300 or so spectators who were following every step of Ballesteros's first round. 'You know, it's an incredible story. But what we want before we do that is not just one tournament, but two or three months of achievement. We're trying to build stability and we don't want anything to get in the way of that.' And he plucked the sleeve of my shirt, dragging me along as he talked.

Three-quarters of an hour later, long after Ballesteros and his partners had left the 18th green, O'Grady was still talking, still plucking my sleeve to emphasize a point, still locking into eye-contact like a doorstep evangelist while his Japanese wife, Fumiko, hovered nearby. In that time he'd gone on and off the record more times than a White House spokesman on Watergate, but the on-the-record stuff more or less told me what I wanted to hear, and anyway, Ballesteros himself later repeated most of the classified stuff during the course of an open conversation.

If you don't know about Mac O'Grady, you'd probably guess that he was a reasonably successful cosmetic surgeon from, oh, Palm Springs, California, with this year's Lexus in the garage and a cheerleader wife at the manicurist. The Palm Springs bit would be right, at least. That lush resort is where O'Grady, who was born forty-three years ago in Minneapolis, now makes his home, researching 'the neuro-biological aspects of the golf swing' in the California desert.

Lots of stories attach themselves to O'Grady. As a golfer, he turned pro in 1972, aged 21, but didn't get through the qualifying school for the US PGA tour until ten years later; somebody told me that he held the record for the number of failures to make the grade. His two victories on the tour came in 1986 and 1987: the Sammy Davis Jr Greater Hartford Open and the MONY Tournament of Champions. Most recently, just before the Ballesteros link became interesting, he made the headlines by claiming, to general annoyance, that many top golfers used beta-blocking drugs to steady their nerves.

He's a bit of a wild card. In the course of our conversation we talked about rotation and take-back and trajectories – the usual technical stuff of the golf swing – but also about zoning, duality, mind and no-mind, the creative instinct and Zen riddles. He'd told me about his father–son relationship with Vic Damone, the crooner, and about the time he spent a year on the US tour in the company of a Zen master, writing a diary that he plans to publish.

Here's the sort of thing he said, delivered with the tongue on rapid-fire, punctuated by sleeve-plucking and eye-locking and scribbled down more or less accurately while following Ballesteros up hill and down dale: 'Seve has one mission. Salvage. That's it. To get things stable. He's the captain of the ship. The bullion's in the hold and it's pulling out of the harbour on the Spanish Main. In his youth he felt invulnerable. He had his adventures and he couldn't wait to get back to give the spoils to Queen Isabelle. But now in his old age of 37 he realizes that he can't carry the whole world on his shoulders. Three years ago he hit the rocks, the ship sank and all the gold went down with it. But it's all still there, at the bottom of the sea, waiting for him. Even the captain's log sank. But he found one bottle of wine floating in the water – and he had the passion to reach out and grab it. To salvage something. That's what he's doing. And building on that. Planting the seed. Waiting for the offspring to come up and blossom. We want substance that's going to survive every tempest and tsunami. In the last two years Seve's learnt from his children how to fall with grace. Now it's time to rise with grace.'

After forty minutes of this sort of thing, I felt that while maybe I didn't know much more about golf, I certainly had a better idea of what being in analysis must be like.

In the clubhouse Ballesteros laughed in an indulgent sort of way when I suggested that O'Grady's ideas on mental preparation must be coming in useful. 'That's the reason why he never really won as many tournaments as he should have,' Ballesteros said, 'because that's the problem he has. I think he's a much better striker of the ball than me, but his problem is that he doesn't have my mind!'

Sitting out the rain-break in the locker room, Ballesteros was talking with charming frankness about the effects of ageing on his game and the importance he now places on consistency – a point reinforced by his fifteen pars on the final day of St Mellion, followed by fourteen more in a level-par first round in Madrid, a major character-change for a man widely loved for his magnificent unpredictability.

'What I find most difficult as I get older is to focus on the game,' he said. 'For me, there's more than just golf now. When I was 20, there was nothing else. Now I have a family, I have businesses … And also, of course, the body doesn't react as well as it did at 20. You slow down a little bit, you don't have as much power, you don't have as much energy or willpower. You cope with that through the thing you do have more of, which is experience.'

So now, at the start of a season, or on the first morning of a tournament, what's your motivation?

'A lot of people follow me. They're pulling for me. When I go to a tournament and I see the people who've come to watch me, that motivates me a lot. I feel like I must do something extra to make sure they enjoy it. Because if I play good, then I know I give a lot of pleasure. This is what they expect from me. When I play bad, I feel bad not only for myself, but because I let people down. And when I'm playing well, I enjoy the game very much. When you enjoy it, the motivation's there.'

And the new consistency is the thing that gives him the means to overcome the depredations of age, to play through the back pain that five weeks of intense physiotherapy in an Arizona clinic has not quite eradicated. 'Consistency is what everybody's after, and the reason for that is that if you're swinging the club well, then your bad shots don't disperse so much. My "missing" shots at the moment aren't as bad as they used to be, so the ball is in play more of the time. I used to miss the green maybe by 30 or 40 yards sometimes. Now it's more like 5 or 10 yards. It's the same from the tee, if you hit more fairways … All of that will make you more relaxed through the round. Because when you go all over the place, it takes a lot from you mentally, which makes it very tough.'

If the idea of Seve Ballesteros hitting fairways with unerring accuracy seems obscurely depressing, then the admirer of golf's most mercurial talent can take comfort in the knowledge that the Spaniard is unlikely to develop a total and permanent immunity to the effects of adrenalin administered by an enthusiastic gallery. 'The crowd helps a lot,' he said. 'The more people are watching, the easier it is for a player to concentrate. But obviously the crowd gets excited and the player sometimes gets a little bit too excited as well, and then things get difficult. Consistency is what gives you the victory. When you're playing consistently, you can have a bad day and still score okay, maybe a 73 or a 74, but when you're inconsistent, you can shoot 78 or 79, which will put you out of the tournament altogether.'

And that's where Mac O'Grady comes in. 'Consistency comes from a consistent swing,' Ballesteros said, 'through repetition. We're working on a lot of things. I'm raising my hands higher, I'm trying not to sway with my head on the backswing, I'm trying to keep the club a little bit more inside the hands on the takeaway, and to turn the shoulders more around with the ball.'

This golf-mechanics stuff didn't sound as much fun as zoning, duality and the sound of one hand clapping, but it was probably what did the business at St Mellion last week and will keep Ballesteros in better heart and form through the summer than his admirers have seen for some years.

What he said about the US Open spoke eloquently of his continuing affection for the game. 'It's a major championship,' he said, 'and I want to be there. If I don't get an invitation, I'll go over there to pre-qualify and we'll see what happens. Why not? You have to be humble in this game.'

And if consistency can get him to Oakmount in mid-June, then the US Open committee will be the people to ask about the sound of one hand clapping. Everyone else will be hearing only the cheers.

WELSH RUGBY
The Dying of the Light

A FEW YARDS FROM where Barry John first kicked a rugby ball, a rock group are practising in the old wooden village hall, their rackety efforts fading into the drizzle that mantles the hills around Cefneithin. No children are playing on the sloping, tussocked pitch where the greatest of all rugby players learnt his craft. On this afternoon a crow perches undisturbed on one of the stunted goalposts, long ago cut and bolted out of steel scaffolding by loving hands, their yellow and green paint – the colours of the village rugby club – now cracked and peeling.

This is where, almost forty years ago, the young Barry John came after school, drawn by the example of an older boy practising his dropkicks alone on the sloping field. Carwyn James, whose family lived down the road, was already the star of the local grammar school team and on the brink of a place in the full Llanelli side over the hills at Stradey Park: a dark, serious, sensitive boy, born – like Barry John – to be a Welsh fly-half, and ultimately one of the great visionaries of British rugby.

Barry John and his friends from the pebble-dashed council houses just below the rugby ground would stand behind the posts to retrieve the ball for their hero. In time they joined in his training routines. And, inexorably, Barry John would go on to follow in the stud-marks of Carwyn James, from the village primary school to Gwendraeth Grammar, from little Cefneithin RFC to Llanelli, the mighty Scarlets, and all the way to the jersey of Wales.

Gwendraeth Grammar, a mile down the old Carmarthen road, was one of the legendary nurseries of Welsh rugby. Every decade a great outside-half emerged from its playing fields. Carwyn James in the 1950s, Barry John in the 1960s, Gareth Davies in the 1970s, Jonathan Davies in the 1980s: as regular as that.

'In those days the boys in the rugby team were the talisman of the school,' Gareth Davies said last week from his office at BBC Wales, where he is Head of Sport. 'We had a real tradition to follow.'

And, of course, there was an inspirational schoolmaster. 'In my case it was Ray Williams, the former Wales and Llanelli winger,' Davies continued. 'A man to be respected. For me, he was the leading light.'

Ray Williams, now retired, sat at home last week and remembered the mass trials they held once a year to produce a side to represent West Wales. 'We'd start with the six schools in the vicinity: Gwendraeth, Llandeilo, Amman Valley, Llanelli, Carmarthen, Gowerton. These schools would all play each other in the first six weeks of the autumn term. Then we'd get together and pick forty-five boys, and we'd try to sort out the sheep from the goats. At the end of that, we'd have a team to represent Carmarthenshire against West Glamorgan. And from that we'd pick a team to play West versus East.'

Like nuggets of good Welsh coal, young boys poured from a smoothly functioning system, adept in the arts of a game that had its distant origins in *cnapan*, the ancient game played from village to village, in which points were scored by grounding the ball in the porch of a school or a chapel.

'At one time,' Ray Williams mused, 'rugby was as important as religion in Welsh schools. Now, I don't think so ….'

It was ten years ago that everything changed. Gwendraeth Grammar became Gwendraeth Valley Comprehensive, absorbing other schools. A year or two later the main teachers' unions ordered their members to work to rule, after which they were presented with contracts that, for the first time, specified their hours of work and at a stroke curtailed their enthusiasm for extra-curricular activities. Satellite dishes began to appear on the council house walls, bringing other cultures and their diversions into Cefneithin's front rooms.

Today, one of Ray Williams's Welsh caps hangs in a case at the school, along with memorabilia of the other past internationals. The sports hall is called the Canolfan Carwyn – the Carwyn Centre, with a bust of the great man in the foyer. Outside, the rugby posts stand tall and underemployed.

'I'm not a fanatical rugby man,' Robert Garrero, the school's headmaster, said last week, 'although I enjoy watching a game now and then. Heritage is important, and the pupils are aware of the tradition. But it's important for people to remember that schools have changed since that time.'

So does Gwendraeth Valley Comprehensive put out a 1st XV every Saturday morning?

'Well, no, we don't,' Robert Garrero said. 'There's quite a lot of interest in the lower school, but there isn't a regular 1st XV. There's a growing diversity of interests these days, you know. Some children might get interested in American football or basketball. It's all part of how life is changing.'

'That's the most heartbreaking thing I've heard in rugby for years,' said Cliff Morgan, another of the heroic figures of Welsh rugby history, when I told him that the school at Gwendraeth no longer had a regular 1st XV. 'I can't believe it. Gwendraeth Grammar School. Once upon a time, just the sound of it was like a bell ringing across Welsh rugby.'

The bell tolls for Welsh rugby again on Saturday, when the national team meets Scotland at Cardiff Arms Park in a meeting of two desperate sides. A few weeks ago Scotland were thrashed by the All Blacks, who were then in turn beaten by England, which cast the Scottish defeat in an even gloomier light. But for Wales, as so often in the past ten years, once again everything – from individual careers to the self-respect of the nation – seems to hang on the outcome of eighty minutes' rugby football.

Twenty years after a golden era that some believed would never end, many reasons are being advanced for the continuing decline of Welsh rugby and for the catalogue of humiliation it has endured – the record defeats (49–6, 55–3, 63–8, 73–8), the first-ever whitewash in the Five Nations' Championship, the losses to minnows such as Romania, Western Samoa and (most recently) Canada, the terrible surrender of Welsh pride and dignity in verbal fights between players and journalists and in actual fist fights between Welsh team-mates feuding in defeat.

As Alan Davies, the national coach, prepares his players for next week's match, he does so against a background of intensified conflict, thanks to the convulsions of the past year, which saw a popular uprising sweep away the committee of the Welsh Rugby Union – a group of men committed to reform – in favour of a return to a more traditional approach, such as a reduction in the unilateral powers of the coach (significantly downgrading his title from 'national coach' to 'coach to the national team') and a return to the system of a selection committee, once known in Wales as the 'Big Five'.

The new committee – a 'Big Six' – features familiar names from the glory years: Elgan Rees, Derek Quinnell and Geoff Evans join Alan Davies, his assistant Gareth Jenkins, and Bob Norster, the team manager. But there are other influences. The new men at the top of the WRU have formed a National Player Development Committee, which called a very strange public trial session at Stradey Park ten days ago, apparently against the wishes of Davies and Norster, who were forced to take the players through training routines and an hour of actual play on the night before they announced their selection to play Scotland.

'It was a farce,' said Brian Price, who captained Wales to the Triple Crown in 1969 and is now among the Greek chorus of former players who ensure that nothing Alan Davies does goes without the minutest scrutiny. 'There's no doubt that Alan Davies doesn't enjoy the confidence of the committee,' Price continued. 'That can only come through results. Last season's game against England is the only match of significance that Wales have won under him, and we were very fortunate to win that. Now he seems to have gone back to a game which we've never been much good at, an English style, for which we haven't got the size of forwards. We've always been good at moving the ball away from the opposition, not taking it back towards them and confronting them physically.'

That is typical of the sort of criticism heaped on Davies's head since his team followed its victory over England in Cardiff at the start of last season – when Ieuan Evans, the captain, caught Rory Underwood napping to score a famous try – with defeats at the hands of Scotland, Ireland and France. Now, particularly since the inept performance against a second-string Canada selection, Davies can do nothing right.

A few days ago the England reserve fly-half Stuart Barnes – who played for Welsh Schoolboys before opting for the land of his birth – used a newspaper column to accuse Davies of confusing his players and dulling their natural flair. The fact that Barnes looks and plays more like a great Welsh outside-half than anyone currently in contention for the role merely heaped insult on injury.

Everyone, of course, has a theory about the plight of Welsh rugby, and the dwindling of rugby in the schools is a part of most of them. Gerald Davies, the prince of wing threequarters, pointed out that the consolidation of grammar schools into comprehensives meant fewer schools and therefore fewer potential opponents.

But there are many other factors, including fundamental changes in society, such as the national identity crisis caused by the destruction of Wales's industrial heart. The number of men working in the coalfields has gone from 250,000 to 700 in four generations. 'We've become a soft nation,' said Ron Waldron, Wales's previous coach. 'We relied on steel workers and miners to play our club rugby. If you went to Cross Keys or Abertillery, you knew you were in for a hard game. That's gone.'

Waldron also pointed to the obvious depredations of the professional thirteen-man game across the border. 'It's not long since eight quality players went over to rugby league in the space of perhaps three years,' he said wistfully, probably thinking that the presence of men like Jonathan Davies, John Devereux and Jonathan Griffiths would have transformed his own brief, unhappy tenure.

And there's the question of size. 'We're a small country,' said Jeff Young, the former Wales hooker who is now the technical director of the Welsh Rugby Union, 'with a relatively small rugby-playing population. We need to travel to expose ourselves more to competition outside Wales, to help us develop outside our own world.'

Most people, though, trace the origins of the ten-year crisis back to the mood that overtook Welsh rugby in the glow of the early 1970s. 'There was hubris,' Gerald Davies said, 'and a certain complacency set in. Those in charge failed to prepare for the future.'

'We felt we had a God-given right to success,' said John Ryan, Waldron's predecessor, 'and no preparation was made for the fact that all those great players would eventually finish. Other countries did prepare for the future. And they've come out stronger.'

'There was no development of international players,' Waldron said. 'They probably thought that the club scene would just go on producing them indefinitely. They didn't realize that more work needed to be put in. It's only now that the union is getting to grips with the problem.'

The man who saw it all coming was the son of Cefneithin, Carwyn James, who coached the British Lions to their greatest triumph in New Zealand in 1971 but was denied the Welsh job because he wanted to take control of the team away from the men in blazers. 'Of course he should have been given it,' Gerald Davies said. 'But he didn't want it under the prevailing conditions. And he knew they couldn't accept his proposals.'

Almost twenty years later, the national coach had just about attained the position of power that James advocated when, at a special meeting in Port Talbot, an entire regime was swept away in a wave of neo-conservatism. It was led by the clubs, who are unwilling to follow the English example and make the sacrifices necessary to establish a successful international XV. The resulting bitterness continues to flavour virtually every aspect of Welsh rugby life.

'Alan Davies, Bobby Norster, Ieuan Evans – they're all lovely people,' Brian Price said witheringly. 'But you've got to have a bit more than that. If they lose on Saturday, Davies's position will be very precarious. He's contracted to the end of the championship, but if I were in his shoes, I'd be contemplating resignation. And perhaps one or two of the committee won't be too sorry to see him go.'

'We're pretty good at fighting each other,' said Davies, who was born forty-nine years ago in Ynysybwl but speaks with a gentle English accent. 'And it may be that it will take a number of Alan Davieses getting their heads chopped off before we get Welsh rugby back where it belongs.'

At the bottom of the village, on the floodlit pitch opened in 1976, the men of Cefneithin RFC are playing a new year game: the over-thirties versus the under-thirties. In the groundsman's shed, spectators shelter from the drizzle and argue the respective merits of the current candidates for the hallowed Welsh number 10 jersey.

It took foresight to create this little ground. For twenty-five years, at the club's behest, the council dumped waste here, until the soil could be tipped over it and the grass sown. Eventually Cefneithin had a setting fit for the heirs of Carwyn James and Barry John. You'd never guess what lies underneath.

Just like Welsh rugby, really. Time, finally, to bury the past.

JAMES HUNT
Lost and Found

HE WOULD HAVE loved it, of course. There was singing and trumpets and laughter and girls and children and a party down the road afterwards. His friends, the ones he had grown up with and the ones he had raced with, told gentle jokes about his quirks of temperament while his two small sons fidgeted in the third pew.

The parish church of St James's, Piccadilly was packed for the memorial service to the one-time golden boy of British motor racing who died of a heart attack on 14 June at the age of 45. The morning rain, reminiscent of the black downpour that washed Mount Fuji that day in 1976 when he won his world championship in a chaotic and climactic Japanese Grand Prix, eased in time for the guests to gather in the churchyard – an exotic crowd including his two former wives, Suzy Miller and Sarah Lomax, and his two long-term companions, Jane Birkbeck and Helen Dawson, who together formed the focal quartet of such a scrum of long-legged blondes that the hallowed precincts began to resemble a casting session for

244 THE VIEW FROM THE HIGH BOARD

Darling or *Blow-Up*, thirty years on. The mourners ranged from Bette Hill and Nina Rindt, widows of other raffish world champions, to a veiled and nose-studded Koo Stark, sharing the front row of the gallery with Becky Few Brown, estranged wife of the errant Marquess of Blandford. Alexander Hesketh and Bubbles Horsley came on from lunch at Wilton's, a reminder of the carefree days in which they respectively bankrolled and managed the little Formula One team that brought Hunt to sudden and unexpected prominence.

Their mechanics reassembled, greeting each other by their old oily-rag nicknames: Beaky, Ferret, Ball-of-String. At the other end of the paddock's hierarchy Ken Tyrrell, Eddie Jordan, Ron Dennis of McLaren, Patrick Head of Williams and Peter Collins of Lotus represented the team owners. Rob Walker and Lord Montagu symbolized the heritage of British motor racing. John Watson stood for the generation of drivers against whom Hunt raced.

The presence of Alain de Cadenet, the playboy-racer-cum-stamp-collector, and Philip Martin, the Mayfair gambler, evoked the highly developed after-hours side of Hunt's life; they were two among dozens of chaps who looked as though they had probably got turfed out of good schools in the early 1960s and then done rather well for themselves.

Hunt's parents read from Ecclesiastes, chapter 3: 'A time to mourn, and a time to dance.' His old music master from Wellington remembered his love of music and, more significantly, how his refusal to join cross-country training had not prevented him winning everything in sight.

Innes Ireland, one of the last of the grand prix cavaliers, read Kipling's 'If', less threadbare than usual in its reference to the spectre of his financial troubles: 'If you can make one heap of all your winnings / And risk it all on one turn of pitch-and-toss …'.

Stirling Moss paid tribute to his combination of wit, intelligence and stubbornness: 'To one of my generation, his behaviour sometimes seemed quite appalling. But then he was James … and whatever else he may have been, he was never boring.' Helen Dyson, the companion of his more tranquil final years, read Psalm 84: 'How amiable are thy tabernacles, O Lord of hosts!'

In a reversal of their usual procedure, the last word went to

Murray Walker, Hunt's co-commentator of thirteen years' standing. 'In today's world most of us stand out like grey against black,' he said. 'James refused to conform to the rules that govern the rest of us. And he made everywhere a more stimulating place to be.'

PAULESBURY, NORTHANTS, THREE MONTHS EARLIER

'**J**AMES COULD ALWAYS get depressed,' Alexander 'Bubbles' Horsley said, looking out over the gentle green acres of Northamptonshire. 'He did have mood swings.'

Ironically, the biggest mood swing of all came in the hour of Hunt's greatest triumph, when he had just taken the prize for which he will be remembered. 'I think when he'd done it,' Horsley continued, 'when he'd won the world championship, when he knew he was the best, there was an element of, "Well, what was that all about?" And that, I think, is the difference between him and a lot of the others.'

Two days after the discovery of Hunt's body at his home in Wimbledon, Bubbles Horsley was still slipping into the present tense as he talked about his friend. Not surprising: they had known each other since the early 1970s, when Horsley and Lord Hesketh had talked Hunt into joining their racing team, which they'd started 'for reasons of boredom, to fill weekends'.

They were raffish young public school boys: Horsley, 28, had been to Dover College; Hesketh, 22, to Ampleforth; Hunt, 24, to Wellington. Kindred spirits flocked around them. 'It was probably the only team,' Horsley said, 'in which the second richest member was the van driver.' Second to Hesketh, of course. The young master of Easton Neston was paying the bills.

The gentleman van driver, Charles Lucas, was a grandson of the man who built St Pancras station, the Albert Hall and the docks at Buenos Aires. The bacon sarnies were cooked by Tom Benson, who had a fashionable restaurant in Beauchamp Place. The team photographer was Christopher Simon Sykes, who later produced opulent picture books of gardens and the English countryside. Together they mixed the amateur spirit – parties, booze, recreational drugs, girls, yachts in the harbour at Monaco – with a carefully disguised professionalism, and were winning grands prix by the time Hesketh ran into cash-flow problems in 1975. Hunt moved on to McLaren and the championship while Horsley, eventually, went into commercial property. But they stayed friends, godparents to each other's children, gossiping about racing, making deals together.

'He kept his mates,' Horsley said. 'That was one of the things. All his mates were from when he was racing his Mini, or playing squash or golf, or from school. He moved in and out of the glamorous world, completely at ease with it, yet it never got inside him. They didn't convert him, if you like. The marketing men convert people – like Nigel Mansell, a Brummie lad struggling for years, now a superstar with his own jet, moving around like royalty. They've converted him. They've got him. He can now be merchandised. They never got James. James never had those desires. No matter how much money he had, he never would have wanted a jet.'

What he ended up with, however, was a rusting Mercedes sedan on blocks in his drive, wheels off, too expensive to run, stranded next to the ancient A35 van and the pushbike that were the transportation of his last years. As it turned out, wanting a bit more might not have been such a bad thing. But once was enough for James Hunt: in his case, the single championship that always leaves room for doubt. Not just in the public's mind, but in his own.

The great champions in any sport are the ones who, having won the thing, go straight back out there and win it again. Niki Lauda, for instance, had won the title in 1975 and was to take it again in 1977 and 1982. But in 1976, when Hunt won it, the Austrian had his bad crash at the Nurburgring, which kept him out of two vital rounds and, even after his astonishingly brave return, reduced his powers. So Lauda's shadow has always hovered over Hunt's title.

'Because of that,' Horsley said, 'I think he felt that his championship wasn't taken as seriously as it should have been, that there were people who said that if Lauda hadn't had the crash, James wouldn't have won it that year. And I think that was a regret. I think that hurt him, because if you actually looked at the facts and figures, it was not true. It was a fair win. You can't take that away from him.'

He had won the title with McLaren and he stayed there for the following season, winning a further three grands prix but finishing only fifth in the championship. In his third season with the team, a solitary third place was his best result and he had fallen to thirteenth place in the final standings. Nevertheless, his two post-title years had set him up financially, and his lack of hard ambition was evident when he turned down the chance to move to Ferrari at a time when the Italian team was still competitive. Instead, for 1979 he went back to a private team, this one run by a Canadian industrialist, Walter Wolf. But the Wolf-Ford could offer him nothing, and by that time the damaging effects of self-indulgence were being compounded by fear.

'Yes, he got frightened,' Horsley said. 'It was demoralizing for him. In the end he said, 'I don't want to kill myself struggling for seventh place.' I think that's what got to him. How it manifested itself, whether as fear or frustration, whether he sought to escape from that in drink, girls, whatever … possibly. He must have known that his career was in decline, that he wasn't in the right team, that it wasn't working for him, and yet his talent hadn't declined. It's rather like a film star who's suddenly getting bum scripts, but he needs to do it because that's what he does, he needs the money and therefore he does it. But in the end the scripts got so bad …'.

So bad that at Monaco, seven races into the season, he got out of his car and quit cold, the first champion to retire in mid-season since Fangio, who at least had the excuse of being 47 years old, with five titles on his mantlepiece

After his death, the newspapers concentrated on his financial misfortunes: 'The hero who died penniless,' the front page of the *Daily Express* said. Which goes back to Horsley's remarks about Hunt's unwillingness to market himself and his championship.

Back in 1973, in his first season with Hesketh in Formula One, Hunt took a retainer of £2,500 – with which he bought a Ford Capri, installing the best sound system he could find – plus 45 per cent of the prize money. The whole season, including seven grands prix, cost Hesketh £78,000. In 1974 Hunt's retainer rose to about £10,000; and, since the team was now building its own cars rather than renting them, the proprietor's liability rose above £200,000. After a handful of races in 1975, including a victory in the Dutch Grand Prix, Hesketh told Horsley that he could no longer support the team.

Things got so tight that Horsley was having to buy a racing engine with the revenue from sales of their famous T-shirts, featuring a helmeted teddy bear and a union jack. To get the team to the French Grand Prix, he had to flog Hesketh's Rolls-Royce. 'We didn't have the money to go, and I saw it parked outside the front of the house, so it went. He came back and said, "Where's my Rolls-Royce?" I said, "It's gone." He wasn't very pleased. He forgave me when we came second, though.'

By that time Hunt was driving for nothing – or at least letting Horsley run a tab. 'He was very good. In fact, he was very good in 1976, too, when he'd gone to McLaren. He gave us lots of time to pay him for the previous year. He was supposed to get £75,000, and eventually he got about half of it. He had a Porsche, too, which he kept.'

So Hunt signed with McLaren and won his title. Horsley and the team took sponsorship from *Penthouse* magazine and Rizla rolling papers and, in Horsley's words, 'went from the front of the grid, from being the glamour boys, to the back of the grid, and being forgotten. But on the other hand, the bank balance went from zero and filled up again.' The carefree amateurs had become grafting pros.

By 1978 the game had lost its joy. 'I think there are those for whom motor racing is an obsession, like Frank Williams. For us, though, while it was fun, while there was still a chance of winning, we'd do it. But when it stopped being attractive, and the alarm would go at five o'clock on a Wednesday morning to tell you to go down to Gatwick and get the charter flight, and you found yourself thinking, "Oh God", then it was time to stop. James stopped, too. And he felt a huge relief. He never regretted it.'

There was a nightclub in Marbella, which went bust. There were relationships that ended and cost him money: the amicable divorce from Suzy Miller, and the split from Jane Birkbeck, to whom he was generous, and the less than amicable divorce from Sarah Lomax, the mother of his two sons, which made a few lawyers a lot wealthier. He was also in Lloyd's – 'not one of the racier syndicates,' Horsley said, 'but he was never very rich, and when you combine all that with a recession …'.

It was a problem of transition, of course. 'When you're a driver in Formula One,' Horsley said, 'your days are completely organized for you. You don't have to think. When that stopped, he was lost for a bit. And I think it led to some of the problems with his relationships. But he'd turned the corner. He was much, much happier in the last year or so. He wasn't drinking, he was getting fitter, he was beginning to see a bit of light at the end of the tunnel. And also, of course, discovering that life doesn't really change if you're driving around in an A35 van and bicycling everywhere. It's actually not that different from driving around in a £70,000 Mercedes.'

Of all that Bubbles Horsley had to tell me about James Hunt, I liked best what he said last. 'James was a very good father,' he remembered. 'He understood people and situations. He could take a small child who was very unhappy about something and walk off with him and talk it all through and really communicate – he was a marvellous communicator, which was why he was so good on TV. And the child would come back grinning and everything would have been solved, just with a few words. That was one of his great strengths. But people who are brilliant at solving other people's problems often struggle with some of their own, don't they?'

ACKNOWLEDGEMENTS

Thanks first of all to Graham Coster, who suggested that these pieces might make a book and then edited the collection with his usual meticulousness and perception. Thanks to various sports editors: Ben Clissitt and Mike Averis at the *Guardian*, Paul Newman and Charlie Burgess at the *Independent*, Simon Kelner and Simon O'Hagan at the *Independent on Sunday*, David Robson at the *Sunday Times*, Norman Fox at *The Times* and Harry Richards at the *Nottingham Evening Post*. Thanks to the sports sub-editors at all those newspapers, and to the specialist correspondents who so generously shared their knowledge, particularly David Davies, Andy Farrell, John Roberts, Stephen Bierley, Mike Selvey, Derek Pringle, David Hopps, David Lacey, Glenn Moore, Phil Shaw, Alan Henry, Robert Kitson, Paul Rees, Chris Hewett, Chris Rea, Duncan Mackay, Mike Rowbottom, William Fotheringham, Sue Montgomery, Greg Wood, Chris Dodd and Hugh Mathieson. Thanks to Mats Olsson of *Expressen* and Hartmut Scherzer of the *Frankfurter Allgemeine*. Thanks to Stephen Wood at *Condé Nast Traveler*. Thanks to Yvonne Fletcher, Kim Doherty, Nicole Wilmshurst and Clare Tomlinson for their patience. Thanks to David Godwin for his encouragement. And thanks, finally, to my father, Ieuan Williams.